An Invitation to Indian Cooking

An Invitation to Indian Cooking

Madhur Jaffrey

JONATHAN CAPE
THIRTY-TWO BEDFORD SQUARE
LONDON

First published in Great Britain 1976
Reissued 1984
This paperback edition first published 1987
Copyright © 1973 by Madhur Jaffrey

Jonathan Cape Ltd, 32 Bedford Square, London WC1B 3EL

British Library Cataloguing in Publication Data

Jaffrey, Madhur
An invitation to Indian cooking.
1. Cookery, Indic
I. Title
641.5954   TX724.5.14

ISBN 0 224 01152 9
0 224 02857 X (pbk)

Printed in Great Britain by
Thomson Litho
East Kilbride, Scotland

To Bauwa and Dadaji
with love

Contents

Acknowledgments

I would like to gratefully acknowledge the help given to me by the following—my grandmother, whose black lemon pickle opened my taste buds at an early age; my mother, who patiently gave me a two-year correspondence course in cooking; K and Motiboo, for unearthing old family recipes; Hussain, for inspiring me with his endless culinary experiments; V, for finding Indeera; Indeera, for her delicious chutney; Maya, for helping out in moments of panic; Zakiya and John, for willingly eating a lunch composed of five different soups; Ved, for showing such positive approval of a banana relish; Virginia, whose enthusiasm for the book in general and specific recipes in particular kept me buoyed up during the agonizing days of remeasuring and retesting; Zia, Chub (especially Chub), and Mitth, for showing a profound understanding of the chapter system and obligingly eating chicken one month, soups and appetizers the next month, vegetables the following, and so on; Sanford, for saying, 'You can do it', when I was convinced I couldn't and each batch of a certain sweet dessert was coming out tasting sour; Ismail, for keeping me striving by calling me the second-best cook; Norma and Mrs S. Matthai, for their expertise in seafood; the Blinkworths, for graciously parting with their recipe for mulligatawny soup before emigrating to Australia; and, most of all, Judith, for her gentle encouragement, unpressured advice, and her very reassuring presence.

Introduction

On a recent visit to London, I was astounded to see Indian restaurants flourishing in practically every neighbourhood. Mistakenly, I took this efflorescence to signify an increased supply of good quality, authentic, regional Indian foods. After all, the Indians who have settled in England—and there are over a million of them—come from some of the remotest areas of the subcontinent. It would not, I thought, be unreasonable to expect the restaurants to mirror this diversity in the foods that they served at their tables.

Upon visiting the restaurants, I found most of them to be second-class establishments that had managed to underplay their own regional uniqueness as well as to underestimate the curiosity and palate of contemporary Britons. Instead of specializing in foods from particular states or districts, they served a generalized Indian food from no area whatsoever; a restaurant calling itself 'Delhi' had no *karhi*, that thick soupy dish with its bobbing flotilla of gram flour dumplings; another, advertising food from the Punjab, was minus those delicious Punjabi mainstays, corn bread and mustard greens; at another called 'Bombay', where were the spongy, cakelike *dhhoklas* or those delicious sweet breads called *puranpoli*? And at all those new Bangalee restaurants I saw no roe fritters, or fish smothered with crushed mustard seeds and cooked gently in mustard oil or *bhapa doi*, that creamy, steamed yogurt.

The greatness of India's cuisine lies in its regional foods and its regional menus. There are several reasons why a great many of the restaurants shy away from them. One is timidity—fear that the diner's unfamiliarity with regional specialities will make certain dishes unpopular. (After all, if *tandoori* chicken and lamb *korma* are selling well, why bother with potatoes cooked with asafetida and cumin or shredded cabbage cooked with mustard seeds and freshly grated coconut?) Another reason is the calibre of the cooks. Good cooks are, in all parts of the world, a rare commodity. And those cooks going in for large-scale restaurant work need, on top of their basic talent, years of apprenticeship and training. The cooks in these proliferating Indian, Pakistani, and Bangalee restaurants are often former seamen or untrained villagers who have come to England in the hopes of making a living, somehow or other, in alien surroundings. Since cooking seems to them to require no unusual skills, a great many become restaurateurs, copying the standardized menus of other Indian restaurants and refusing to experiment with dishes from their own villages and home towns which they perhaps know much better. The result is that sauces in such eating places inevitably have the same colour, taste, and consistency; the dishes generally come 'mild, medium or hot', which is an indication that the food is not being cooked with the spices, as it should be, but that something is being ladled on; mediocre chutneys and relishes are piled on the table to fake an appearance of 'a lot for your money'; appetizers are suggested not because Indians eat them but because it is felt that the Western world cannot do without them.

This is, of course, not true of *all* Indian restaurants. There are a few *very* good ones, specializing generally in certain types of North Indian food. But even here, the menus are stubbornly limited to the tried and the true. Since the introduction of *tandoori* foods over a decade ago, nothing new has been added. The same menu repeats itself over and over again. The only difference between restaurants is that some cook the general run of *kormas* and *biryanis* well, while others do not. One restaurant owner, however, proudly presented me with a *new* dish which he alone served—*niramish* vegetables cooked with the typically Bengali five-spice combination of cumin, fennel, fenugreek, mustard, and onion seeds. Unfortunately, the vegetables he had used were from a frozen packet of 'mixed vegetables', thus completely negating all his own sincere and well-meaning efforts at authenticity.

The only way to eat superb Indian food, with a guarantee of variety, quality and freshness of ingredients, is to learn to cook it for yourself. And that is the purpose of this book—to open up the infinite possibilities offered by a cuisine that is over a thousand years old! Most of the recipes here have been adapted to the English kitchen. Some, like the fried aubergines, are very easy and quick to make. Others require a little time and patience. Just as you cannot expect to turn out a home-made apple pie in two minutes, you cannot expect the stuffed green peppers to be ready for eating with just two turns of the spatula. Good food cannot always be rushed.

I realize that many of you may be cooking Indian food for the first time. I have tried to write the recipes in great detail, describing how the food should look at the end of each major step as well as when it is fully cooked. This may make the recipes a bit long, but don't let that put you off. My intention is merely to lessen the chances for error. Also, don't be discouraged by a long list of spices. Once you have them on your shelf, it is just as easy to sprinkle in five of them as it is to add two.

It may, perhaps, encourage you to know that I myself learned to cook not from observation and practice in our family's kitchen in Delhi but from recipes written on flimsy air-letters, mailed to me by my mother. As a teenager growing up in India I was preoccupied with the usual teenage concerns —boys (whom we saw only at a distance and therefore coveted), my ambitions (why can't *I* play Hamlet?), and other such nonsense. I went into the kitchen only as a dilettante, more to taste than to help or learn.

It was when I was twenty and went to England as a student that I started to learn how to cook. I was extremely homesick, and this homesickness took the form of a longing for Indian food.

The canteen at my drama school served a see-through slice of roast beef accompanied by some watery potatoes and cabbage which no amount of H.P. sauce could improve. My limited scholarship funds did not allow me to eat out at the Indian restaurants. So I decided to learn how to cook, and I wrote to my mother in India for recipes. She would answer with long letters in Hindi which I would take with me to school. As I ate my roast and two vegetables, I would ponder her advice ... put in a pinch of asafetida—don't let it burn—now put in the cumin and stir for a second or two ... add the chopped-up tomatoes and fry ... my mouth would water and the cabbage would stick in my throat. At this point I couldn't even make tea.

But with expert long-distance help from my mother, I started learning. I began adapting her recipes to the ingredients and appliances that I found in Britain. Over the years I discovered that the electric blender could do much of what the Indian grinding stone did, and much faster; that instead of roasting aubergines in hot ashes as my mother recommended, I could do it directly over a gas burner; that English meats just couldn't be fried the Indian way because they contained too much water and that it was often better to cook with tinned tomatoes than fresh ones because they had more taste and colour. Slowly I began changing the recipes to suit the conditions. I managed to arrive at the genuine taste of traditional dishes, but often had to take quite a circuitous and unorthodox route to get there.

I'm sure by now you want to know what special ingredients are required to produce that genuine flavour, what special spices you need before you embark on this culinary adventure. Let me start negatively by saying that what you don't need is curry powder, which many of you may already realize. But for those who don't, let me explain.

To me the word 'curry' is as degrading to India's great

cuisine as the term 'chop suey' was to China's. But just as the English are learning to distinguish between the different styles of Chinese cooking and between the different dishes, I fervently hope that they will soon do the same with Indian food instead of lumping it all under the dubious catchall title of 'curry'. 'Curry' is just a vague, inaccurate word which the world has picked up from the British, who, in turn, got it mistakenly from us. It seems to mean different things to different people. Sometimes it is used synonymously with all Indian food. In America it can mean either Indian food or curry powder. To add to this confusion, Indians writing or speaking in English use the word themselves to distinguish dishes with a sauce, i.e., stew-like dishes. Of course when Indians speak in their own languages, they never use the word at all, instead identifying each dish by its own name.

The origin of this English word could be *kari*, a Tamil word meaning 'sauce', it could be a spice called the *kari* leaf, or it could be *karhi*, a North Indian dish made with buttermilk and chickpea flour. Who knows where some wandering sixteenth-century Englishman found his inspiration! Whatever its source, the word is obviously a British oversimplification for what is universally recognized as a richly varied cuisine.

If 'curry' is an oversimplified name for an ancient cuisine, then 'curry powder' attempts to oversimplify (and destroy) the cuisine itself. Curry powders are standard blends of several spices, including cumin, coriander, fenugreek, red peppers, and tumeric — standard blends which Indians themselves never use. Here again I am sure the British are responsible for its creation. This is how I imagine it happened:

A British officer in full uniform (possibly a young David Niven) is standing under a palm tree and looking fondly at his bungalow as Indian servants go back and forth carrying heavy trunks from the house into a waiting carriage. When the carriage is loaded, the servants line up on the veranda with tears in their eyes. The officer, overcome with emotion, turns to khansamah (cook).

OFFICER: How I shall miss your delicious cooking. My good man, why don't you mix me a box of those wonderful spices that you have been using. I will carry it back with me to Surrey, and there, whenever I feel nostalgic about India, I will take out this box and sprinkle some of your aromatic spice mixture into my bubbling pot.

KHANSAMAH: Yes, sa'ab, as you say, sa'ab. (*Runs off to kitchen.*)

Scene shifts to kitchen, where cook is seen hastily throwing spices into box. He runs back with it to officer.

KHANSAMAH: Here is the box, sa'ab. Sa'ab, if your friends also like, for a sum of two rupees each, I can make more boxes for them as well ...

Several years later: Former cook is now successful exporter. He is seen filling boxes marked 'Best Curry Powder'. When boxes are filled, he puts them in a large crate and stamps it in black: FOR EXPORT ONLY. Then he goes to his money box, opens it, takes out his money, and gleefully counts it. As scene fades away, former cook and present exporter is doing Dance of Joy ...

So much for my scenario. The point is that no Indian ever uses curry powder in his cooking. Nor do we mix our own, because if we did we would end up with our own blend of collective spices. Cooking again and again with the same blend of spices would make all dishes taste alike. It would be the same as taking a tablespoon each of dried thyme, basil, rosemary, tarragon, bay leaves, and allspice, putting them in a jar, shaking the jar, labelling it 'French Spices', and then using a portion of this mixture for every French dish one made, from soup to salad. Also, since 'curry powder' is a blend of *ground* spices, it tends to get stale very quickly and lose its flavour. So one ends up with something that has the negative aspects of being standardized and somewhat rancid at the same time.

And it isn't just Britons and Americans who are misguided.

The Chinese, who insist on the freshest herbs and vegetables for all their own food, use some of the stalest curry powder for the curried dumplings they serve in Hong Kong's best tea rooms. The Japanese, who are probably the world's greatest culinary aesthetes, don't hesitate to serve a greenish-yellow glutinous mess over their rice and label it 'curry', and the Frenchman, who insists on a perfect *velouté*, also eats the most ghastly 'shrimp Indienne' in a curry-tinted cream sauce.

But eating habits are changing, and today's English populace seems to have a great desire to experience the 'real' thing, an authentic taste, a different life style. Anything fake is deplored, fake foods included. It is a hopeful trend and leads me to believe that if the variety of authentic Indian food is ever going to be discovered, this is perhaps the time for it.

What is it then that gives Indian food its particular range of flavours? It may surprise you to know that a great many of the spices we use are ones that you probably have on your kitchen shelves already—cloves, cinnamon, bay leaves, black pepper, nutmeg and mace. These, along with cardamom, are what we call *garam masalas*, 'hot spices'. They are hot only inasmuch as they are supposed to provide heat for the body. The spices which you may not have would include cumin, coriander, turmeric, fenugreek, black mustard seeds, fennel, and dried hot peppers. All these, I find, are readily available on the spice racks of most large supermarkets and delicatessens.

There is a slight problem with supermarket spices which you might as well be aware of. Those spices which do not 'move'—i.e., sell fast—tend to stay on the shelves and get stale. A few lose their aroma, others fade in the light, some get oily and rancid. Therefore, try to buy only whole spices and grind them yourself in small quantities. The grinding is best done in a coffee-grinder, or, if the spices are slightly roasted first, some can be crushed between waxed paper with a rolling pin. The electric blender will grind spices, if you do them in sufficiently large quantities. If all else fails, you could use a mortar and pestle, though that tends to crush spices rather than grind them. Whole spices retain their flavours for very long periods. Make sure you store them in jars with tightly screwed lids, well away from dampness and sunlight. Ground cumin and coriander are fine if bought from Indian spice dealers in small quantities.

Even though the Indian styles of cooking require, in general, a fair number of spices, we do not, of course, use all of them for each dish we cook. Cauliflower, for example, may be cooked with just turmeric, fresh ginger, fresh green coriander, and ground cumin. A chicken dish I make requires only whole cloves, black peppercorns, cinnamon sticks, bay leaves, and cardamom pods. One potato dish needs just a pinch of asafetida, whole cumin seeds, and turmeric.

Sometimes, as you glance at a couple of recipes, the spices used might look identical, which may lead you to the conclusion that the two dishes will taste the same. But that's not necessarily true. It is not only *what* spices you use but also *how* you use them that gives dishes their special taste and appearance. Take cumin, for instance. If it is roasted whole and crushed, its coffee colour will darken the looks of any food and its strong aroma will fill not just your kitchen but your entire house. This way it has a sharp, nutty taste. Whole cumin, when it is 'popped' in very hot fat, has a mild aroma and a gentle, liquorice-like taste. Ground unroasted cumin provides a third flavour and has perhaps the mildest taste of the three.

Different spices require different treatment during cooking. Turmeric burns easily and becomes bitter, so it is generally used in conjunction with some liquid. Saffron gives off its best colour when lightly roasted, crushed, and then left to soak in warm milk. Too many fenugreek seeds can make a dish bitter, so while you can play around with the number of peppercorns or cardamom pods you put into a dish, you cannot do the same with fenugreek.

Spices, herbs, and other seasonings are always added to the cooking pot in a specific order, and this again changes the taste of the dish. For example, if a hot, dried red pepper is browned in oil and then mixed in with cooked lentils, the lentils will not be very hot but will have gained the subtle flavour of the pepper. On the other hand, if the pepper is browned in oil first and then cooked *with* the lentils, you will end up with a fairly hot dish. This applies to nearly all the spices, as each has its own peculiarities. The order in which they are put into a pot is extremely important. All this may sound confusing, but it is really easier to master than, say, a French custard. If you follow the recipes carefully, you will soon begin to understand the properties and idiosyncrasies of each spice.

Not all Indian dishes are stew-like, as some people imagine. We distinguish between 'wet' and 'dry' dishes, and of course we have every category in between. Sometimes we start cooking a meat dish like a stew, then boil down the liquid and end up by frying the meat. At other times we fry a fresh ginger paste with turmeric, sauté a vegetable in this mixture briefly, sprinkle a little water over it, and let it cook, covered, in its own steam. Potatoes can be cooked in a variety of sauces, or they can be boiled, diced, and cooked 'dry' with a little oil, fennel, and cumin seed. We deep-fry vegetables in batter and eat them with a fresh green coriander chutney, and we roast chicken and fish whole in clay ovens. Just as there is no one spice used for every single Indian dish, there is really no single technique that is common to all Indian foods.

A great many people stay away from Indian food because they assume it is hot. This 'heat', when it exists, is generally provided by the red or green pepper (or chili), spices which can easily be omitted without any loss of authenticity. In fact, in my own family, we rarely ate hot food, because it didn't 'agree' with my father. Being perverse, I naturally developed a very strong liking for it, but there is no reason why you must do the same. Some Englishmen feel that they lose face if they are confronted with very hot food and then cannot eat it. Perhaps they will relax when they know that there are also many Indians who prefer their food 'mild'. It is not the chili pepper which makes Indian food Indian. After all, the Thais,

Mexicans, Nigerians, and many others use it as well. It is the preparation and combination of whole or freshly ground spices which makes Indian foods unique.

There is another slight misconception even among knowledgeable Englishmen, which is that most Indian food is cooked in *ghee*, and that *ghee* is clarified butter. Actually, there are two kinds of *ghee*. The *usli ghee*, or 'real ghee', is indeed clarified butter, but if you consider India as a whole, it is very rarely used. In a nation where milk and butter are luxuries, cooking in *usli ghee* for the masses is unthinkable. Most people keep a small jar of *usli ghee* in their kitchen and use it occasionally on *chapatis* or *dal*, for cooking special dishes, or for religious and medicinal purposes. (I remember when at the age of twelve I had my ears pierced, for a month my mother applied hot fomentations of *usli ghee* and turmeric to my tortured earlobes!) In the western state of Punjab, however, *usli ghee*, butter, buttermilk, and milk are used much more frequently. The Punjabis, a tall, strong people, tend to believe that their enterprising spirit and immense energy come from the meat, corn bread, mustard greens, and dairy products they consume, and in some households it is quite common to give each child a daily spoonful of *usli ghee* pretty much in the same way that English parents pop vitamin pills into their children's mouths.

The other *ghee*, the one that is more commonly used, is made up of various vegetable oils. It is sold under various brand names—Dalda and Palm being the most popular—and can be purchased in large cans. In my own family we always used this vegetable *ghee* because my father insisted that *usli ghee* was too rich for a daily diet.

The cooking medium that is used almost as frequently as vegetable *ghee* is oil. It is cheap and excellent for deep frying. Also, different states show their individuality by using local oils—coconut oil in Kerala, mustard oil in Bengal, and peanut or sesame oil in various parts of North India.

In the last few years India, like most other nations, has become increasingly aware of the possible harm that can be caused by saturated fats. They are said to contain saturated oils and are therefore being rejected in favour of peanut oil, mustard oil, and other unsaturated oil mixtures. For this reason, I have used vegetable oil as the cooking medium in most of my recipes. You can use peanut oil or any other unsaturated oil mixture that you prefer. If, however, you wish to use *usli ghee*, directions for making it can be found on page 42.

Newborn Indian infants do not, of course, start off life on spicy foods (I have been asked this question several times.) They thrive on mother's milk, like most other infants. I do remember one particular custom in our family, however. As soon as an infant is born, whether at home or in the hospital, my grandmother would come and write the sacred syllable 'OM' (I am) on its tongue, with a finger dipped in honey. Children develop the taste and desire for spicy foods rather slowly. Our standard excuse, as six-year-olds, when we didn't want to eat was that the cook had put some red pepper in our food by mistake. If my mother was the only one presiding at the table, we would generally get away with it, but sometimes my father would arrive and insist on tasting the food and then our ruse was discovered. At the age of six, I loved to put sugar on my bread, but by nine I had graduated to a thick layer of hot mango pickle.

Children in Britain are always being told not to eat too many sweets. We were always being told not to eat too many sour things like tamarinds, raw mangoes, and *aam papar* (*aam papar* is made with sour mangoes, and the tastiest variety looks like thick, dirty brown leather). Even though our garden was full of fruit trees, the only ones that bore fruit were the mulberry and mango trees. We weren't interested in the mulberries because they were sweet; we left those to the old folks. But the raw mangoes were attacked and seldom given a chance to ripen. The best time to steal the mangoes was mid-afternoon when the temperature was 110 degrees and most of the household napped in air-cooled comfort. Often we would climb the mango tree equipped with knife, salt, and pepper. We would then picnic on the boughs, along with the twittering sparrows.

My father and mother were both born in the heart of the old city of Delhi, where the streets are so narrow that a man and a cow can barely pass each other. Most of the old town houses there are three or four floors high and are built around an inner courtyard. They have many small rooms, niches for closets, and no view, except other houses, other courtyards, other floors. On all the floors are balconies, running around the courtyard. When my paternal grandfather had become a successful barrister and had returned from his travels abroad, being an adventurous and ambitious man, he decided to move out of the area and bought himself a garden estate on the banks of the Jumna. But my mother's people stayed on in the old city. Every now and then my mother would take us to visit her family. Here I must rather shamefacedly admit that I felt, in those days, that I had very little in common with my old-city cousins. I loved to go there because of the food, which was superb—the best Kayasth (the name of my community) food one could ever hope to have. There were not many servants in this house, and all the cooking was done by the women, squatting on the kitchen floor. The odours would draw me to the kitchen door, where I would stand, first on one foot, then another, watching and sniffing. I wanted to go inside, but the kitchen was tiny and I would have had to take my shoes off— which was always difficult because of my mother's tight, well-knotted shoe-lacing techniques. So I would stand, peering from the outside, until my aunt, a gentle woman with large teeth, would tell me to go and play on the roof. I would do as she said, but eventually the odour of mushrooms cooking would draw me down again.

Sunset signalled the approach of dinner. A large cotton rug was unfolded in the courtyard. On this was spread a clean cotton sheet. Food was brought in on serving plates and placed in the centre of the sheet. I always liked to carry in my favourite dishes, so I could look at them longer. Everyone sat around the food. Unfortunately, the men ate first and the women served them. I would watch my favourite dish of mushrooms, which I *loved*, being devoured by greedy males. As I took the empty plate ro refill it for them, I would pray that at least *some* would be left for us. Finally our turn came. Fresh food was put on the serving plates and the women and girls would eat. We ate directly from the serving plate, breaking off a piece of bread from one plate and dipping it into another. My favourite mushrooms were obtainable only briefly during the rainy season. They were cooked with onions, garlic, tomatoes, cumin, coriander, turmeric, and a lot of hot red pepper. We ate them with *pooris*, an unleavened whole-wheat bread, round and puffed with hot air. We would also have potatoes, boiled first and then cooked with coriander, cumin, fenugreek, turmeric, onions, garlic, ginger, and yogurt. There would be lamb, prepared in the best Moghul tradition—with saffron, cardamoms, and nutmeg. And there were always pickles called water pickles because the pickling base in not oil or vinegar but water. To make them, green marrows (long and pale green), turnips, carrots, or watermelon rinds are blanched or put raw into a large earthenware container, together with crushed mustard seeds, salt, and, of course, water. The container is lightly covered, and the pickle is allowed to mature for one to two weeks. Even the liquid is totally irresistible.

Childhood taste habits never completely die out. They seem to leave their mark on us and often dictate the areas that we are willing to explore or not explore as adults. That is why I feel, rather strongly, that children should be exposed to not only the best foods but also foods of as many different countries as possible. Culinary insularity is really nothing more than a set of stubborn taste habits. And the best way to break these habits is through enlightened exposure at an early age. You'd be surprised at what some children are willing to try if adults are not sitting there looking apprehensive. I've had my daughters' non-Indian friends drop by and eat, with great relish, all sorts of Indian foods, including betel nuts! I keep

23

my brass betel box in the living room. By now I am quite accustomed to seeing my daughters' friends come through the front door, say hello, walk straight to the betel box, rifle it, scattering seeds all over the floor, and then calmly walk on to the children's room, munching away like any Indian child. They seem to love the cauliflower cooked with fresh ginger and the chicken cooked with whole spices, and the marinated butterflied leg of lamb is, of course, an all-time favourite. One group of girls astonished me by eating (and enjoying) some hot mango pickle! All these children are under twelve years of age and belong to a pizza-Coke sorority that I have long despaired of.

I have tried to begin each chapter with simpler recipes which are easier to make and not too surprising to the palate.

At the end of each recipe I give serving suggestions in which I sometimes indicate if the dish is one which is likely to find popularity with children. Don't underestimate them. They'll surprise you. I remember so well one of our trips to Paris. We were seated in a restaurant slightly beyond our means, studying our menus, when my husband asked the children what appetizer they wanted. The eldest, who was supposed to be studying French, didn't want to admit that she couldn't understand a word of the menu, so she countered with, 'Well, what are *you* having?' My husband translated that section of the menu and said he was having snails and would they like to try that. Two children immediately turned up their noses and said, 'Eeeu', a favourite word in school that year. The third, whose glasses always seem to rest halfway down her nose, peered over them at my husband and asked, 'Do you *like* snails?' My husband said he liked them very much. She looked up at the ceiling for a good minute as if consulting someone in that direction and then said, 'Okay, I'll try 'em'. Well, she loved them and now orders snails at every opportunity she gets.

Try out these Indian dishes on your whole family. Take some of them with you on picnics. You'll be amazed to see how fast they are eaten up.

There is another group of people for whom this book should prove very useful. And they are vegetarians. One of the hardest things to find in this country is a good, balanced, fresh vegetarian meal. The choice seems to lie between macaroni and cheese, salads, raw or boiled vegetables, cheeses and fruit. The reason is that the English menu is planned around meat, poultry, or fish, the vegetables being just accessories. This country has not developed a vegetarian cuisine because, until now, there seemed to be no need for it. But a lot of young people are turning to vegetarianism because of a horror of all forms of killing, and many of the middle-aged are turning to it out of despair—they are wary of beef, pork, and lamb because of cholesterol, wary of fish because of mercury pollution, veal is ridiculously expensive, and just how many days a week can you eat chicken?

I happen to feel that Indian vegetarian food is perhaps the best in the world. It almost has to be. Our vegetarian population goes into the hundred millions! The Brahmins, upper-caste Hindus from both North and South India, rarely touch meat, fish, or eggs. The Buddhists and Jains abhor all killing, orthodox Jains going so far as to wear masks over their noses and mouths so as not to accidentally entrap some minute victim that strays in as they inhale. The poor in India are also generally vegetarian because meat is simply beyond their means.

The result of all this is that in the last few thousand years, Indians have developed a most balanced and varied vegetarian cuisine. The essential proteins in these meals are provided by the many *dals* (lentils, split peas, black-eyed peas, chickpeas, etc.) and by yogurt relishes and milk desserts. The variety is provided by the sheer number of vegetable dishes. Each is cooked with a different combination of spices—some with sauces, others 'dry', some vegetables cooked in combination with others, like potatoes, peas, and cauliflower, others grated and stuffed in bread, some boiled, some sautéed, some fried, some pickled and some puréed into fresh chutneys.

The longest chapter in this book is the one on vegetables. That, as well as the chapters on Rice; Breads; Chutneys, Pickles, and Other Relishes; and Desserts should provide enough material for vegetarians to make interesting and wholesome menus.

I also give, a little later, a list of sample menus both vegetarian and non-vegetarian. Use them if you feel you need initial guidance, but experiment and try any combination that strikes your fancy. Also, don't feel compelled to plunge into Indian cooking with a full-scale banquet. An Indian soup with your meal one day, a tomato chutney with your roast lamb the next, some sweet rice with your duck at the weekend—these are good beginnings. If you are in the habit of serving spaghetti and meat sauce quite often, try rice and *kheema* instead. It is a pleasant variation and equally simple.

All the dishes in this book can be made in standard English pots, saucepans, and frying-pans. It does help, however, to use good-quality heavy-bottomed pots, especially for rice. For making Indian bread a *tava*, a rounded iron plate, is very convenient, but you can use instead a cast-iron frying-pan. For deep frying we use a *karhai*, which is similar to a Chinese wok. Many kitchenware stores carry woks. If you can find one easily, do buy it. It is a worthwhile investment. If you cannot find one, don't be discouraged, as I will suggest substitutes whenever a *karhai* (or wok) is called for.

A word about the limitations of this book. If you are looking for an encyclopedic tome encompassing *all* Indian food, you certainly won't find it here. Such a task would have taken me at least twenty years, as I would have had to approach it slowly, region by region. What this book does offer you is the chance to understand and cook the food of one specific area—the region in and around Delhi, including the adjacent sections of Uttar Pradesh.

Since Delhi is a city and not a large province, you might consider knowing the food of this area alone as being rather limited. But that is not so. First of all, the best Indian food is that which is specifically regional. I would rather that you started with a thorough understanding of the cuisine and eating habits of one region than with a vague superficial understanding of the cuisines of the entire subcontinent. Second, even though Delhi is just one city, it is the capital and was, until the British threw them out in the nineteenth century, the seat of the great Moghul emperors. And it was in their royal kitchens that the Delhi cuisine was conceived. Because of the Moghuls' power and prestige, their cuisine was then aped, with interesting local variations, in the courts of the lesser maharajahs, rajahs, generals, and governors scattered across the nation.

The Moghuls were originally nomadic Tartars from the plains of Mongolia. They were so unused to living in permanent structures that the first palaces they built in India in the sixteenth and seventeenth centuries resembled gigantic tents but were made of red sandstone and marble. They were also unused to the heat, so they immediately set about building canals everywhere—they even had canals going through their bedrooms! They sent runners up to the Himalayas to bring them ice for their drinks, and in the summers the entire city—to the last courtesan—moved up to the royal gardens in the cool vale of Kashmir. The country they admired most was Persia. They had passed it on their way to India and had been awed by the glitter of courtly robes and the delicacy of the miniature paintings, and by the exquisite food they had been served. Much of it they introduced into their own courts, sending off to Persia and Afghanistan regularly for melons, pomegranates, plums, grapes, dates, and nuts.

But India has a way of influencing, if not overpowering, everything it comes in contact with. Very soon the mighty Moghuls were chewing the betel leaf, crying in ecstasy over the mango, adding more spices to their Persian meats, and relishing the vegetarian dishes prepared for them by their Hindu wives and mistresses. It was this combination of richly cooked Persian meats and rice (sometimes called Moghul food) with the local vegetarian styles that gave birth to what I call the Delhi cuisine.

Although this book basically contains the food of the Delhi region, I have, I must confess, cheated slightly to include a few recipes for foods which were cooked in our home but which originated in other states. I feel very attached to these dishes, and as this is essentially a personal book, I had no compunction about including things that have been adapted in my own kitchen.

I'm sure many readers are curious about just how different the other Indian cuisines really are. One tends to think of India as one large subcontinent almost the size of Europe (without Russia). It is divided into about twenty states and territories. (I say 'about' because the number keeps changing.) Each state has its own language, history, literature, dress, and culinary traditions. Transportation of fresh produce isn't particularly efficient, reliable, or cheap, so each area tends to eat what it produces locally. In some states like Kerala, Bengal, and Andhra Pradesh, the staple is rice, whereas in others like Punjab and Uttar Pradesh, the staple is wheat. Along the coast fish and seafood are eaten extensively and are often cooked in coconut milk. In the northern interior, where people see neither the sea nor coconut palms, they usually eat an unleavened whole-wheat bread with *dal* and vegetables.

In Bengal, I've had an entire meal consisting of five different lobster dishes served with rice, the most delicious being one in which the lobster was cooked with mustard seeds and freshly grated coconut. This was followed by Bengali sweets — tiny squares, rectangles, and balls, no bigger than a sugar lump, coloured pink, green, and yellow and made with milk, cheese, and sugar.

In Kashmir, where the people are often red-haired, green-eyed, and freckled, the staple diet is meat, fish, and rice. Meat and vegetables are dried during the summer months and stored to be used once the snow begins to fall and movement becomes restricted. The spices used are those which are thought to provide heat for the body—cardamom, cinnamon, cloves, black peppers, chilies. Even their tea is delicately spiced. Kashmiri food often has a red appearance owing to the liberal use of the Kashmiri chili, which is not very hot but provides flavour and colour. I've had meals in Srinagar in which every course was meat, including a mincemeat dessert.

Modern Bombay boasts of hundreds of instant products; the label on one reads: 'Instant Dal. SAVE time, labour, money. By adding only water, READY within three minutes'. Side by side with this evidence of 'progress', Gujarati-speaking people of Bombay still relish more traditional foods. One great favourite is a paper-thin bread, eaten with the pulp of the best seasonal mangoes. This bread is made by dipping two balls of whole-wheat dough into fat and flour, rolling them out together very thinly, and toasting them on a hot griddle. The two layers are then separated, making an even finer, lighter bread. Another favourite is *undhya* (meaning upside down). Whole, often unpeeled vegetables, coated with oil, red pepper, garlic, ginger, fenugreek, coriander, fennel, and cumin, are put into an earthenware pot and covered with moistened hay. The pot is then turned upside down over smouldering cinders.

In Madras, it is customary to eat on the floor, out of a banana leaf, which serves as a plate. A mountain of rice is piled on the leaf, and a visitor unaccustomed to the southern ways begins to wonder how he can ever find room for all that rice. The host's deft hands quickly make a crater-like hole in the mountaintop, and into this is poured the highly spiced hot *sambar* (yellow lentils, cooked with asafetida, fenugreek, coriander, cumin, turmeric, chilies, mustard seed, and tamarind, to which have been added sliced vegetables such as tomatoes, onions, and aubergine). This is eaten with great relish, the entire palm of the right hand, from fingertips to wrist, being used to transport the food from leaf to mouth. The Northerners tend to look down on the Southerners for what they consider to be rather messy eating habits. In the

North, the finicky pale when they see anyone soiling more than the top section of his fingers with food. I remember being scolded by my mother for letting the food slip from fingertip to mid-finger. Whenever that happened, she would say, 'Chhi, chhi, chhi' (dirty, dirty, dirty) and make me wash my hand. Whether we soil the digital end or the whole palm, one thing at least is generally true of all Indians: we like to eat with our hands. For this reason we have strict rules about washing hands and mouths before and after meals. This rule is followed meticulously by the poorest villager and the richest urbanite.

Some day, I hope, books will be written about all of India's cuisines—Gujarati food, Malayali food, Assamese food, Punjabi food, Maharashtrian food, Sindhi food, Bengali food, Goan food, Kashmiri food, Hyderabadi food, to name just a few. But until that happens, my book can introduce you to the smells and tastes which *I* grew up with as a child in Delhi and which I have struggled over the years to re-create in an English kitchen. These dishes, some traditional and some adapted to the produce in English supermarkets, you can now cook in your own homes instead of having to rely on second-rate eating places or the mercy of Indian acquaintances.

Two words of advice

Avoid using aluminium pans when cooking with any ingredients that have acidity.

If you aren't familiar with Indian cooking, it is wise to grind, measure, and set out *all* your ingredients before starting the cooking because so often parts of a recipe require that you work without interruption.

Sample menus

Kheema with fried onions
Green beans with onion paste
Moong dal
Rice with potatoes and cumin seeds
Yogurt with spinach
Chopped onions in vinegar
Gulab jamun · Fruit

Koftas (Indian meatballs)
Potatoes with asafetida and cumin
Rice with peas and whole spices or *Parathas*
Chana masaledar
Yogurt with tiny dumplings (boondi-ka-dahi)
Cucumber and tomato with lemon juice
Kheer · Fruit

Chicken cutlets
Sookhe aloo ('dry' potatoes)
Green beans with ginger
Rice with cauliflower and cumin seeds
Gulab jamun · Fruit

Chicken with tomato sauce and butter
Whole pea pods with cumin
Maya's potatoes
Chapati or Plain boiled rice
Cucumber *raita*
Malpua · Fruit

Prawn with dill and ginger
Crisp fried okra
Rice with spinach cooked in aromatic broth
Yogurt with potatoes
Tamarind chutney with bananas
Kheer · Fruit

'Butterflied' leg of lamb, marinated and barbecued
Green beans with onion paste
Rice with spinach
Cucumber and tomato with lemon juice
Kheer · Fruit

Pullao (rice with lamb)
Shrimp with peas and green coriander
Cauliflower with onion and tomato
Aubergine *bharta* (smoked aubergine)
Yogurt with potatoes
Chopped onions in vinegar
Kheer · Fruit

Tandoori chicken
Rice with cauliflower and cumin seeds
Naan
Whole unhulled *urad* and *rajma dal*
Onions pickled in vinegar
Cucumber and tomato with lemon juice
Kulfi · Fruit

Sea bass in green chutney
Cauliflower with ginger and green coriander
Buttered saffron rice
Sweet tomato chutney
Kulfi · Fruit

Pork chops à la Jaffrey
Green beans with onion paste
Sweet rice with carrots and raisins
Cucumber and tomato with lemon juice
Gajar-ka-halva · Fruit

Green peppers stuffed with kheema
Okra with onions
Plain boiled rice
Karhi (with *pakoris*)
Carrots pickled in oil
Gulab jamun · Fruit

Sindhi gosht (Sindhi meat)
Fried aubergines with sour green chutney
Cabbage with onions
Pooris or *Parathas*
Tomato and onion with lemon juice
Malpua · Fruit

Menu for a party

Koftas (Indian meatballs)
Pullao (rice with lamb)
Prawn with brown sauce
Cauliflower with ginger and green coriander
Whole unhulled *urad* and *rajma dal*
Yogurt with spinach
Cucumber and tomato with lemon juice
Tamarind chutney with bananas
Kheer · Fruit

Vegetarian

Green beans with onion paste
Fried aubergines with sour green chutney
Chickpeas with garlic and ginger
Rice with peas and whole spices
Cucumber and tomato with lemon juice
Kulfi · Fruit

Cabbage leaves stuffed with potatoes
Green beans with ginger
Black-eyed peas (*lobhia*)
Rice with spinach
Yogurt with tiny dumplings (*boondi-ka-dahi*)
Kheer · Fruit

Okra with onions
Cauliflower with onion and tomato
Pyazwale sookhe aloo ('dry' potatoes with onions)
Lentils
Parathas
Fresh mint chutney with fruit
Cucumber and tomato with lemon juice
Fried dates · Fruit

Cauliflower with ginger and green coriander
Aubergine *bharta* (smoked aubergine)
Mushrooms with cumin and asafetida
Sookhe aloo ('dry' potatoes)
Moong dal
Pooris
Cucumber *raita*
Gulab jamun · Fruit

Potatoes in thick sauce
Green beans with onion paste
Mushrooms with cumin and asafetida
Basmati rice with spices and saffron
Masoor dal with vegetables
Yogurt with roasted aubergine (*baigan-ka-bharta*)
Tamarind chutney with bananas
Fruit

Chickpeas with garlic and ginger
Cauliflower with onion and tomato
Bhaturas
Yogurt with potatoes
Carrot 'water' pickle or Onions pickled in
   vinegar
Yogurt with spinach
Malpua

Karhi (with *pakoris*)
Cauliflower with ginger and green coriander
Stuffed whole okra
Plain boiled rice or Plain *basmati* rice
Tomato and onion with lemon juice
Tamarind chutney with bananas
Gajar-ka-halva · Fruit

Menu for a party

Cauliflower with ginger and green coriander
Whole pea pods with cumin
Cabbage with onions
Mushrooms with cumin and asafetida
New potatoes cooked in their jackets
Fried aubergines with sour green chutney
Rice with spinach
Whole unhulled *urad* and *rajma dal* with Fried
   onion rings for garnishing
Yogurt with tiny dumplings (*boondi-ka-dahi*)
Sweet tomato chutney
Cucumber raita
Kheer · Fruit

A note on flavourings

Most of the spices used for Indian cooking are available in English supermarkets. It is best to buy spices whole, as they tend to retain their flavour for longer periods. They can be ground at home in an electric blender or coffee-grinder in small quantities and then stored in tightly covered containers. (A mortar and pestle can be used to crush spices, but it will not grind them finely.)

There are, however, certain spices and ingredients which are unavailable in local supermarkets. These can generally be found in or obtained by mail from the Bombay Emporium, Radiant House, Pegamoid Road, London N18, telephone 01-803 4271.

There are also some special herbs which give Indian foods their characteristic flavours—like green coriander and ginger. The best places to find such ingredients are Chinese, Middle Eastern, or Indian grocery stores.

AMCHOOR   Raw mango, dried and ground. It makes food tangy and sour. In North India it is used as freely as lemon is in American cooking. It also comes in dried slices.

ASAFETIDA   A smelly resin which is used in very small quantities for vegetarian foods. It is available as a lump, or broken into pebbles, or powdered. The lump variety is generally the purest. Break off tiny chips (with a hammer, if necessary) and keep the rest in a tightly covered jar.

CARDAMOM   Three varieties are available in England: the greenish pod and the slightly plumper whitish pod are the most common. The seeds in the greenish pod are generally more fragrant. The cardamom pod is sometimes used whole, and at other times the skin is discarded and the seeds are ground (a clean pepper mill is excellent for this) and sprinkled over meats and desserts. There is also a large black cardomom which is used for certain rice and meat dishes. When this is unavailable, either variety of the smaller cardamom can be substituted. For cardamom as a mouth freshener, see page 335.

CAYENNE PEPPER   Same as ground red pepper. Use with discretion.

CINNAMON   Indians use both stick and ground cinnamon. Stick cinnamon is used whole in certain meat and rice dishes, whereas ground cinnamon is used in meat sauces and vegetables.

COCONUT   When you buy a coconut, make sure it is not cracked. Shake it to make sure it contains liquid. Even though this liquid is later discarded, it ensures a moist inside. To open, hit the coconut with a hammer and pry it apart. Get the meat out by sliding a sharp knife between the shell and the meat. Before grating the coconut, cut off the dark brown crust on the meat. To roast grated coconut, place it in a heavy frying-pan (iron is best) over a medium flame. Stir for 3 to 4 minutes or until it begins to turn brown.

CORIANDER   Coriander seeds can be used whole, ground, or roasted. To roast coriander, place desired amount of ground coriander in a heavy frying-pan (iron is best) over a medium flame. Stir for 2 to 3 minutes or until coriander turns a few shades darker. Be careful not to burn it. When buying ground coriander, purchase in small quantities.

CORIANDER LEAVES   Called small *cilantro* in Spanish shops, fresh coriander or fresh *dhania* in Indian food shops, and Chinese parsley in Chinese shops, it is used in our food as a herb and a garnish. If unavailable, Italian or ordinary parsley can be substituted. If you have a herb garden, you can grow your own fresh coriander by planting coriander seeds and waiting until the plants are about 10 inches high. Keep the leaves refrigerated in a plastic bag. *N.B.* Dried coriander powder cannot be substituted for fresh green coriander.

CUMIN Indians use this spice whole, ground, or roasted. To roast cumin, place desired amount of whole seeds in heavy frying-pan (iron is best) over a medium flame. Stir 2 or 3 minutes or until seeds turn a darker brown. Remove from heat. The cumin can now be ground on an Indian grinding stone if you happen to have one, or it can be crushed just as easily with a mortar and pestle or with a rolling pin. It is best when freshly roasted, but you could keep it a few days in a tightly covered jar. In North India, ground roasted cumin is sprinkled over many yogurt relishes, snacks, and cooked vegetables. When buying ground cumin, purchase in small quantities. There is also an expensive, aromatic, black cumin seed.

DRY RED PEPPERS Dry red peppers or dry red chilies are available in many sizes with just as many variations in their degrees of potency. The kind I have used in my recipes are about an inch long and *very* hot. I generally use them whole. Remember that red peppers are not essential to Indian food. If you don't like them you can use fewer than suggested or none at all. If whole red peppers are used in cooking, it is a good idea to remove them before serving. They are deadly if bitten into!

FENNEL The fennel seed is really a larger, plumper sister of the anise seed. It is excellent in vegetables. It is also roasted and used as an after-dinner freshener—see page 335.

FENUGREEK Fenugreek seeds are yellow in colour and rather flat. Since their taste borders on bitterness, very few are used at a time. They are excellent with aubergine and potatoes.

GARAM MASALA This is a mixture of several 'hot' spices, generally prepared ahead of time in small quantities and used as needed to flavour meats and vegetables. It can be bought in delicatessens, but has a fresher taste if you grind it yourself. To make about 3 tablespoons, you will need:

- **1 tablespoon cardamom seeds**
- **1 2-inch stick cinnamon**
- **1 teaspoon black peppercorns**
- **1 teaspoon black cumin seeds**
- **1 teaspoon whole cloves**
- **¼ of an average-sized nutmeg**

Combine all ingredients and grind very fine, in a coffee-grinder reserved for spices. (If you want to make your *garam masala* less hot, decrease the amount of black peppercorns and increase the cumin proportionately.) Store in a tightly covered container, away from sunlight and dampness. If carefully stored, this *garam masala* can be kept for a couple of months.

GHEE *Ghee* is the cooking medium used in many parts of India. There are two kinds of *ghee*. *Usli ghee* or clarified butter is used rarely, partly because of its expense and partly because many Indians consider it 'heavy'. The more commonly used *ghee* is a mixture of various vegetable oils. See page 20 in the Introduction. I tend to use unsaturated oils for most of my cooking. Many Indians use peanut oil or mustard oil. Use whatever you prefer. If you wish to make *usli ghee* or clarified butter, here is how you do it: Melt butter. Pour off the clear liquid, discarding the milky residue. Boil the clear liquid for a minute or two. Cool. Store, covered, in the refrigerator.

GINGER This is a tan-skinned, knobbly rhizome with a sharp, pungent taste, available in Indian and Chinese food shops. Some delicatessens carry it as well. It is used for making meat dishes, vegetables, and chutneys. Ginger is generally peeled and then grated or ground. It is easier to grate it if you don't break off the needed section but rather grate it off the whole piece instead. To grind it, chop it coarsely and place in electric blender with a little water. To store ginger, cover it well with plastic wrap and keep in the refrigerator. It is good until it begins to mould. Another way to keep it is to plant it (bury it) in sandy soil. Water it infrequently. It not only stays fresh this way but also sprouts fresh knobs. Cut off what you need and put the rest back in the soil. Dried ginger 'root' (called so mistakenly) is bottled and put out by major spice companies. This can be used as a second-best substitute. It is preferable to powdered ginger, which in India is considered to be so different from fresh ginger that it is called by another name altogether. Follow the instructions on the bottle for presoaking, which must be done a few hours before you plan to cook.

GREEN CHILIES Fresh, hot green peppers or chilies are available in some Chinese, Indian, Spanish, and Italian shops. Since chilies vary in their strength, caution must be exercised in using them. The hottest part of the chilies is their seeds, and there are more seeds near the stem. Ideally, each chili should be sampled before being used. You can cut it in half and take the tiniest bite from its centre. If it is hot use it sparingly. Most Indians can generally gauge the hotness of a chili by breaking it in two and just smelling it. As a substitute, tinned Mexican *jalapeños* or cayenne pepper can be used. Neither has the taste of a green chili, but both are hot. (See instructions for substitutions in individual recipes.)

KALONJI These are black onion seeds which are used occasionally for meat dishes and often for vegetables. If you can't find them, leave them out of the recipe.

KARI LEAVES Fresh leaves from the *Kari* tree, used as flavouring. There are really no substitutes for this. The dried leaves, more freely available, seem to lack both aroma and flavour.

MUSTARD SEEDS We generally use black mustard seeds, but if you cannot find them, yellow mustard seeds may be substituted. For some recipes, mustard seeds need to be crushed. This is best done with a heavy mortar and pestle or an electric coffee-grinder.

NUTMEG Buy whole nutmeg and store it in a tightly closed jar. Use a nutmeg grater and grate whenever needed.

POPPY SEEDS We use the white poppy seeds. They are generally ground before being cooked. To facilitate grinding, roast them first. Place them in a heavy frying pan (iron is best) over a medium flame. Stir them around for 3 to 4 minutes. Now they can be ground with an Indian grinding stone or in a coffee-grinder. If white poppy seeds cannot be found, do without them.

SAFFRON This very expensive stigma of the crocus flower is used in Moghlai meat and rice dishes as well as in desserts. Ideally, saffron stigmas or 'leaf' saffron should be lightly roasted in a hot frying-pan, crumbled, and allowed to soak in a tablespoon or so of warm milk before being used.

TAMARIND PASTE The tamarind is a kind of bean, which grows on large trees. For commercial use it is peeled, seeded, and pressed into a lump. Indians use its paste to add a special kind of tartness to their foods. Lump tamarind is available in Indian and Middle Eastern groceries in Britain. These shops also sell a bottled tamarind paste, but this is often extremely fermented. To make your own tamarind paste, break or pull a golf-ball-sized piece from the lump tamarind and soak it in $\frac{1}{4}$ pint hot water for 3 to 4 hours or overnight. Use a small, non-metallic cup or bowl. Press pulp through a strainer and reserve. (You may need to add extra water to the strainer in order to dislodge all the pulp.) Discard whatever is left in the strainer. Covered tamarind pulp can be stored several days in the refrigerator. Lump tamarind should be wrapped in a plastic bag and stored in the refrigerator. It will last for months.

TURMERIC This spice is really a boiled-down root which is

available in small lumps in India but only in its ground form in Britain. It is this yellow spice which gives colouring to a lot of our foods. It burns easily, so care should be taken when cooking with it.

VARK These are extremely fine, delicate sheets of real silver (or gold) foil, used for garnishing. (They *are* eaten.) When you buy them, generally each sheet is between 2 layers of tissue paper. *You cannot lift a sheet by picking it up with your hands:* it will disintegrate or fly away. Remove one layer of tissue paper carefully, leaving the *vark* on the other sheet. Slide your hand under the paper and invert the *vark* on the food. Garnish thinly, as you should not really be able to taste the *vark*. The effect is prettier when the *vark* lies on the food in an unbroken sheet, but it's all right if it disintegrates slightly. *Vark* is available only at Indian stores. Since it can tarnish, like any real silver, it should be stored in a dark, airtight container.

Kitchen utensils &
other equipment

Here is a list of some utensils which are found only in Indian kitchens.

CHIMTA These flat, smooth-edged, long tongs are used for everything from picking up live coals to turning over bread.

KARHAI This is a utensil for deep frying. Like the Chinese wok, it is curved at the bottom and very wide at the top, resembling half-moon. It can be made of cast iron, aluminium, stainless steel, or brass.

KATORI Small bowl made out of gold, silver, stainless steel, or aluminium, used to serve individual portions of meat, vegetables, and *dals*. Often several filled *katoris* are arranged on a *thali* and the *thali* is then placed before the diner.

MUTKA Round pot of half-baked clay used for storing water and excellent for making 'water pickles'.

PARAAT This is a large, wide-rimmed brass tray, used for kneading bread. It is also used as a serving tray at weddings.

SIL BATTA The North Indian grinding stone comes in 2 sections. The *sil*, or larger stone, is about a foot long, 9 inches wide, and 2 inches high. It is pockmarked with tiny, shallow ridges. Food is placed on this larger stone for grinding. The grinding is done by the *batta*, the second, smaller, half-moon-shaped stone, which is about 6 inches long and $1\frac{1}{2}$ inches thick. (*N.B.* The sizes and shapes of Indian grinding stones vary in the different states.)

TANDOOR   A large clay oven utilizing coal or wood as fuel and used for baking chicken, fish, meat, lentils, and breads. Very popular in the Punjab.

TAVA   This is a slightly curved, cast-iron plate, useful for making breads and patties.

THALI OR THAL   Gold, silver, brass, or aluminium tray used both for serving and as a plate. The Bohris of Gujarat place a large *thal* on a stool and use it as a table.

Soups &
Appetizers

SOUPS

Mulligatawny soup
White soup (safed sarvo)
Dal soup
Potato soup
Cold yogurt soup

APPETIZERS

Khatte aloo (sour potatoes)
Vegetable pakoris
Pappadums, or papars
Seekh kabab flat style
Left-over ham on toast
Pacific king prawns on toothpicks
Whole-wheat samosas
Cocktail koftas
Grilled chicken strips

SEE ALSO

Vegetables stuffed with kheema (pages 80–82)

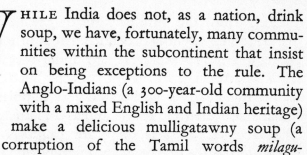

WHILE India does not, as a nation, drink soup, we have, fortunately, many communities within the subcontinent that insist on being exceptions to the rule. The Anglo-Indians (a 300-year-old community with a mixed English and Indian heritage) make a delicious mulligatawny soup (a corruption of the Tamil words *milagu-tannir*, meaning 'pepper water') with meat and chickpea flour, and the Bohris of Gujarat make a superb 'white soup' (*safed sarvo*) with goat's meat and milk.

The appetizers you will find in this chapter are those among the Indian 'snack' foods that can be most conveniently eaten with drinks—triangular *samosas*, filled with meat or potatoes, vegetable fritters, and minced meat *kababs*. *Kababs*, often sprinkled with finely sliced onion rings, are favourites among Indian Scotch drinkers. The North Indian word for alcoholic beverages is *sharab*, and it is very interesting that the North Indian label for a man who drinks and eats well is *sharabi-kababi*!

Mulligatawny soup

Serves 4

Judging from the Tamil origin of the name 'mulligatawny' (see page 51), one might deduce that it originated in the Madras region 100 to 300 years ago under the benevolent gaze of British patronage. British in concept but Indian in its ingredients, this hearty soup became very popular with the Anglo-Indians scattered all across India, and there are probably as many recipes for it as there are Anglo-Indian families. My favourite was the one made by a family who eventually decided to migrate to Australia. The day before their departure they came to our house to say goodbye. I remember that we all sat out on the lawn and I begged them to leave their recipe for mulligatawny soup with me. This is their recipe.

4 cloves garlic, peeled and chopped

a piece of fresh ginger, about ½-inch cube, peeled and chopped

½ lb boneless lamb (from shoulder or leg), with fat removed, and cut into ¾-inch cubes

2 tbs vegetable oil

1 tbs white poppy seeds, roasted and ground (see page 44)

½ tsp ground coriander

½ tsp ground cumin

¼ tsp ground turmeric

½ tsp salt (more if the broth is unsalted)

⅛ tsp cayenne pepper (optional)

⅛ tsp freshly ground black pepper

2 tbs chickpea flour (*besan*)

1 pint chicken broth (tinned or homemade)

1 tbs lemon juice

2–3 tbs cooked rice, or 1–1½ tbs uncooked rice (optional)

Put the garlic and ginger into the container of an electric blender with 3 tablespoons of water. Blend at high speed until you have a smooth paste. Set aside.

Pat dry the pieces of lamb. Heat the oil in a 2-quart pot over medium-high flame, and add the meat. Turn, and fry until the pieces are lightly browned on all sides. Remove with slotted spoon and set aside. Turn the heat off.

To the same pot, add the paste from the blender, the roasted and ground poppy seeds, the coriander, cumin, and turmeric. Turn the heat to medium, and fry, stirring constantly, for about a minute. Turn heat to low.

Now add the browned meat and any juice that may have accumulated, the salt, cayenne, and black pepper. Stir and leave on low flame.

Combine chickpea flour and 4 tablespoons water in a bowl, mixing thoroughly until you have a smooth paste. Slowly add the chicken broth, stirring as you do so. Pour this mixture over the meat in the pot. Turn heat to high and bring soup to the boil. Add uncooked rice if you are using it. Cover, lower heat, and simmer gently for half an hour or until meat is tender. Stir in the lemon juice.

If you are using cooked rice, mix it into the soup just before serving. Pour the soup into a tureen or into individual bowls. Mulligatawny soup can be served with both Indian and Western-style meals. Since it is thick and fairly filling, it can be a main course for lunch or a light supper followed by a green salad and fruit.

White soup
(safed sarvo)

Serves 4–6

This relatively unknown but delicious soup is made by the Bohris of Gujarat. It is brought to the table in a large serving bowl. The eldest lady of the house then asks how many people want their soup flavoured with lemon, and she squeezes fresh lemon over one section, leaving the rest plain. Next, she ladles the soup into small Chinese-style bowls, the lemony part of the soup going to those who asked for it. The white colour comes from the milk and almonds (or cashews, if you like).

4 cloves garlic, peeled and chopped

a piece of fresh ginger, about $\frac{1}{2}$-inch cube

$1\frac{1}{2}$ lbs neck of lamb, with bone left in, cut into 1–$1\frac{1}{2}$-inch cubes

1 medium-sized onion, finely chopped

$1\frac{3}{4}$ pints beef broth (tinned or fresh; do not use bouillon)

$\frac{1}{2}$ tsp salt (more if beef broth is unsalted)

1 bay leaf

1 tbs blanched slivered almonds (or unroasted cashews)

$\frac{1}{2}$ pint milk

4 tbs whole-wheat flour (use plain flour as substitute)

$\frac{1}{8}$ tsp cayenne pepper (optional)

1 tbs vegetable oil

$\frac{1}{8}$ tsp whole cumin seeds

Garnish

2 tbs fresh mint leaves, chopped (parsley may be substituted)

1 lemon cut into 6 wedges

Put the garlic and ginger into the container of an electric blender, along with 4 tablespoons water. Blend at high speed until you have a smooth paste.

In a largish pot, combine the meat, chopped onions, garlic and ginger paste, beef broth, salt, and bay leaf. Bring to the boil. Cover, and simmer gently for $1\frac{1}{2}$ hours.

Meanwhile, soak the blanched almonds in the milk.

In a small, heavy-bottomed frying-pan, dry-roast the whole-wheat flour over a medium flame, stirring constantly until the flour is 2 or 3 shades darker (this should take about 3 minutes). Then turn off flame and pour flour into a medium-sized bowl.

When the soup has cooked for an hour and a half, take out a teacup of the boiling liquid and mix it well with the roasted whole-wheat flour in the bowl. When the mixture is smooth, pour it back into the pot of soup.

Put the milk and almonds into the blender and blend at high speed until you have a thin, smooth paste. Add to the simmering soup.

Taste the soup. Add cayenne if you desire.

Heat the oil in a small frying-pan over a medium flame. When hot, put in the whole cumin seeds, stirring for a few seconds until seeds begin to pop and darken, then add to the soup. Stir soup again. Turn off heat and leave soup covered.

To serve: This soup can be served with or without the pieces of meat (remove bay leaf though!). Garnish with chopped mint leaves and serve lemon wedges on the side.

Dal soup

Serves 8

My mother used to make this mild-flavoured 'split-pea' soup. The only spices in it were cloves, peppercorns, and turmeric. It was served with lemon wedges and homemade croutons.

10 oz green or yellow split
  peas, washed
2½ pints chicken broth
  (tinned or homemade)
24 black peppercorns and

15 whole cloves (tied in
  cheesecloth)
½ tsp ground turmeric
½–¾ tsp salt (more if broth
  is unsalted)

Garnish

8 lemon wedges
croutons made from 6 slices
  of slightly stale bread and

enough vegetable oil to
cover ½–¾ inch in a 10-inch
frying-pan

Combine the split peas and chicken broth in a pot and bring to the boil. Remove scum from the top.

Add the spices in the cheesecloth, the turmeric, and the salt. Cover, lower heat, and simmer gently for 1 to 1½ hours or until peas are tender. Remove cheesecloth from soup, squeeze its juices into soup, and discard. Check salt.

Press the soup through a strainer, using the back of a wooden spoon, or put it through a food mill. If the soup seems too thick, add a little water.

To serve: Heat soup. Serve in bowls, garnished with a lemon wedge. Pass around croutons on the side.

To make croutons: (These can be prepared ahead of time.)
Remove crusts and cut slices of bread into ½-inch cubes.

Heat oil in frying-pan over medium flame, and put in a third of the croutons. Fry for 3 or 4 minutes, turning them around, until they are golden brown. Lift out with slotted spoon and leave to drain on paper towels. Prepare the rest of the croutons in two more batches, and leave to drain.

Potato soup

Serves 4

1 tbs vegetable oil
a pinch of ground asafetida
  or a $\frac{1}{16}$-inch pebble broken
  from the chunk asafetida
¼ tsp whole cumin seeds
2 medium-sized potatoes,
  peeled and quartered

2 tbs tomato purée
¼ tsp ground turmeric
1¼ tsp salt
⅛ tsp cayenne pepper
  (optional)

Heat the oil in a 3-quart pot over a medium flame, put in the asafetida and the cumin, and stir once. In a few seconds, when the cumin seeds begin to sizzle, add the quartered potatoes, tomato purée, turmeric, salt, and cayenne. Stir, and continue to fry for 2 minutes.

Add 1¾ pints of water and bring to the boil. Cover and simmer gently for 45 minutes.

Turn off heat and lift cover. Mash potatoes coarsely with a potato masher or with the back of a slotted spoon.

To serve: Pour soup into small bowls or *katoris* (see page 47) and serve.

Cold yogurt soup

Serves 4

Here is a very refreshing summer soup.

½ pint plain yogurt
¼ pint double cream
⅓–½ tsp salt
a sprinkling of freshly
  ground black pepper

4 tbs peeled and grated
  cucumber
10–12 fresh mint leaves,
  finely chopped

Combine all ingredients in bowl with ¼ pint of cold water.
Mix well. Cover and chill for several hours until ready to serve.

To serve: Serve on hot days in small chilled bowls or *katoris*
(see page 47).

Khatte aloo
(sour potatoes)

Serves 10–12

This is an adaptation of a street-side snack to be found in
different forms all over North India.

7 medium-sized potatoes,
  boiled ahead of time, and
  set aside for at least 2
  hours to cool
1½ tsp salt (or to taste)
2–3 tbs lemon juice (or to
  taste)

2 tsp ground roasted cumin
  (see page 41)
¼ tsp freshly ground pepper
¼–½ tsp cayenne pepper
2 tbs finely chopped fresh
  green coriander

Peel the cooled potatoes and dice them into ½-inch cubes.
Place in large bowl. Add remaining ingredients. Mix well.
Check to see if salt and lemon juice are in correct proportion.

To serve: Place potatoes on platter and stick with toothpicks.
Serve with drinks.

Vegetable pakoris

Serves 6–8

These *pakoris* are vegetable fritters—similar to Japanese tempura. They are generally eaten with tea, but there is no reason why they cannot be served with drinks. I have specified potatoes in this recipe, but you could use any of the following instead:

1-inch flowerets of cauliflower (a small head), or $\frac{1}{16}$-inch-thick onion rings (4 medium-sized onions), or Italian peppers, cut in half lengthwise ($\frac{1}{2}$-$\frac{3}{4}$ lb)

You can also make a plate of mixed *pakoris*, using different vegetables. Chickpea flour is very light, so do weigh it.

The batter

4 oz chickpea flour (*besan*), sifted
$\frac{1}{4}$ tsp salt
$\frac{1}{4}$ tsp ground turmeric
$\frac{1}{4}$ tsp ground cumin

$\frac{1}{4}$ tsp baking soda
$\frac{1}{8}$ tsp freshly ground pepper
$\frac{1}{8}$ tsp cayenne pepper (optional)

The filling

3 medium-sized potatoes, peeled (or other vegetables —see above)
vegetable oil, enough for $2\frac{1}{2}$–3 inches in wok,

karhai (see page 47), or other utensil for deep frying
salt and pepper for sprinkling on cooked pakoris

Put the chickpea flour in a bowl. Gradually mix in about 7 fl. oz. water, until you have a thickish batter—thick enough to coat the vegetables. Add the other batter ingredients and mix well.

Cut the potatoes into rounds $\frac{1}{16}$ inch thick, and put into a bowl of cold water.

Heat oil over a low flame until hot but not smoking. Take a few potato slices at a time, wipe them dry, and dip them in the batter. Now drop them into the oil. Fry slowly, 7 to 10 minutes on each side, until they are cooked through and have turned a golden-brown. Remove with slotted spoon and drain on paper towels. Sprinkle with salt and pepper. Do all *pakoris* this way, never putting in more at one time than your deep-frying utensil will hold in one layer.

To serve: Serve *pakoris* while they are crisp and hot with either the Fresh Green Chutney with Coriander Leaves and Yogurt or Fresh Mint Chutney with Fruit. The chutney is used as a dip. If you're feeling lazy, tomato ketchup or Chinese duck sauce or a combination of soy sauce, white vinegar, grated fresh ginger, and a dash of Tabasco can be used as alternative dips.

Pappadums, or papars

Serves 8–10

Pappadums (as they are called in the South) or *papars* (as they are called in the North) are wafers, usually made out of a *dal* dough which is rolled out and dried. (You can also buy *sago* wafers and potato wafers, but they are less popular.) *Papars* can be bought in delicatessens in two basic varieties—spiced and unspiced. The spiced ones often have a liberal sprinkling of crushed black pepper in them. They are deep-fried in hot oil and served at cocktail parties. The frying takes just a few seconds. *Papars* cannot be fried too far in advance, as any moisture in the air tends to make them go limp and they should be crisp. *Papars* come in several sizes. The large ones can be broken in half and then fried. They expand a bit as they are cooked. Before you set out to make them, put a large platter, well lined with paper towels, beside the stove to drain the *papars*.

10 papars or pappadums
oil for deep-frying, enough
    for 2 inches in 10-inch
    frying-pan

Heat oil in frying-pan over medium flame. When hot, put in one *papar*. It should sizzle and expand immediately. (If it doesn't, your oil is not hot enough!) Turn it over, leave for a few seconds, and remove with slotted spoon. Place on platter with paper towels and drain. Do all *papars* this way, one at a time. If they begin to brown, your oil is too hot. Turn down the heat. The *papars* should retain their yellow colour.

To serve: Serve warm or at room temperature with drinks.

Seekh kabab,
flat style

Serves 8–10

This version of the ground meat *kabab* is excellent to serve with drinks and to take out on picnics. The meat and spices can be combined a night in advance and left, covered, in the refrigerator.

½ **medium-sized onion,**
    peeled and chopped
4 cloves garlic, peeled and
    chopped

3 tbs lemon juice
4 tbs chickpea flour (*besan*)
2½ lbs minced lamb or beef,
    minced three times

a piece of fresh ginger,
  about 1-inch cube, peeled
  and chopped
20 whole black peppercorns
10 whole cloves
seeds from 8 cardamom pods
1 fresh hot green chili,
  sliced (optional)
½ tsp ground nutmeg
½ tsp ground cinnamon

1 teacup (loosely packed)
  chopped fresh green
  coriander
1 tsp ground cumin
1 tsp ground coriander
1½ tsp salt
½ tsp cayenne pepper
  (optional – use as desired)
1 egg, beaten
5 tbs melted butter

In the container of an electric blender, combine the chopped onions, garlic, ginger, peppercorns, cloves, cardamom seeds, green chili, nutmeg, cinnamon, and lemon juice. Blend at high speed until you have a smooth paste.

Heat a small iron frying-pan over medium flame. Put in the chickpea flour and stir until it is 2 or 3 shades darker. Remove from heat.

In a large bowl, combine the meat, the chopped green coriander, the contents of the blender container, the cumin, coriander, salt, cayenne, and roasted chickpea flour. Mix well with your hands. Cover and refrigerate until ready to grill (overnight if convenient).

Take meat out of refrigerator 45 minutes before serving.

Preheat grill.

Add beaten egg to meat and mix well.

Line 10-by-15-inch baking tray with aluminium foil, and brush it with half the melted butter.

Spread the meat mixture in the tray: it should be ⅓ to ½ inch thick. Brush the top with the rest of the melted butter. Place under grill, 3 to 4 inches away from heat. Grill until golden brown, about 15 to 20 minutes. Remove with a bulb baster any liquid that may accumulate.

Cut meat into 1½–2-inch squares.

Serve hot, or cold, with Raw Onion Rings and Fresh Green Chutney with Coriander Leaves and Yogurt or Fresh Mint Chutney with Fruit.

Left-over ham on toast

Serves 8–10

This dish of my own devising can be made with any left-over roasts. I have used ham, but you could use lamb or beef or pork, in which case salt should be added.

2 teacups (well packed) diced cooked ham

1 medium-sized potato, boiled, peeled, and diced

½ medium-sized onion, peeled and chopped

1 tsp fresh ginger, peeled and grated

2 cloves garlic, peeled and chopped finely

½ teacup washed fresh green coriander

⅛ tsp freshly ground pepper

¼ tsp cayenne pepper (optional – use as desired)

⅛ tsp ground cloves

⅛ tsp ground nutmeg

⅛ tsp ground cinnamon

3 tbs tamarind paste (see page 44) or 1½ tbs lemon juice

rounds of small cocktail rye bread, or Melba toasts, or any firm bread slices, crust removed, cut into 4 rectangles

3 tbs melted butter

Put the ham, potato, onion, ginger, garlic, and green coriander through the fine blade of a meat grinder. Add black pepper, cayenne pepper, cloves, nutmeg, cinnamon, and tamarind paste or lemon juice. Mix well with hands. You can do this much ahead of time and keep it covered in refrigerator.

Twenty-five minutes before serving time, preheat grill.

If using bread, spread out as many slices as will fit on a large baking sheet, and lightly toast one side. Remove from grill.

Spread other side with the ham paste ¼–⅓ inch thick. (Melba toasts do not need to be browned. You can just spread ham mixture on them directly.) Make sure the edges of bread or Melba toast are covered or you will burn them. Brush with melted butter. Grill 7 to 8 minutes or until golden-brown. Do as many batches as you need.

To serve: Place on platter and serve hot with drinks.

Pacific king prawns on toothpicks

Serves 4

5 cloves garlic, peeled and chopped	3 tbs vegetable oil
a piece of fresh ginger, about 1-inch cube, peeled and chopped	3 tbs tomato purée
	$\frac{1}{2}$ tsp ground turmeric
	1 tbs lemon juice
1$\frac{1}{2}$ lbs Pacific king prawns peeled and deveined (see page 147)	$\frac{3}{4}$ tsp salt
	$\frac{1}{8}$–$\frac{1}{4}$ tsp cayenne pepper

Put the garlic and ginger in the container of an electric blender along with 3 tablespoons water. Blend at high speed until you have a smooth paste.

Wash prawns well and pat them dry. Cut each prawn into 3 sections. Set aside.

Heat oil in 10–12-inch frying-pan over medium flame. When hot, pour in the paste from blender and fry, stirring constantly, for 2 minutes. Add tomato purée and turmeric. Fry and stir another 2 minutes. Add 4 tablespoons water, the lemon juice, salt, and cayenne pepper. Cover, and simmer gently for 2 to 3 minutes. (This much can be done in advance.)

Five minutes before serving time, lift off cover, put in the prawns, and turn heat to high. Stir and fry the prawns for about 5 minutes or until they just turn opaque.

To serve: Place on platter and stick toothpicks into each prawn piece. Serve hot.

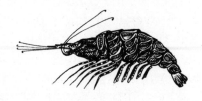

Whole-wheat samosas

Serves 8–10

Samosas are deep-fried patties, filled with potatoes or ground meat. I have a simple version of them. This is how they are made. (For stuffing use recipe for *Sookhe Aloo*, page 214, or *Kheema*, page 76.)

8 oz whole-wheat flour	**½ tsp salt**
3 tbs vegetable oil (plus a little extra for brushing on dough)	**vegetable oil for deep frying, enough for 3–3½ inches in pot**

Combine oil and flour and rub together. Add salt and mix. Add about 8 fl. oz. water, a little at a time, until you have a firm dough. Knead the dough well for 7 to 10 minutes, until smooth. Form into a ball. Brush with a little oil, and cover with a damp cloth. Set aside until ready for use.

If using *Sookhe Aloo* for stuffing, cook it according to the recipe and then crush potatoes coarsely with the back of a slotted spoon.

If using *Kheema* for stuffing, cook *Kheema* until it is very dry, with no liquid left at all. If any fat has accumulated, it should be discarded.

Divide dough into 28 to 30 equal balls. (Each ball makes 2 *samosas*, so you'll end up with about 60.) Flatten each ball and roll it out on a floured surface until it is 3½ to 4 inches in diameter. Cut each round in half. Taking one semicircle at a time, moisten half the length of the cut edge with a finger dipped in water. Form a wide cone with the semicircle, using the moist section to overlap ¼ inch and hold it closed. Fill *samosa* three-fourths full with the stuffing. Moisten the inside edges of the opening and press it shut. Seal this end by pressing down on the outside with the tip of a fork, as you would a pie crust. Prepare the *samosas* this way and keep them covered with a plastic wrap.

When you are ready to fry them, heat the oil in a wok, *karhai* (see page 47), or a utensil for deep frying. Keep the heat at medium. When oil is hot, drop a *samosa* in to check the temperature. It should start sizzling immediately. Fry 2 to 3 minutes, or until it looks a warm brown. Remove with slotted spoon and drain on paper towels. Do all *samosas* this way. If they brown too fast, lower your heat.

They can be reheated in a 300°F., Mark 3 oven.

To serve: Place *samosas* on platter and serve hot or warm with either Fresh Green Chutney with Coriander Leaves and Yogurt or Fresh Mint Chutney with Fruit. The chutney is used as a dip.

Cocktail koftas

Serves 15

Follow recipe on page 82. Make the *koftas* smaller, about $\frac{3}{4}$ inch in diameter. They can be made a day in advance, and then reheated.

When serving, keep *koftas* warm in chafing dish. Place toothpicks nearby to aid self-service.

Grilled chicken strips

Serves 8–10

See recipe on page 131. Instead of cutting chicken breasts into strips $1\frac{1}{2}$ to 2 inches long, cut them into strips that are 1 inch long and $\frac{1}{2}$ inch wide. Follow the rest of the recipe.

To serve: Place on warm platter and stick with toothpicks. Serve with drinks.

Meat

Khare masale ka gosht (meat with whole spices)
Pyazwala khare masale ka gosht (meat with whole spices and onions)
Kheema (minced meat)
Kheema with fried onions
Kheema with fried onions and peas
Kheema used as stuffing: for green peppers and long Italian peppers,
*   for tomatoes, for aubergines*
Koftas (Indian meatballs)
Nargisi koftas (large meatballs stuffed with hard-boiled eggs)
Cubed lamb with onions and raisins
Lamb with onions and mushrooms, or lamb do pyaza
Lamb korma
Lamb (or beef) korma with almonds, pecans, and sour cream
Lamb cooked in dark almond sauce (badami roghan josh)
Lamb with vinegar and mint
Lamb with spinach
Sindhi gosht (Sindhi meat)
Lamb chops with whole spices and yogurt
Pork chops cooked with whole spices and tamarind juice
Pork chops cooked with cabbage
Pork chops à la Jaffrey
Sweetbreads with fresh green coriander

SEE ALSO

Mulligatawny soup (page 52)
White soup (page 53)
Seekh kabab, flat style (page 60)
Left-over ham on toast (page 62)
'Butterflied' leg of lamb, marinated and barbecued (page 170)
Cubed leg of lamb, barbecued (page 173)
Boti kabab (cubed meat kabab) (page 173)
Kidney kabab (page 175)
Seekh kabab (page 175)
Marinated pork chops (page 178)
Pullao (page 255)
Chana dal cooked with lamb (page 274)

WHEN an Indian sits down to eat meat, it is nearly always goat meat. The English have translated the meat as mutton, but it is not to be confused with the aged sheep meat available in England, Australia, and New Zealand. Perhaps the English in India didn't know what else to call it—or perhaps they found a dish called 'mutton chops' more palatable than if it was called plain old 'goat chops'. Who knows!

At any rate, 'mutton' in India is not old sheep meat—far from it. It is usually *very* fresh goat meat and therefore not always very tender. Because of the lack of proper refrigeration facilities in India (most butchers cannot afford any) the animals are slaughtered daily and the meat is sold within 24 hours. In the richer homes it is then washed and refrigerated or frozen. But in the poorer homes it is cooked immediately. Since the meat is fairly tough, it is cooked slowly, over a longish period of time. For quicker fried and grilled dishes, the meat has to be tenderized first. The cheapest and most common tenderizer is crushed green papaya, but marinades of vinegar and yoghurt are also used.

Not only is Indian goat meat a little on the tough side; it is also very lean. The result is that we use a great deal of cooking fat to brown our meats. We tend to like this 'browned' look. When I buy lamb in Britain (lamb is the best substitute for the Indian 'mutton'), I first trim away all signs of fat. Then, to make it taste like the food I have in India, I cook it in lots of oil. This cooking fat can, of course, be removed later, once the dish is completely cooked, by spooning it off the top just before serving.

There is another significant difference in the quality of Indian meat which influences cooking techniques. In India, meat dropped into fat can be expected to fry, slowly or quickly, as the cook desires. Here, in Britain, if a pound of meat is put into oil to fry, unless one has taken careful preliminary steps, it will start boiling. The meat here gives off a lot of water, possibly because of prior freezing or because of the water-injecting habits of some butchers. There is no really good way to avoid this extra water, but defrosting frozen meat completely and wiping it well before cooking will be somewhat helpful. You can also fry the meat over a high flame in small quantities or boil off the extra liquid towards the end of the cooking time. As I go along I will tell you, in each recipe, which step to follow. What I want you to understand here is *why* an Indian meat dish cooked in Britain will never taste quite the same as it does in India.

Contrary to what most outsiders think, beef *is* eaten in India. About 80 per cent of India is Hindu (those who, technically, do not eat beef) but the other 20 per cent includes 60 million Muslims and 12 million Christians, i.e., 72 million people who can eat beef without battling with their consciences first. Every now and then, when it seems politic, there is a rousing debate in our parliament on the subject of cow slaughter. But while cows ('The cow is your mother', they say) are being heatedly discussed, no one is saying much about the buffalo (a kind of poor relation, I suppose), so this creature is being slaughtered and sold—though not always in the open market. A very popular dish in most 'Western'-style Indian restaurants is the 'sizzling' steak (alas—buffalo), and I must say I have seen many a Hindu devour this with great relish. It does not taste as good as the best English steak, but it is served very attractively right on the platter on which it is cooked, accompanied by a lot of hissing and sizzling vegetables.

When beef is cooked in the Indian manner, it is cooked like mutton, slowly, over a period of time. In some areas, beef is dried and then fried with onions and served at breakfast. I have also eaten it cooked with spinach and with potatoes. One strange thing that I have noticed about us Indians is that although many Hindus will eat beef in restaurants, in Muslim and Christian homes, and when they are abroad, very few will cook it in their own kitchens. Each country has its own varieties of national hypocrisy. Self-righteously proclaimed rules on diet and cleanliness seem to be part of our heritage.

Besides 'mutton' and beef, pork, lamb, and venison are also eaten in the areas where they are found. *Dumba*, a fan-tailed sheep, is used for a special *pullao* (a rice and meat dish) cooked at the Muslim festival *Id*. Venison, considered rather dry, is often made into *koftas* (meatballs) or *shami kababs* (ground meat patties).

Meat is, of course, cooked very differently in the different regions of India. Most of my recipes are for dishes eaten in and around my hometown, Delhi. I will start with the easier recipes. My aim is to interest you first, and then entice you on—slowly.

Cuts of meat to use

Generally, when Indians cook a simple, everyday meat dish, they use meat with bone. This could come from the neck, shoulder, shank, ribs, or elsewhere from the goat or sheep. Often they combine these different parts, add some chunks from the leg, and throw in a few extra dark marrow bones for good measure. (These coveted marrow bones, once cooked, are fought over by the children with the winner gleefully digging out the delicious marrow with long, slim spoons!) When I buy lamb in Britain for stew-type dishes, I use all the cuts just mentioned. But I find that the English, eating with a knife and and fork, do not seem to be much attracted to cubes of meat that are often three-fourths bone and one-fourth meat. When you eat with your hands, there is a great deal of pleasure to be derived from tearing meat off a bone with your teeth, and from sucking the bones. Since this is seldom done in Britain, I have limited myself a great deal to cubed, boned meat from shoulder of lamb. Any butcher will bone and trim the meat, but if you do not have access to a butcher you can buy shoulder chops from the supermarket and cut and trim them yourself. Just cut around the bones (these can be saved for soup), trim off the big concentrations of fat, and then cut the meat into 1–1½ inch cubes. Generally, you can assume a waste of about 40 to 50 per cent—so if you buy 4 lbs of shoulder chops, you are likely to end up with about 2 lbs of meat or a bit more.

Leg of lamb can be used for a great many of the following recipes that require cubed meat, but it tends to get rather dry when cooked in a stew-like manner. It should be saved for grills and barbecues (see the chapter on summer cooking, pages 165–84). However, if you wish to use it, cook it for the same length of time as meat from the shoulder—about an hour and fifteen minutes.

Neck and shank are excellent for stews but require longer cooking time—about 1½ to 2 hours. Serve them to people who like bones. You will need to buy about 4 lbs to serve 4–6 since so much of it will be bone. You will also need to increase the salt a bit as some of it will be absorbed by the marrow.

Stewing beef may be substituted for cubed lamb. Here again, increase the cooking time, in this case to about 2½ hours, and adjust the recipes accordingly.

Khare masale ka gosht
(meat with whole spices)

Serves 4–6

Here is my first meat recipe for this book. It is very easy to make and has a delicately flavoured taste. By placing it first, I hope to lure you all towards the more complicated and the more heavily spiced meat recipes. This dish is normally made with goat meat, using either the leg or the neck and shoulders, cubed into 1-inch pieces. If the neck and shoulders are used, the bones are always left in. Since we eat with our hands, none of the meat is wasted, the fingers making their way around the oddly shaped bones more easily than a knife and fork. You can, however, use either beef or lamb. If you use beef, get cubed stewing beef. If you use lamb, and don't want bones, get the butcher to give you 2 lbs of meat from the shoulder. Trim the larger chunks of fat from the meat, and cut it into 1-inch cubes.

8 tbs vegetable oil
1 stick cinnamon, 2 inches long
20 whole black peppercorns
15 whole cloves
10 whole cardamom pods
2 bay leaves
1–4 whole dried hot peppers (or more, according to taste)

2 lbs boneless meat from shoulder of lamb, cut into 1-inch cubes, with fat and tissues removed
1–1½ tsp salt (according to taste)
1 tsp garam masala (optional)

Garnish

1 tbs trimmed, chopped fresh green coriander

Pat the meat dry on paper towels.

Heat the oil in a heavy-bottomed pot over medium heat. When it is very hot, put the spices in quickly in this order: first

73

the cinnamon, then black peppercorns, cloves, cardamom pods, and bay leaves, and finally the hot peppers.

When the hot peppers begin to change colour and darken, add the pieces of meat and the salt. Stir for 5 minutes or until the pot begins to make boiling noises. Cover, lower heat, and cook for approximately 1 hour and 10 minutes—or until the meat is tender.

Remove the cover and continue cooking on medium heat for a final 3 to 5 minutes, gently stirring the meat pieces. Take care not to break them. The meat is done now. It should look a nice brown, be tender, and have no sauce other than what is clinging to it and the fat it cooked in.

To serve: In India the contents of the pot are put into a serving bowl, 1 teaspoon of *garam masala* is sprinkled on the top, and the dish is served with hot *chapatis* or Rice with Spinach. I tend to think the English would be rather put off if they saw so much fat lining the serving dish, so I suggest that you lift the meat and spices out with a slotted spoon (the spices, though not to be eaten, make an attractive garnish). Place them on a serving platter and serve them sprinkled with chopped green coriander. You could serve almost any vegetable or *dal* as an accompaniment—for example, green beans and *urad dal*. Plain rice or hot *chapatis* are also good. This dish can be made a day before, cooled, covered, and refrigerated. Reheat gently and serve.

Pyazwala khare masale ka gosht
(meat with whole spices and onions)

Serves 4–6

When I was a student in London and had written home begging my mother to teach me how to cook, one of the earliest letters I received from her was dated March 9th, 1956, and said, 'I received your letter. I am glad to know you have gained weight. I miss you and cannot wait to see you in your new "plump" state. Your younger sister is supposed to be studying for her exams and your father has even given up his room for her, but she spends all her time reading novels. Here is the recipe for the *Khare Masale Ka Gosht* that you asked for. Write and tell me how it works out … ' It worked out very well!

Here it is. It's very much like the preceding recipe, with the addition of onions, ginger, and cumin seeds, and it has one extra step.

2 lbs boneless meat from shoulder of lamb, with extra fat removed, cut into 1–1½ inch cubes
4 onions
9 tbs vegetable oil
10 whole cardamom pods
4 whole large black cardamom pods (if available)

6–7 bay leaves
1 tsp whole cumin seed
1–4 whole hot dried red peppers (optional)
5 whole black peppercorns
1 piece fresh ginger, 1½ inches by 1½ inches, peeled and minced or grated
1 tsp salt (according to taste)

Prepare all the ingredients first. Pat dry the meat pieces thoroughly with paper towel. Peel the onions, cut them in half, then slice in very thin half-circles.

Heat the oil in a 10–12-inch heavy-bottomed pot over medium heat. When it is very hot, put in the onions. Fry, stirring occasionally, for about 15 minutes or until the onions are a darkish brown and crisp, but not burned and black. Lift out

75

the onions with slotted spoon, taking care that the fat drains back into the cooking pot first. Spread the onions on paper towels, and leave uncovered.

In the same pot, put in the small and large cardamoms, bay leaves, cumin, red peppers, peppercorns, and finally the ginger. Stir for a minute until bay leaves turn dark and ginger sizzles awhile. Now add the wiped meat and the salt.

Stir for about 5 minutes or until the pot begins to make boiling noises. Cover, lower heat, and simmer very gently for 1 hour and 10 minutes or until meat is tender.

Take cover off, add onions, and let the meat cook over medium heat a final 3 to 5 minutes, stirring gently. Take care not to break the meat. All extra liquid should be boiled away, and the meat should look a nice brown and have no sauce other than what is clinging to it and the fat left in the pot.

To serve: See suggestions for preceding recipe.

Kheema
(minced meat)

Serves 6

This is the first Indian dish all Indian students abroad learn to make. It can be cooked plain or with potatoes, peas, or mushrooms.

2 medium-sized onions,
  peeled and coarsely
  chopped
4 cloves garlic, peeled and
  coarsely chopped
1 piece fresh ginger, 2 inches
  long and 1 inch wide,
  peeled and coarsely
  chopped
4 tbs vegetable oil
1 stick cinnamon, about
  2 inches long
4 whole cloves
4 black peppercorns

1 bay leaf
1–2 hot red peppers to taste
  (optional)
1 tbs ground coriander
1 tsp ground cumin
½ tsp ground turmeric
1 large tinned tomato or 2
  small ones, coarsely
  chopped
2 lbs finely minced lamb or
  minced beef
¾–1 tsp salt (or to taste)
1 tsp lemon juice

Place chopped onions, garlic, and ginger in blender with 3 tablespoons water and blend to smooth paste (1 minute). Set aside.

Heat oil in a 10–12-inch frying-pan over medium heat. When hot, add cinnamon stick, cloves, black peppercorns, bay leaf, and then the red peppers. In about 10 seconds, when the peppers turn dark, add paste from blender, keeping your face averted. Fry for about 10 minutes, adding a sprinkling of water if the food sticks to the bottom. Add the coriander, cumin, and turmeric, and fry another 5 minutes. Now put the chopped tomato in, fry for another 2 to 3 minutes, and add the minced meat and the salt. Fry on high heat about 5 minutes. Break up all the lumps in the meat and brown it as much as you can. Add ¼ pint water and the lemon juice. Bring to the boil and cover. Lower flame and let it simmer for 1 hour.

To serve: Spoon off any accumulated fat and discard. Serve the *kheema* with rice, or *chapatis*, or *parathas*, and any vegetables you like. If serving it with a rice dish, e.g., Rice with Potatoes and Cumin Seed, serve a *moong* or *masoor dal* with it.

77

Kheema with fried onions

Serves 6

This is easily my favourite *kheema* recipe. Nutmeg, mace, and yogurt are added to the meat for a slight variation.

1 medium-sized onion, peeled and cut into very thin rings
4 tbs vegetable oil
2 bay leaves
1 cinnamon stick, 3 inches long
6 whole cloves
2 medium-sized onions, finely chopped
a piece of fresh ginger, 1 inch long and 1 inch wide, finely chopped
5 cloves garlic, minced

1 tbs ground coriander
1 tbs ground cumin
1 tbs ground turmeric
2 tbs plain yogurt
1 medium-sized tomato (tinned or fresh), peeled and chopped
2 lbs minced lamb or minced beef
$\frac{1}{4}$ tsp ground mace
$\frac{1}{4}$ tsp ground nutmeg
1 tsp salt
$\frac{1}{4}$–$\frac{1}{2}$ tsp cayenne (optional)

Halve the onion rings and separate. Heat the oil in a heavy-bottomed 10–12-inch frying-pan over medium heat. When hot, add the halved onion rings and fry them for about 5 minutes until they are dark brown but not burned. Remove with a slotted spoon and spread on paper towels. They will not be needed until the meat is almost cooked.

Put the bay leaves, cinnamon, and cloves in the hot oil. When the bay leaves begin to darken and the cinnamon starts uncurling slightly, add the finely chopped onions, ginger, and garlic. Fry, stirring, for 10 to 12 minutes, until the onions darken to a medium brown with darkish edges. Lower flame a bit and add the coriander, cumin, and turmeric. Fry for about 2 minutes, stirring all the time. Add the yogurt and cook, stirring, another minute. Now put in the chopped tomato, and keep frying and stirring for 2 to 3 minutes.

Add the meat. Raise the flame to medium (medium high if

the meat is very watery) and fry, breaking up all the lumps with the back of a slotted spoon, for about 7 or 8 minutes. Next, put in the mace, nutmeg, salt, cayenne, and ¼ pint water, and stir. Bring to the boil, cover, turn flame down to low, and let it simmer for 1 hour. Stir every 10 minutes or so. After an hour, mix in the browned onion half-rings and remove the cinnamon.

To serve: Serve with Rice with Spinach, Potatoes with Asafetida and Cumin, Green Beans with Ginger, and Yoghurt with Tiny Dumplings. Or serve with plain boiled rice, *moong dal*, and a cauliflower dish. This *kheema* is also excellent served with *chapatis* and *pooris* instead of rice.

Kheema with fried onions and peas

Serves 6

Follow the preceding recipe. Instead of cooking the minced meat for 1 hour, cook it for 50 minutes. Add 1 cup freshly shelled (or frozen) peas to it, mix, cover, and let cook another 5 to 10 minutes or until peas are tender. Add the fried onion half-rings and serve as in the previous recipe.

Kheema used as stuffing

Minced meat, *kheema*, is used very often as stuffing for vegetables. If the *kheema* is cooked well, and the sauce used over the vegetable is flavourful, these dishes can be superb. Sometimes, when serving four people, I have bought two large aubergines, stuffed them, and bought them to the table covered with a red tomato and tarmarind chutney. They have created a sensation.

The vegetables easiest to stuff are green peppers, long Italian peppers, tomatoes, and, of course, aubergines. (The discarded inside of the aubergine can be used for an unsmoked version of Aubergine Bharta, page 206.) These vegetables come in different sizes, so it will be up to you to decide how many you need. Pick your vegetables of a uniform size.

For the stuffing I use *Kheema* with Fried Onions (page 78). You can use any *kheema* left-overs as well. The stuffing can, if necessary, be made the day before and refrigerated. You could also make the chutney a night before and store it in a closed jar in the refrigerator. It will keep well.

To stuff green peppers and long Italian peppers: Preheat oven to 350°F., Mark 4.

Wash the peppers, then with a small sharp pointed knife cut a small cap around the stem of each pepper. Pull off the cap by the stem. Scoop out and discard the seeds inside the pepper and cut off seeds attached to the cap. Be sure to keep track of which cap belongs to which pepper.

Using a teaspoon, stuff each pepper with the prepared *kheema* and stick the cap back on. Lay or stand the peppers in one layer in an ovenproof baking dish. Pour Tomato Tamarind Chutney (page 294) over them, reserving a little chutney to pour over peppers just before you serve them. Cover the baking dish with a lid or aluminium foil, making sure it is tightly covered.

Bake in the preheated oven 45 to 55 minutes, or until peppers are tender.

To serve: Transfer peppers and chutney onto warm serving platter and spoon fresh chutney over them. Serve with *Sookhe Aloo*, Cucumber *Raita*, and *parathas*. Or you could serve them with rice, a chicken or shrimp dish, a vegetable, and a salad type of relish, e.g., Cucumber and Tomato with Lemon Juice. Or serve the peppers alone as an appetizer.

To stuff tomatoes. Preheat oven to 400°F., Mark 6.

Wash the tomatoes, then with a small sharp pointed knife cut a cap off at the stem end of each tomato. Reserve the caps. Remove the seeds and pulp from each tomato. (A grapefruit knife or serrated spoon is useful for this.)

Using a teaspoon, stuff each tomato with the prepared *kheema*. Replace the caps.

Stand the tomatoes in a single layer in an ovenproof baking dish. Pour Tomato Tamarind Chutney (page 294) over them, reserving a little chutney to pour over tomatoes just before you serve them. Cover the baking dish tightly with a lid or aluminium foil.

Place in preheated oven, and bake 15 to 20 minutes or until tomatoes wrinkle slightly.

To serve: Lift the tomatoes gently with large kitchen spoon and place on serving platter. Pour extra chutney over them, and serve as an appetizer or as in the preceding recipe for stuffed peppers.

To stuff aubergines: Pick medium or large aubergines. Wash them.

Bring water to which 1 teaspoon of salt has been added to the boil in a pot large enough to hold the aubergines. Since the aubergines will float, you can half-fill the pot with water. When the water comes to the boil, put in the aubergines and boil 15 minutes. Turn them over halfway through boiling time.

Preheat oven to 350°F., Mark 4.

Pour water carefully out of the pot, so as not to bruise the aubergines, and leave them to cool. Prepare each aubergine this way: when it is cool, cut off a cap at the stem area, and reserve. Now scoop out the inside, leaving only ½ inch of flesh all around. This is not easy. Use a grapefruit knife, a long sharp knife, spoons, a spoon handle—anything that will help you gouge out the inside—holding the aubergine carefully so you don't break the skin. (If you begin to despair, cut the aubergine in half lengthwise and scoop out the inside, leaving ½ inch around the skin, then proceed with the recipe.) When the pulp is out, the aubergine will shrink into itself and look like a very sad sack. Fatten it back into shape by stuffing it with lots of *kheema*. If it is still whole, put its cap on, pour Tomato Tamarind Chutney (page 294) over it, and bake, covered, for 45 minutes to 1 hour or until the aubergine is tender. Turn over once halfway during baking time. (If you had to halve the aubergines and stuff them that way, place snugly, skin side down, covered, in a baking dish.)

Follow serving directions for stuffed peppers (page 81).

Koftas
(Indian meatballs)

Serves 6–8. Makes about 48 meatballs

Koftas take a fairly long time to make, so I suggest that you prepare them a day in advance. They can be covered and left in the refrigerator overnight (they will taste even better) and can be reheated before serving. Take care not to break them while stirring and serving.

For the meatballs

2 lbs finely minced meat from a leg of lamb, or minced beef (put meat twice through fine blade of grinder, or ask your butcher to do so)	**¾ tsp salt**
	¼ tsp freshly ground pepper
	1 tbs garam masala
	1 tsp ground coriander
	½ tsp ground cumin

For the stuffing

1–2 fresh hot green chilies (optional), finely chopped

2 cloves garlic, peeled and minced

a piece of fresh ginger, about 1 inch square, peeled and minced

6 spring onions, minced, or 1 medium-sized onion, peeled and minced

3 tbs lemon juice

a dash of salt and freshly ground pepper

For browning the meatballs

7 tbs vegetable oil

1 cinnamon stick, 2 inches long

2 dried red peppers (optional)

4 whole cardamom pods

6 whole black peppercorns

4 whole cloves

For the sauce

vegetable oil (as needed to make up 5 tbs)

4 medium-sized onions, peeled and coarsely chopped

6 cloves of garlic, peeled and coarsely chopped

a piece of ginger, 1 inch square, peeled and coarsely chopped

2 tbs ground coriander

2 tsp ground cumin

1 tsp ground turmeric

2 medium-sized tomatoes (tinned or fresh), drained and chopped

1 tbs paprika

1 tbs garam masala

1 tsp salt

Garnish

1 tbs chopped fresh green coriander

1 onion, peeled and fried in rings (see page 258)

$\frac{1}{4}$ tsp freshly ground cardamom seeds (see page 40)

Mix all the ingredients for meatballs and keep covered in a bowl.

Mix all the ingredients for the stuffing in another bowl.

Preparing the *koftas* takes a little time, so you might as well make yourself comfortable. If you have a table and chair in your kitchen, sit down there. Otherwise, spread a newspaper on any handy table and pull up a chair. Place before you the bowls of minced meat and stuffing, a platter with a cover, and a bowl of warm water.

Two lbs of meat will make about 48 *koftas* about 1 to 1½ inches in diameter. To simplify, portion the meat into 8 equal sections and then make 6 *koftas* out of each section.

Pick up enough meat for one *kofta* and form into a rough ball. Depress the ball and place a generous pinch of stuffing in its centre. Cover the stuffing by bringing around the meat from the outer edges and making it into a ball again. Smooth out the ball by moistening your palms and fingertips slightly and by working it in your hand. As each ball is made, place it on the platter and cover. Continue this way until you have used up all the meat and stuffing.

Heat the oil in a 10-12-inch frying-pan over medium heat, and put in the cinnamon, red peppers, cardamom pods, peppercorns, and cloves. Stir once. In 10 seconds or so when the cloves begin to expand and the red peppers swell and turn dark, add the meatballs, just enough of them so they don't overcrowd the frying-pan. Brown them on all sides, remove with slotted spoon, and return to platter. (Remember, you are just browning the *koftas*, not cooking them through.) When all the *koftas* are browned, cover the platter and set aside.

The last step is making the sauce: Lift out the whole spices from the oil used for browning the *koftas* and place them with the *koftas*. Pour the oil into a very large and wide heavy-bottomed pot. Add more oil, if needed, to make 5 tablespoons.

Place the chopped onions, garlic, and ginger in a blender with 4 tablespoons water and blend at high speed until you have a smooth paste.

Heat the oil, then pour in the paste from the blender. Fry over medium heat for about 15 minutes or until all the liquid has evaporated, stirring frequently. Add the coriander, cumin, and turmeric, and keep frying another 5 minutes. If the spices stick at the bottom of the pan, add 1 teaspoon of warm water at a time and keep stirring. (Never put too much water in. The idea is to fry the spices and onions, not to boil them.)

Add the chopped tomatoes, and continue to stir and fry 2 to 3 minutes. Add 1 tablespoon water, cover pan, and let the tomatoes simmer 3 to 5 minutes, lifting the cover two or three times to make sure they are not burning. Remove cover, stir again, and fry for 1 more minute.

Now add 12 fl. oz. water, the *koftas*, the spices used in frying meatballs, the paprika, the *garam masala*, and the teaspoon of salt. Mix gently, and bring to the boil. Cover, and simmer slowly for half an hour.

To serve: Gently spoon out the *koftas* into a heated serving dish, taking care not to break them. Stir the sauce and pour it over them.

Sprinkle the green coriander and onion and cardamom on top. This dish can be served with plain boiled rice, *moong dal*, and a cucumber and tomato salad, at its simplest. (As a child I used to love this combination. On Sundays, we very often substituted *Karhi* for the *dal*.) At a banquet, you could garnish it with *vark* and serve it with Chicken *Biryani*, Carrots and Peas with Ginger and Green Coriander, and Yogurt with Spinach.

At picnics, it goes well with 'stale' *pooris* or *parathas* and pickles.

Made a little smaller, the *koftas* can be served with drinks.

Warn diners not to eat the whole spices, but to leave them delicately on one side of their plate!

Nargisi koftas
(large meatballs stuffed with hard-boiled eggs)

Serves 4

Koftas, as you know by now, are meatballs. *Nargis* is the Indian word for the narcissus flower. Why these particular meatballs are considered narcissus-like, I am not too sure. I can only guess that when cut in half (they are nearly always served that way) these egg-filled *koftas* remind some people of the yellow and white spring flower.

Nargisi koftas are definitely not an everyday dish in India. It may be *my* particular experience, but I have eaten them only at weddings and banquets. You, of course, need not limit yourself this way! They are not difficult to make, look beautiful, and taste quite marvellous. They are actually meatballs stuffed with whole hard-boiled eggs and cooked in a thick sauce.

$1\frac{1}{4}$ lbs minced lamb or minced beef (put through the mincer 3 times)

$\frac{1}{4}$ tsp ground cloves

$\frac{1}{4}$ tsp cayenne pepper (optional)

$\frac{1}{8}$ tsp ground cinnamon

$\frac{1}{8}$ tsp ground mace

$\frac{1}{8}$ tsp freshly ground pepper

$1\frac{1}{2}$ tsp ground cumin

$1\frac{1}{2}$ tsp salt (or a little more if needed)

8 tbs plain yogurt

2 tbs finely chopped fresh green coriander

2 medium-sized onions, peeled and coarsely chopped

3 cloves garlic, peeled and coarsely chopped

a piece of fresh ginger, about 1-inch cube, peeled and coarsely chopped

4 medium-sized eggs, hard-boiled and peeled

6 tbs vegetable oil

6 lightly crushed cardamom pods

2 bay leaves

2 whole dried hot red peppers (optional)

2 tsp ground coriander

$\frac{1}{2}$ tsp ground turmeric

1 tsp paprika (for colour)

1 medium-sized tomato (tinned or fresh), peeled and finely chopped

86

If your butcher has not minced the meat 3 times, do it yourself at home. It should be *very* finely minced.

In a large bowl combine the meat, cloves, cayenne pepper, cinnamon, mace, black pepper, ½ teaspoon of the cumin, 1 teaspoon of the salt, 2 tablespoons of the yogurt, and the chopped green coriander. Mix well, cover bowl, and leave aside.

Place onion, garlic, and ginger in container of an electric blender with 6 tablespoons water and blend to a smooth paste.

Divide the minced meat into 4 portions. Wrap one portion around each peeled hard-boiled egg, covering it well.

Heat the vegetable oil in a 10-12-inch frying-pan over a medium-high flame, and put in the cardamom pods and bay leaves, and the red peppers if you want them. The spices will darken in a few seconds. Now put in the four meatballs and brown them all over. Turn them carefully so as not to break them. They will brown unevenly, but don't let that worry you. When they have browned, lift them out gently with a slotted spoon and place them on a plate.

To the same oil, add the paste from the blender container, keeping face averted, and fry, stirring, for about 10 minutes.

Now turn the flame to medium and add the coriander, the remaining 1 teaspoon cumin, and the turmeric. Keep frying and stirring for a minute. Add 1 tablespoon yogurt and stir for ½ minute. Add another tablespoon yogurt and stir for ½ minute. Repeat this process until all the yogurt has been added. Now put in the remaining ½ teaspoon salt, the paprika, the chopped tomato, and 6 fl. oz. water. Bring to the boil. Cover and simmer gently for 10 minutes.

Lift up lid and add the *koftas*. Cover and simmer gently for ½ hour. Turn the *koftas* every 7 or 8 minutes and spoon sauce over them.

To serve: Cut *koftas* in half and place on a warm platter. Spoon sauce over them and serve with almost any rice dish or with hot *chapatis*. Any yogurt *raita* and a pea or green bean dish would also go well with them.

Cubed lamb with onions and raisins

Serves 6-8

This dish is an adaptation I have made from *mullah do pyaza*, a Moghul favourite in which the meat is served with a lot of fried onions. These onions are cooked separately but are added to the meat for the last 5 minutes of cooking time. I brown the lamb pieces before I cook them, because, as I explained earlier, the meat in Britain seems to have a very high water content and will not brown with the spices, as it does in India. The raisins I add are optional. You could omit them if you do not like raisins or add more if you really like them.

3 lbs boneless meat from shoulder of lamb (stewing beef may be substituted)	1 tsp ground turmeric
	3 heaped tbs plain yogurt
	1 medium-sized tomato (tinned or fresh) peeled and finely chopped
11 tbs vegetable oil	1½ tsp salt
10 medium-sized onions	½ tsp ground cloves
5 cloves garlic, peeled and coarsely chopped	½ tsp ground nutmeg
a piece of fresh ginger, 2 inches long and 1 inch wide, peeled and coarsely chopped	½ tsp ground cinnamon
	⅛–¼ tsp cayenne pepper (optional)
1 tbs ground coriander	⅛ tsp freshly ground black pepper
2 tsp ground cumin	2 tbs golden seedless raisins

Trim fat off the cubes of lamb. Pat dry with paper towels.

Heat 5 tablespoons of oil in a wide, heavy-bottomed pot. When oil is very hot, fry 7 or 8 pieces of meat at a time, browning well on all sides, and then remove with a slotted spoon. When all the meat has browned, turn off the heat.

Peel and coarsely chop 2 of the onions and place them with the garlic, ginger, and 5 tablespoons of water in the container of an electric blender. Blend at high speed until you have a smooth paste.

Turn on the heat to medium under the pot in which you

browned the meat. Pour in the paste from the blender and fry, stirring constantly, for about 5 minutes. Add the coriander, cumin, and turmeric, and fry, stirring, for 1 minute. Add the yogurt, a tablespoon at a time, and keep stirring and frying. Then add the peeled and finely chopped tomato, and keep stirring. (In all, this should take about 10 minutes.) If after you have added the tomato some sticks to the bottom of your pot, add warm water, a teaspoon at a time, scraping the bottom and continuing to cook. The paste should turn a rich brown colour.

Put in the browned pieces of lamb along with any liquid that has accumulated, $\frac{1}{2}$ pint of water, the salt, cloves, nutmeg, cinnamon, cayenne (if desired), and black pepper. Mix well. Bring to the boil. Cover, lower heat, and allow to simmer gently for 1 hour. (The beef should cook for $2\frac{1}{2}$ hours.)

Meanwhile peel the other 8 onions, cut them in half lengthwise, and slice them into half-rings $\frac{1}{8}$ inch thick.

Heat 3 tablespoons of oil in each of two frying-pans over medium heat. (It is quicker and easier to use two frying-pans, frying half the onions in each simultaneously. You can also do them in two batches.) When the oil is hot, fry the onion slices 10 to 12 minutes, until they are browned but not crisp. If the lamb has cooked 55 minutes to an hour by this time, remove onions with a slotted spoon and add them to the meat. If not, remove with a slotted spoon to a bowl and set aside. Turn off the heat under one frying-pan. Into the other put the raisins and fry for a few seconds until they turn brown and puff up, then add to the meat pot if the meat is done or hold in the bowl with the fried onions. Once the onions and raisins have been added to the meat, simmer for 5 minutes.

To serve: Serve with *pooris* or *chapatis*, a yoghurt dish, a relish —Sweet Tomato Chutney or Cucumber and Tomato with Lemon Juice—and a vegetable: cabbage or cauliflower would be good. Almost any plain rice or vegetable and rice dish can be served with it as well. I often serve it with Rice with Whole Spices and *Karhi*.

Lamb with onions and mushrooms,
or lamb do pyaza

Serves 4–6

Any meat *do pyaza* usually means meat cooked with an equal weight of fried onions, *pyaz* being the North Indian word for onions. I have modified the traditional recipe slightly by adding mushrooms and by cooking with fenugreek, fennel, and onion seeds instead of the more commonly used cardamom, cloves, peppercorns, and cinnamon.

This is a mild-tasting dish, relatively easy to make and very popular with both children and adults.

2 lbs boned meat from shoulder of lamb, trimmed of excess fat, and cut into 1-inch cubes

5 medium-sized onions

vegetable oil (enough for $\frac{1}{8}$ inch in bottom of frying-pan)

$\frac{1}{4}$ tsp whole black onion seeds (kalonji), if available

$\frac{1}{2}$ tsp whole fennel seeds

$\frac{1}{4}$ tsp whole cumin seeds

15 fenugreek seeds

$\frac{1}{2}$ cup plain yogurt

1 tsp salt (more if needed)

$\frac{1}{8}$ tsp freshly ground pepper

$\frac{1}{8}$–$\frac{1}{4}$ tsp cayenne pepper (optional)

$\frac{1}{2}$ lb fresh mushrooms

Dry the meat thoroughly with paper towels and leave at room temperature while preparing the other ingredients.

Peel and halve the onions lengthwise. Slice them into $\frac{1}{8}$-inch-thick half-rings. In a 12-inch frying-pan, heat the oil. Fry the onions over a high flame 8 to 10 minutes, until they turn dark brown in spots and soften. Stir as you do this.

Remove onions with a slotted spoon and set aside in a bowl or dish.

In the same frying-pan put the onion seeds, fennel seeds, cumin seeds, and fenugreek seeds. Within a few seconds the fennel seeds will begin to darken. As soon as this happens, put in the cubes of meat and fry 5 to 10 minutes until well browned on all sides. While the meat is browning, put the yogurt in a bowl. Add ¼ pint water to it very gradually, a tablespoon at a time, beating with a fork. Once the meat has browned, beat the yogurt mixture again and pour it into the frying-pan. Add salt, pepper, and cayenne, bring to the boil, cover, lower heat to medium low, and cook for 25–35 minutes. Clean the mushrooms. Cut off the hard ends of the stems. If the mushrooms are largish, quarter them whole (stem and all); if they are of medium size, halve them; if they are of button size, leave them whole. After the meat has cooked 25 minutes, add the mushrooms. Stir well. Cover again and cook another 25 minutes or until meat is tender.

Lift off the cover and add the fried onions. Raise heat to medium high and boil away most of the liquid. (The only 'sauce' should be what clings to the meat. At the bottom of the pan you should see just the fat.) This should take 5 minutes or less. Check the salt.

To serve: Here is an Indian dish that can be served as part of a traditional Indian dinner or as the main course of a Western-style meal.

At an Indian meal, you could serve it as we did very often on Sundays—with plain rice, *Karhi*, green beans, and Tomato and Onion with Lemon Juice.

I serve it often to my family with Rice and Peas and a fresh green salad.

91

Lamb korma

Serves 6–8

3 tbs ground coriander
1 tbs ground cumin
1 tbs desiccated unsweetened coconut
4 medium-sized onions, peeled and coarsely chopped
5 cloves garlic, peeled and coarsely chopped
a piece of ginger, about 1½ inches long and 1 inch wide, peeled and coarsely chopped
1 large tomato (tinned or fresh) or 2 small ones, peeled and coarsely chopped
1 tsp ground turmeric

6 tbs vegetable oil
5 whole cardamom pods
6 whole cloves
7 whole black peppercorns
2 bay leaves
1 cinnamon stick, 2 inches long
2 or more dried hot red peppers (optional)
3 lbs boneless meat from lamb shoulder, cut into 1-inch cubes (or shank, neck, or leg—see page 72 for proportions), thoroughly dried
1 tbs plain yogurt
2 tsp salt
1 tsp garam masala

Garnish

fried onion rings (page 258)
¼ tsp freshly ground cardamom seeds (page 40)

sliced hot green chilies
chopped fresh green coriander

Heat a small heavy frying-pan over medium flame, and dry-roast the coriander, cumin, and coconut, tossing them around with a spoon. Roast for 2 to 3 minutes until the spices turn a few shades darker, and set aside. Remove frying-pan from heat. Place onions, garlic, and ginger in blender with tomato and turmeric. Blend at high speed for 1 minute or until you have a smooth paste, and set aside.

In a large, heavy-bottomed pot heat 4 tablespoons of the oil over medium flame. When hot, add the cardamom, cloves, peppercorns, bay leaves, cinnamon, and red peppers. Stir. As soon as the peppercorns begin to expand and the red peppers turn dark, put in a few pieces of meat at a time. Turn the flame higher and brown the meat on all sides. As each batch browns, remove it to a side plate. When all the lamb is browned, cover it and set it aside. Remove the whole spices from the pot with a slotted spoon and keep with lamb.

To make the sauce: Keep flame on medium high, and add 2 tablespoons of oil to what is left in the pot. While it is heating, add the paste from the blender, keeping face averted. Stir from time to time. As the water evaporates and the paste starts to stick to the bottom, lower heat and stir continuously, for about 5 minutes in all, sprinkling in a little water now and then to prevent scorching. Add the roasted spices and cook for another 5 minutes, then stir in the yogurt, a little at a time, to prevent scorching.

Now put in the meat, the salt, and enough water to barely cover the lamb. Bring to the boil, cover, and simmer about 1 hour or until done. Lift cover. Sprinkle in 1 teaspoon *garam masala*, and cook, stirring, for another 5 minutes.

To serve: Spoon out into serving dish and garnish with one or all of the items suggested. Serve with boiled rice, *pooris* or *chapatis*, and okra or cauliflower or Aubergine *Bharta*. This dish is also good served with sweet rice, a yogurt dish, and Sweet Tomato Chutney.

Lamb (or beef) korma
with almonds, pecans, and sour cream

Serves 4–6

This dish can be made with shoulder or leg of lamb or stewing beef. Stewing beef generally takes much longer to cook, so adjust your time accordingly (see page 72).

5 medium-sized onions

5 cloves garlic, peeled and
coarsely chopped

a piece of fresh ginger,
about 1-inch cube, peeled
and coarsely chopped

vegetable oil, enough to
have $\frac{1}{16}$ inch in frying-pan

2 lbs boned meat from
shoulder of lamb, trimmed
of excess fat, and cut into
1–1$\frac{1}{2}$-inch cubes

1 tbs ground coriander

2 tsp ground cumin

1 tsp ground turmeric

2 medium-sized tomatoes
(tinned or fresh), peeled
and finely chopped

$\frac{1}{4}$ tsp ground mace

$\frac{1}{4}$ tsp ground nutmeg

$\frac{1}{4}$ tsp ground cinnamon

$\frac{1}{4}$ tsp ground cloves

1 tsp salt (or as desired)

$\frac{1}{8}$ tsp freshly ground black
pepper

$\frac{1}{8}$–$\frac{1}{4}$ tsp cayenne pepper
(optional)

10 pecan halves

$\frac{1}{4}$ cup blanched almonds

2 tbs sour cream

Garnish

5 cardamom pods

2 tbs chopped fresh green
coriander

the fried onions

Peel the onions. Cut 4 of them into halves lengthwise, and then slice them into very thin half-rings.

Chop the fifth onion coarsely. Put it along with the garlic and ginger in the container of an electric blender. Add 4 tablespoons of water and blend at high speed until you have a smooth paste.

Heat oil in a 10–12-inch frying-pan (use a deep, heavy-bottomed frying-pan with lid or a wide casserole-type dish) over medium-high heat. Put in the sliced onions and fry, stirring, for 15 to 20 minutes or until they are dark brown and crisp, not black and burned. Remove them with a slotted spoon and spread on paper towels to drain. (You will not need them until serving time.)

Dry the pieces of meat thoroughly and brown them well, about 8 pieces at a time, in the onion-flavoured oil. As each batch gets done, remove with slotted spoon to a platter. When all the meat is browned, turn off the heat.

94

When the frying-pan has cooled a bit, pour in the paste from the electric blender. Stir it well, mixing it with the coagulated pan juices. Turn the heat on medium high and fry the paste, stirring all the time, for 8 to 10 minutes, or until it has browned. Now lower heat and add the coriander, cumin, and turmeric. Mix and fry, stirring, for a minute or two. Add the chopped tomatoes and fry another minute.

Next add the mace, nutmeg, cinnamon, and cloves. Mix and cook slowly for 5 minutes. Stir every now and then.

Now add $\frac{1}{4}$ pint water, the salt, black pepper, cayenne pepper, and browned meat, as well as the juices that have accumulated. Bring to the boil, cover, lower heat and simmer gently for 30 minutes.

If you want to remove the fat, skim it off as it rises to the top.

Put the pecans and almonds in a blender with 3 tablespoons of water, and blend at high speed until you have a smooth paste. You may need to stop and push down with a rubber spatula a few times.

Add the nut paste, then the sour cream, to the meat. Stir and check the salt. Bring to the boil, cover, lower heat, and simmer gently for 25 to 30 minutes or until meat is tender.

Peel the cardamoms, discarding the skin. Crush the seeds with a heavy mortar and pestle or put them through a clean pepper grinder.

To serve: Place the meat and gravy in a wide bowl. Garnish with ground cardamom seeds, chopped green coriander, and the fried onions. Serve with hot *chapatis* or *parathas*, or almost any rice dish. Cabbage, green beans, and carrot dishes would go well with this *korma*. For a relish, choose something with raw onions and tomato.

Lamb cooked in dark almond sauce
(badami roghan josh)

Serves 4–6

Roghan josh is a traditional North Indian Muslim dish. It has a thick, dark, nutty sauce made with almonds and roasted cumin, coriander, and coconut. Even though shoulder of lamb is used here, you could use leg, neck, or shank (see page 72 for directions). Stewing beef may also be substituted.

2 lbs boned meat from shoulder of lamb, cubed into 1-inch pieces
6 tbs vegetable oil
10 whole cloves
1–2 whole dried hot red peppers (optional)
12 peppercorns
6 whole cardamom pods
1 tbs ground cumin
2 tbs ground coriander
1 tbs desiccated unsweetened coconut
3 tbs blanched almonds, coarsely chopped
6 cloves garlic, peeled and coarsely chopped
a piece of fresh ginger, about 1-inch cube, peeled and coarsely chopped
$\frac{1}{2}$ tsp ground turmeric
$\frac{1}{4}$ tsp ground nutmeg
$\frac{1}{4}$ tsp ground mace
2 medium-sized onions, peeled and finely minced
3 tbs plain yogurt
3 medium-sized tomatoes (tinned or fresh), peeled and coarsely chopped
$1\frac{1}{2}$ tsp salt

Wipe the meat well with paper towels.

Heat the oil in a 10–12-inch frying-pan. When the oil is hot, add the cloves, red peppers, peppercorns, and cardamom. Stir them for a few seconds until they puff up and darken.

Now put in 7 or 8 pieces of meat at a time to brown. When each lot is brown on all sides, remove with a slotted spoon to a large flameproof covered casserole, taking care to leave the spices in the frying-pan. Continue to brown all the meat this way and set aside. Turn off flame under frying-pan.

You have to roast some spices now, so take out your heaviest iron-type frying-pan (I keep a small one just for this purpose). Put the cumin, coriander, coconut, and almonds in it. Turn heat on medium and roast, stirring, for about 5 minutes or until spices turn a coffee colour. Turn off heat and pour roasted spices and nuts into container of electric blender. Add chopped garlic and ginger.

With a slotted spoon, lift out the fried spices in the oil and put them in the blender container too. Add the turmeric, nutmeg, mace, and 8 tablespoons water. Blend at high speed until you have a smooth, thick paste. You may need to stop the blender and push down with a rubber spatula.

In the same frying-pan in which the lamb cooked, fry the onions over high heat, stirring and scraping up the juices for about 5 minutes, or until they turn dark in spots. Then lower heat to medium and add paste from blender. Stir and fry for another 5 minutes, gradually adding the yogurt, a tablespoon at a time. Put in the chopped tomatoes. Stir and fry another 2-3 minutes.

Now add ½ pint water. Bring to the boil. Cover, lower heat, and simmer gently for 15 minutes.

Put the meat into this sauce. Add the salt and stir. Bring to the boil, cover, lower heat, and simmer gently for 1 hour. Stir a few times as it cooks.

To serve: Place in a warm dish, cover, and take to the table. *Rogham josh* goes very well with *pooris* or *chapatis* and Rice with Peas or Rice with Spinach. Serve a yogurt dish with it, and cauliflower, or carrots.

Lamb with vinegar and mint

Serves 4–6

This is a very refreshing way of cooking lamb. I like to make this dish fairly hot, but you could use fewer red peppers or none at all, as you prefer. Fresh mint is available from the greengrocer, but as this dish requires a whole bunch of mint it would certainly be easier if you cooked it in the summer months. As a substitute, you could use dried mint flakes, but I find all dried herbs seem impregnated with a rather undesirable musty flavour.

There are three ways you could serve this meat. You could dish it out with all its sauce – in which case you should serve the meat either on rice, to soak up the sauce – or in a little bowl, like a stew, set on the dinner plate. Or you could use the last 5 minutes of cooking time to reduce the sauce by about half by cooking it uncovered over a high flame – you will then be left with a thick sauce which can be served directly on the plates with the meat. The third alternative is to use the last 10 minutes of the cooking time to dry up almost *all* the sauce and serve the meat as a 'dry' dish. The recipe given here is for the 'dry dish', which I happen to prefer.

2 lbs boneless meat from
    shoulder of lamb, cut into
    1-inch cubes (or shank,
    neck, or leg – see page 72
    for proportions)
6 tbs vegetable oil
1½ tbs ground cumin
½ tsp ground cloves
¼ tsp ground cinnamon
½ tsp ground turmeric
1 tsp dry English mustard
1–2 whole dried hot red
    peppers (optional)
6 cloves garlic, peeled and coarsely chopped

a piece of fresh ginger,
    about 1-inch cube,
    peeled and coarsely
    chopped
5 tbs red wine vinegar
2 medium-sized onions,
    peeled and minced
1½ tsp salt
4 tbs well-packed finely
    minced fresh mint, or
    1 tbs dried mint plus 2 tbs
    trimmed, chopped parsley

Wipe lamb cubes well.

Put oil in a 10–12-inch frying-pan and turn the flame on high. When hot, put in 7 or 8 cubes of meat at a time and brown them on all sides. As each lot gets browned, remove it with a slotted spoon to a heavy-bottomed pot and cover. Brown all the cubes of meat this way. Turn flame off under frying-pan and set aside to use later.

Put the cumin, cloves, cinnamon, turmeric, and mustard powder, as well as the 2 (or less) red peppers and the chopped garlic and ginger, into the container of an electric blender. Add the vinegar and blend at high speed, until you have a smooth paste.

Put the minced onions in the frying-pan in which you browned the meat. Turn the heat to high and fry the onions for 5 minutes, scraping up the meat juices in the frying-pan as you do so. The onions must turn brown in spots. Turn heat down to medium and pour in the thick blended paste. Stir and fry for 5 minutes, adding a teaspoon of water every minute.

Now put in ½ pint of water and bring to the boil. Cover, lower heat, and simmer gently for 10 minutes.

When the sauce has cooked, pour it over the meat. Add the salt and mint, bring to the boil, cover, lower heat, and simmer gently for about an hour.

Remove the cover and raise the flame to high. Cook, stirring frequently, for about 10 minutes until the sauce is almost dried up, leaving only a few tablespoons in the pot and what is coating the meat. You will need to lower the heat the last few minutes so that the sauce does not stick.

To serve: Serve with *pooris*, a potato dish, and a green vegetable dish. You could also serve it with a rice dish and a green vegetable. As part of a Western-style meal, serve it with wild rice and a green salad.

Lamb with spinach

Serves 6–8

This is a traditional Moghul recipe. I use lamb for the recipe, but you could use beef (chuck or round) if you like.

3 lbs fresh spinach (or three 12 oz packages of frozen spinach)

3 medium-sized onions, peeled and coarsely chopped

a piece of fresh ginger, 2 inches long and 1 inch wide, peeled and coarsely chopped

7–8 cloves garlic, peeled and coarsely chopped

1 fresh hot green chili, chopped (optional), or $\frac{1}{8}$–$\frac{1}{2}$ tsp cayenne pepper

8 tbs vegetable oil

3 lbs boneless meat from shoulder of lamb, cut into 1-inch cubes (or shank, neck, or leg – see page 72 for proportions)

1 cinnamon stick, 3 inches long

7 whole cloves

7 whole cardamom pods

2 bay leaves

2 tbs ground coriander

1 tbs ground cumin

1 tsp ground turmeric

1 medium-sized tomato (tinned or fresh), peeled and finely chopped

2 tbs plain yogurt

$1\frac{1}{2}$ tsp salt

1 tbs garam masala

In a large pot, bring about 4 quarts of water to boil.

Meanwhile, trim and wash the fresh spinach thoroughly in cold water. Make sure you get all the sand out.

Drop the spinach in the boiling water, a pound batch at a time, and let it boil until the leaves wilt. You may need to push it down occasionally. As each batch wilts, scoop it out into a colander and run cold water over it. (If you are using frozen spinach, cook according to directions and drain.) When all the spinach is done, squeeze out most of the water and mince it. Keep aside in bowl.

Place the chopped onions, chopped ginger, garlic, green

chili, and 5 tablespoons of water in the blender container and blend at high speed until you have a smooth paste (about 1 minute).

Heat the oil in a 4–5-quart heavy-bottomed pot over medium heat. Pat dry the cubes of meat thoroughly on paper towels. Put 7 or 8 pieces at a time into the hot oil and brown them on all sides. Remove with a slotted spoon and set aside.

Put the cinnamon stick, cloves, cardamom pods, and bay leaves in the same hot oil. Stir. When the bay leaves begin to darken (10 to 20 seconds), add the paste from the blender (keep face averted). Keep stirring and frying for 10 minutes until the mixture darkens (if it sticks to the bottom, sprinkle a teaspoon of water at a time, and keep frying).

Now lower the flame and, continuing to stir and fry constantly, add at intervals first the coriander, cumin, and turmeric, 2 minutes later the chopped tomato, then about 5 minutes later the yogurt, and finally 2 minutes later the browned meat cubes. When meat and spices are well mixed put in the spinach. Add salt, bring to the boil, then cover and lower the heat to allow the mixture to simmer gently for 50 minutes. (Most meat gives out enough water for it to cook in its own juice, as it were. If you find that the meat is sticking, you can add up to $\frac{1}{4}$ pint of warm water.) Stir occasionally as it cooks.

At the end of the cooking time, uncover, increase heat, and cook rapidly until most of the liquid evaporates, leaving a thick sauce. Put in the *garam masala* and stir gently, being careful not to break meat pieces.

To serve: Place in warm dish and serve with *chapatis*, Potatoes with Asafetida and Cumin and Yogurt with Roasted Aubergine. Or you could serve it with plain boiled rice, any lentils, and a cauliflower dish if you like.

Sindhi gosht
(Sindhi meat)

Serves 6

This is a marvellous dish from Sindh, a state on the western coast of India. I first encountered it at a friend's house in Bombay, and insisted on leaving with the recipe in my pocket.

The meat (lamb) is marinated for 3 to 4 hours in a paste of onions, garlic, ginger, coriander, cumin, turmeric, red pepper, salt, pepper, and vinegar. It is then cooked in this marinade, with the addition of onion and fennel seeds.

$2\frac{1}{2}$ lbs boneless meat from lamb shoulder, cut into 1-inch cubes (or shank, neck, or leg – see page 72 for proportions)

2 medium-sized onions, peeled and coarsely chopped

a piece of fresh ginger, 2 inches long and 1 inch wide, coarsely chopped

6 cloves garlic, peeled and coarsely chopped

1 tbs ground coriander

2 tsp ground cumin

1 tsp ground turmeric

$\frac{1}{8}$–$\frac{1}{2}$ tsp cayenne pepper (optional; use desired amount)

4 fl. oz red wine vinegar

1 tsp salt

2 tsp whole fennel seeds

1 tsp whole black onion seeds (kalonji), if available

5 tbs vegetable oil

Remove fat and tissue from the cubes of meat.

In the container of an electric blender, place the chopped onions, ginger, garlic, coriander, cumin, turmeric, cayenne pepper (if used), vinegar, and salt. Blend at high speed until you have a smooth paste.

Pour paste into a bowl large enough to contain the meat. Prick the meat with a fork or with the point of a sharp knife and place in marinade. Mix well, cover, and leave for 3 to 4 hours. (Refrigerate if it is a very hot day; otherwise leave at room temperature.)

After the meat has marinated, pour contents of bowl into a wide 4-quart cooking pot. Add the fennel and onion seeds. Bring to the boil. Cover, lower heat, and simmer about 1 hour.

Lift off cover. Taste to check the salt (you may want to add a little more). Raise the heat and boil rapidly until most of the liquid evaporates. You will need to stir more frequently as the liquid diminishes. Now add the oil and keep stirring and frying over a medium flame. This dish must be 'dry', i.e., a thickish sauce should cling to the meat, which browns as the liquid cooks down. Be careful not to break meat pieces as you stir.

To serve: Place in a warmed dish and serve with *chapatis*, *parathas*, or *pooris*. You could also serve it with almost any kind of rice. With it, serve peas, okra, beans, or cabbage, and some yogurt dish, perhaps Yogurt with Potatoes.

Lamb chops with whole spices and yogurt

Serves 4

In this dish, lamb chops are cooked with whole spices, garlic, ginger, green coriander and yogurt. It is simple to make and very delicious in its final blend of flavours.

8 lamb chops
4 heaped tbs plain yogurt
3 tbs vegetable oil
10 whole black peppercorns
10 whole cloves
2 bay leaves
8 cardamom pods
2 cinnamon sticks, 2 inches long
2 whole dried hot red peppers (optional)

a piece of fresh ginger, about 1-inch cube, peeled and minced
2 cloves garlic, peeled and minced
4 tbs chopped fresh green coriander, or use fresh mint, watercress, or regular parsley as a substitute
1 tsp salt

Trim lamb chops of excess fat, leaving ⅛ inch along the sides. Pat dry with paper towels.

Mix the yogurt with 8 fl. oz of water and set aside in a non-metallic bowl.

Heat the oil in a 10–12-inch heavy-bottomed pot. When oil is very hot, put in 4 chops at a time, brown well on both sides, and remove with slotted spoon. Turn heat down to medium and fry the whole spices (peppercorns, cloves, bay leaves, cardamom, cinnamon, and red peppers) for about 20 seconds or until the bay leaves turn darker. Now add minced ginger and garlic, and fry, stirring, for a minute. Add the parsley and keep stirring for another minute.

Now put lamb chops back into the pot along with any liquid that may have collected in the bowl. Stir the yogurt water once again and pour over chops. Add salt, bring to the boil, cover, and simmer one hour. Stir gently every 10 minutes.

To Serve: Serve with Rice with Peas, Cucumber *Raita*, and any of the green bean recipes. Or serve with plain boiled potatoes and a green salad.

Pork chops cooked with whole spices and tamarind juice

Serves 4

Indians sometimes use Western cuts of meat to cook local dishes. We did not eat pork very often in our home, but every now and then my father would drive down to a special butcher to buy pork chops. Here is one of the ways we ate them.

N.B. This dish should be cooked in a stainless steel pan or a pan lined with porcelain, enamel or teflon.

1 tamarind lump about the
  size of a walnut
8 loin or rib pork chops
2 tbs vegetable oil
12 whole black peppercorns
10 whole cloves
2 cinnamon sticks, each
  2½ inches long

8 whole cardamom pods
2 cloves of garlic, peeled
2 whole dried hot red
  peppers (optional)
1½ tsp salt
1 tsp granulated sugar

Soak the tamarind lump in 6 fl. oz hot water for at least 2 hours.

Pat dry the eight pork chops with paper towels. Trim off all but ⅛ inch fat along the sides.

Heat oil in a 10–12-inch heavy-bottomed pot over medium-high heat. When oil is very hot, put in 4 pork chops at a time and brown them on both sides. This should take 3 to 4 minutes on each side.

Once the pork chops have browned, remove them to a side dish and keep covered. Lower flame to medium.

In the same oil place first the peppercorns, then the cloves, the cinnamon, the cardamom pods, the garlic, and finally the red pepper. Stir and fry these ingredients for about a minute or less until the red peppers darken and the garlic is a bit browned.

Now return the pork chops to the frying-pan and add ½ pint warm water and 1 teaspoon salt. Bring to the boil, cover, lower heat, and allow to cook very gently for ½ hour. Turn the chops over a few times as they cook.

Meanwhile, press the tamarind juice and pulp through a strainer into a non-metallic bowl. Discard tamarind fibres, skins, seeds, etc. (see page 44).

When the pork chops have cooked for 30 minutes, add 2 tablespoons tamarind juice, 1 teaspoon sugar, and ½ teaspoon salt. Mix well, turning the chops. Cover and keep cooking slowly another 20 to 30 minutes. By this time most of the liquid will have been absorbed, leaving just the fat behind.

To serve: In India, the fat and the spices would be served with the meat. Here, in Britain, I suggest you lift the chops from the pot with a slotted spoon, leaving all the oil and spices behind.

Place on a warm platter and serve with Rice with Peas or any other vegetable rice dish. You could also serve it with *Sookhe Aloo* ('Dry' Potatoes) instead. For a vegetable, the Cabbage with Onions would be a good idea. If you are not up to cooking a complicated vegetable dish (as I am sometimes not), serve just a salad, or sliced tomatoes.

Pork chops cooked with cabbage

Serves 4

This is another recipe for pork chops which is relatively simple and quite delicious. The chops and cabbage are cooked separately first and then combined to cook together for the last 10 minutes. At home we considered this a 'Western' dish and ate it with mashed or boiled potatoes. The combination of spices used is actually very Indian, even though the dish does lend itself to being served in a Western style.

1 medium-sized cabbage (2½ lbs or so)	10 whole cloves
1 medium-sized onion	12 whole black peppercorns
8 pork chops (loin or rib)	2 dried hot red peppers (optional)
5 tbs vegetable oil	1½ tsp salt
2 bay leaves	1 tsp sugar
2 cinnamon sticks, each 2½ inches long	½ tsp whole cumin seeds
8 cardamom pods	3 heaped tbs plain yogurt
	2 tbs lemon juice

Remove outer leaves of cabbage. Wash, quarter, remove core, and shred cabbage into long, fine slices.

Peel onion, cut into half lengthwise, and slice into thin half-rings.

Wipe the pork chops dry and trim away all the fat except about ⅛ inch along the sides.

Heat 2 tablespoons of the oil in a 10–12-inch heavy-bottomed pot over a medium-high flame. When oil is hot, put in 4 chops at a time and brown them well on both sides. This will take 3 to 4 minutes on each side. When all the chops have been browned, remove them to a plate or bowl.

In the same pot, over medium-high heat, fry the bay leaves, cinnamon, cardamom pods, cloves, peppercorns, and whole red peppers for about a minute or until red peppers darken. Now add ½ pint water, the pork chops, 1 teaspoon salt, and 1 teaspoon sugar. Bring to the boil, cover, turn down flame to very low, and simmer gently for about 35 minutes.

Meanwhile, heat the remaining 3 tablespoons of oil in a large wide pot over medium-high heat. When hot, put in the cumin seed. When the cumin seed darkens—in about 20 seconds —add the sliced onion and fry for about 5 minutes, stirring all the time. Turn the heat to medium and add the cabbage. Fry, stirring for a minute. Cover, lower flame, and allow cabbage to steam in its own liquid for 5 minutes.

Uncover and raise flame again to medium. Add ½ teaspoon salt. Now fry, stirring, for about 20 minutes until the cabbage is slightly browned. Turn off flame.

Put the yoghurt in a cup and add enough cold water to make 4 fl. oz. Mix well.

When the pork chops have cooked about 45 minutes, uncover and add the cabbage, the yogurt mixture, and the lemon juice. Mix well, cover, and simmer another 10 minutes.

To serve: Arrange pork chops and cabbage on a warm platter and serve with boiled or mashed potatoes. Some of my friends like to serve a spiced apple ring or other fruit relish with this dish.

Pork chops à la Jaffrey

Serves 2

I apologize for this name. The dish is really my very own concoction and unlikely to be served in any Indian home other than mine. Indians almost never use celery in their cooking. Nor do they often use soy sauce, though I must say that in the major cities the influence of an overcooked version of Chinese cuisine is certainly making itself felt. This recipe acknowledges its debt to that cuisine, but tastes, in the last analysis, rather Indian. The dish is simple to make and quite delicious. The recipe here serves 2 people (2 chops each). If you wish to serve 4, just double the ingredients.

N.B. This dish should be cooked in a stainless steel pan or a pan lined with porcelain, enamel or teflon.

4 pork chops (loin or rib)	a piece of fresh ginger, 1
2 tbs vegetable oil	inch long and $\frac{1}{2}$ inch wide,
2 bay leaves	sliced into 3 rounds
1 hot dried red pepper	2 cloves garlic, peeled
(optional)	$\frac{1}{8}$ tsp ground cinnamon
8 whole cloves	$\frac{1}{8}$ tsp ground mace
1 large stick of celery, diced	3 tbs soy sauce
1 medium-sized onion,	$1\frac{1}{2}$ tsp granulated sugar
coarsely chopped	$\frac{1}{2}$ lemon

Try to get pork chops that are evenly cut, so that they may brown evenly. Pat the chops dry and trim all but $\frac{1}{4}$ inch of the fat. Place them in a large frying-pan and turn heat on high. The chops should brown in their own fat. When they are a golden colour on both sides (press down areas that refuse to touch the frying-pan), remove them from frying-pan and place in bowl or plate. Turn off the heat and pour off only the accumulated fat in the frying-pan.

Heat the vegetable oil along with the coagulated juices in the same frying-pan over a medium flame, and put in the bay leaves, red pepper, and cloves. Stir. When the bay leaves change colour (this should take a few seconds) add celery, onions, ginger, and garlic. Stirring, fry over medium flame for 4 to 5 minutes or until everything is slightly browned. Add the browned pork chops, cinnamon, mace, soy sauce, sugar, and 2 fl. oz. water. Cut the lemon into 4 round slices (skin and all — remove pips though) and place over chops. Bring to the boil. Cover, lower heat, and simmer gently 50 minutes to 1 hour or until tender. Turn and mix gently every 10 to 15 minutes.

To serve: Place contents of frying-pan on platter and serve with Plain *Basmati* Rice and a green salad. A yogurt type of relish would be a good side dish. If you like you can remove the pieces of ginger and garlic before you serve.

Sweetbreads with fresh green coriander

Serves 6

If you like sweetbreads, you will enjoy this dish. I happen to love it, but my children are nearly always reduced to remarks like 'I like it, but I don't want it' — remarks which I counteract by drawing my eyebrows close together and staring at the wall in a hurt kind of way. This induces some polite nibbling which I try to make easier by saying, 'It's good for you'. My mother did the same kind of thing to me, so I see no reason to break tradition. Here is my recipe for sweetbreads. Try it. It's good for you!

2 lbs sweetbreads
2 medium-sized onions
4 cloves garlic, peeled and coarsely chopped
a piece of fresh ginger, 2½ inches long and 1 inch wide, peeled and coarsely chopped
5 tbs vegetable oil
1 hot green chili, finely sliced (more or less as desired), or ⅛–½ tsp cayenne pepper (as desired)

4 tbs chopped fresh green coriander
2 tsp ground coriander
1 tsp ground cumin
½ tsp ground turmeric
1 medium-sized tomato (tinned or fresh), peeled and finely chopped
2 tbs plain yogurt
1¾ tsp salt
2 tbs white vinegar
1 tbs lemon juice

Soak the sweetbreads in ice water for 1 hour.

Meanwhile, peel the onions. Slice one into fine rings and halve the rings. Set aside. Chop the other onion coarsely.

Put the chopped onion, garlic, and ginger in container of electric blender, add 3 tablespoons of water, and blend at high speed until you have a smooth paste (about 1 minute). Leave in container.

Heat the oil in a 10–12-inch frying-pan over medium heat. When hot, put in the halved onion rings and fry them, stirring, for about 5 minutes until they are crisp, dark brown, but not burned. With a slotted spoon, remove them and spread on paper towels.

Pour the paste from blender into the onion-flavoured oil. Fry, stirring, for 6 to 8 minutes, or until mixture turns a medium golden-brown. Add at intervals, stirring continuously, the green chili (or cayenne) and the green coriander; then, after 1 minute, lower the flame and add the coriander, cumin, turmeric; after another minute, the chopped tomato; and then the yogurt, continuing to fry and stir, for 2 to 3 minutes; finally ¾ teaspoon salt and 4 tablespoons warm water. Bring to the boil, cover, lower heat, and allow the mixture to simmer for 15 minutes.

In a large pot, bring 3 quarts of water to boil. Add 1 teaspoon salt and the vinegar. Remove the sweetbreads from the ice water and drain. Plunge them into the boiling water, drain, and plunge again into the ice water. Remove connecting tissue carefully (you can almost peel it off) and break sweetbreads into 1–1½-inch pieces.

After the sauce has cooked about 15 minutes, add the sweetbread pieces and lemon juice; stir, cover again, and cook gently for another 15 minutes.

To serve: Place in a warm dish. Sprinkle with the browned onions, and serve with hot *chapatis* and a vegetable and a yogurt dish of your choice. You could also serve any tomato or onion relish.

Chicken,
Other Birds,
& Eggs

Chicken cooked with yogurt
Chicken in light sauce
Chicken with potatoes
Chicken with sliced lemon and fried onions
Chicken with tomato sauce and butter
Chicken cutlets
Marinated grilled chicken
Grilled chicken strips
Roast chicken stuffed with spiced rice
Murgh mussallam (whole chicken with spices)
Duck—stuffed and roasted
Khitcherie unda (scrambled eggs, Indian style)
Chicken Moghlai
Eggs Moghlai

SEE ALSO

Tandoori chicken (page 179)
Chicken biryani (page 252)

 NTIL a few years ago there were only two ways one could buy poultry in India. Either you went up to the poultry market where live birds were kept in coops and you selected one, or you would wait at home for the poultry man to come around, hawking his wares. If he was somewhat affluent, he would arrive on a bicycle, but more often than not he came at a half-run, on his own two feet. On his humped shoulders he carried a bamboo, bent by the weight of a large basket dangling at each end. The lower section of these baskets was wicker, while the top was made of a rope mesh which could be opened and closed like an old-fashioned pouch. The occupants of these swaying baskets were the indignant birds—chickens and ducks mostly—which could not be seen except for a head here, a foot there, and a tail sticking out of the rope mesh; but they could be heard from a distance, squawking, quacking, and cackling. One had to know how to pick a bird by feeling its flesh. Experts like my father could even tell the age of the bird by prodding and squeezing in the right places.

In the last few years refrigeration and freezing have increased tremendously. The result is that poultry farms have mushroomed all over the country. The birds are sent, cleaned and plucked, to speciality stores where they can be bought much as they are in Britain. Of course, this is true only of the larger cities. The small towns and villages still rely on the old system.

The chickens in India seem to me to have more flavour than chickens here, though they can frequently be fairly tough, requiring a much longer cooking time. The only chicken that can be grilled in India is the $1\frac{1}{2}$–$2\frac{1}{2}$-lb spring chicken, and even then the bird must first be tenderized in a marinade containing green papaya or yogurt.

The Moghul miniature painters of the seventeenth century often showed royalty at the hunt, the *shikar*. Seated on cushioned, throne-like howdahs atop elephants or camels, they hunted anything from tigers to quail. The *shikar* still goes on, and although big game is generally left to the very rich, duck, geese, partridge, and quail can still be had by the ordinary Mr Singh on the street. Many restaurants have partridges on their daily menu, and many homes, like mine, serve roast duck frequently during the winter season.

The chicken available in British markets is so tender that it begins to fall apart well before it can go through the several stages required in most Indian recipes. Very often the chicken is cooked before the spices have permeated the meat. I have tried to adjust the chicken recipes to the tenderness of the English supermarket birds.

Most Indian chicken recipes require the removal of the skin before the bird is cooked. My English butcher shakes his head in despair every time I request this. To spare his feelings, I have now taken to doing the task myself. It is really quite easy and can be accomplished with a sharp, pointed knife and a bit of tugging in certain places.

Also, Indians generally cut their chicken into small pieces but rarely remove the bones. Legs are separated into drumsticks and thighs, breasts are cut into four or six pieces, backs into two or three, and wings into two. The reason is to allow the spices to penetrate the meat and bones as much as possible. I often serve just legs and breasts. They are easier to handle with knife and fork, and no one is stuck with the back. Backs and wings necessitate digital manipulation. They are to be avoided if you have finicky eaters.

While chicken is considered rather ordinary fare in this country, in India it is still regarded as an indulgence reserved for the rich. To be served chicken in someone's house definitely means that you are getting special treatment. In restaurants it is always one of the more expensive items on the menu.

In my recipes you will notice that I often brown the chicken quickly before I leave it to cook. In India this browning is done either with the paste of onions, garlic, ginger, and spices or at the end, when the chicken is cooked and the sauce has been reduced over high heat. Since the bird cooks very quickly here, any attempt at browning during these two stages leaves my chicken a disintegrated, shattered mess. I have discovered that an initial browning of the chicken provides the right colour and the bird does not fall apart.

Chicken cooked with yogurt

Serves 4–6

Here is a simple chicken recipe using very few of the spices generally associated with Indian cuisine. Yet the dish is typically North Indian. It is easy to make and very popular with children and adults alike.

4 chicken legs
1 whole chicken breast
¼ pint plus 2 tbs plain yogurt
5 medium-sized onions
2 cloves garlic, peeled and
   coarsely chopped

a piece of fresh ginger, about
   1-inch cube, peeled and
   coarsely chopped
7 tbs vegetable oil
1 tsp salt
⅛–¼ tsp cayenne pepper (as
   and if desired)

Skin all the chicken pieces. Divide each leg into 2 pieces (drumstick and thigh). Quarter the chicken breast. Pat dry the chicken pieces and set aside.

Put ¼ pint yogurt in a bowl. Add 6 fl. oz water, a little at a time, beating with a fork as you do so.

Peel all the onions. Cut 4 in half, lengthwise, then slice them into half-rings, about ⅛ inch thick. Chop the other onion coarsely.

Put the chopped onion, garlic, and ginger in the container of an electric blender. Add 6 tablespoons of water and blend to a smooth paste.

Heat 5 tablespoons of the oil in a 10-inch pot over medium heat. Put in the sliced onions and fry them, stirring, 8 to 10 minutes or until they have turned dark brown at the edges but are still limp. Remove them with a slotted spoon to a small bowl and set aside.

Add the remaining 2 tablespoons of oil to the pot and put in about 4 pieces of chicken at a time. Fry them, at medium-high heat, 7 to 8 minutes or until they are browned on all sides. Remove chicken pieces to plate with a slotted spoon.

Turn heat to low and pour paste from the blender into the pot, keeping your face averted. Scrape the bottom of the pot for browned meat juices and mix in scrapings with the paste. Now raise the heat to medium and fry, stirring, 4 to 5 minutes. Add 1 tablespoon plain yogurt, scraping bottom of pot and continuing to fry and stir another minute. Then add 1 more tablespoon yogurt, stirring for another minute.

Now put into the pot the chicken pieces, the well-blended yogurt and water mixture, the salt, and the cayenne pepper (if you desire it). Stir and bring to the boil. Cover, lower heat, and simmer 20 minutes.

Remove lid, raise heat to medium, and cook for 5 minutes to boil down some of the liquid, turning the chicken pieces carefully. (You should be left with a thick sauce.)

Mix in reserved fried onions, and cook at same heat another 2 minutes, stirring occasionally.

To serve: Place contents of pot in warmed dish and serve with hot *pooris* or hot *chapatis* or almost any kind of rice. You might serve okra or aubergine or green beans as a vegetable. Since this dish is cooked with yogurt, serve a non-yogurt relish, such as Cucumber and Tomato with Lemon Juice. A fresh green chutney (mint or coriander) might also be refreshing.

Chicken in light sauce

Serves 4–6

Here is another relatively uncomplicated chicken dish made with whole spices (*khara masala*), ginger, and garlic. In India a whole chicken is used, skinned and cut into small serving portions. I often serve just legs and breasts since they are easier to handle with fork and knife and no one is stuck with the back.

This dish tastes particularly good if you make it a day in advance and let it sit in its sauce, covered and refrigerated, overnight. It can be reheated easily on top of the stove over a low flame.

1 tbs tomato purée	1 cinnamon stick, about 2½ inches long
3 tbs plain yogurt	
4 cloves garlic, peeled and coarsely chopped	2 bay leaves
	5 whole cardamom pods
a piece of fresh ginger, about 1-inch cube, peeled and coarsely chopped	5 whole cloves
	2 hot dried red peppers (optional)
4 chicken legs	1 tsp ground turmeric
1 whole chicken breast	1 tsp salt
6 tbs vegetable oil	⅛ tsp freshly ground pepper
	1 tbs lemon juice

In a small bowl, combine tomato purée, yogurt, and ½ pint of water. Mix well and set aside.

Put chopped garlic and ginger into the container of an electric blender, along with 2 tablespoons of water. Blend until you have a smooth paste.

Cut chicken into serving portions: divide legs into drumstick and thigh, and quarter the breast. Remove skin from pieces of chicken and pat dry.

Heat oil in heavy-bottomed 10–12-inch casserole-type pot over medium-high heat. Put in chicken pieces, a few at a time, and brown on all sides. When each batch turns a golden-brown, remove with slotted spoon and do the next batch. When all chicken pieces have been done, put the cinnamon, bay leaves, cardamom, cloves, and red pepper into the same oil. Stir once. The spices will darken immediately. Now pour in the paste from the blender (keep face averted as you do this) and add the turmeric. Stir and fry for about a minute.

Next, put in the browned chicken pieces, the mixture of tomato purée sauce, yogurt, and water, salt, pepper, and lemon juice. Bring to the boil. Cover, lower heat, and simmer gently 20 to 25 minutes, turning chicken pieces a few times.

Uncover pot, raise flame to medium, and cook 5 to 7 minutes or until sauce is reduced to half, turning the chicken pieces over gently.

To serve: Put contents of pot into a hot bowl and serve with plain boiled rice or hot *pooris*. Serve at least one vegetable — green beans, aubergine, or cauliflower might be nice. As a relish, Tamarind Chutney with Bananas or Cucumber and Tomato with Lemon Juice could be served.

Chicken with potatoes

Serves 2–3

This dish is fairly similar to the preceding one. No yogurt is used, however, and the addition of boiled potatoes gives it a rather thickish gravy. If you wish to double this recipe, double all ingredients except the oil. Instead of 5, use 6 tablespoons of oil. Your cooking time will not change much, except that of course you will have to fry the chicken in two batches. You will also need a bigger pot. (In this recipe I use a frying-pan.)

3 medium-sized potatoes
 for boiling
1 medium-sized onion,
 peeled and coarsely
 chopped
3 cloves garlic, peeled and
 coarsely chopped
a piece of fresh ginger, about
 1-inch cube, peeled and
 coarsely chopped
1½ lbs chicken sections
5 tbs vegetable oil

1 cinnamon stick, 2½–3
 inches long
1 bay leaf
4 whole cardamom pods
2 whole hot dried red
 peppers (optional)
2 whole black peppercorns
½ tsp ground turmeric
1 tbs tomato purée
1 pint chicken broth (tinned
 or homemade)
½ tsp salt

Put your potatoes to boil. When done, drain off water and leave potatoes to cool. (Do not use boiled potatoes which have been refrigerated for this recipe.)

Place onion, garlic, and ginger in container of blender with 5 tablespoons water and blend to smooth paste.

Remove skin from chicken pieces and pat them dry.

Heat oil in a 12-inch frying-pan over medium-high flame, then add the cinnamon, bay leaf, cardamom, red peppers, peppercorns, and chicken pieces. Fry chicken pieces quickly on all sides until golden-brown. Remove chicken with slotted spoon and set aside.

Pour the paste from blender into frying-pan, averting your face. Add turmeric and fry, stirring, for about 3 minutes. Now add the tomato purée and the chicken broth. Mix. Bring to the boil. Cover, lower heat, and simmer gently for 15 minutes.

Peel and quarter the potatoes. Add salt, the browned chicken pieces, and the potatoes to the sauce. Stir, bring to the boil, cover, lower heat, and simmer gently for 20 to 25 minutes or until chicken is tender. Turn chicken and potatoes a few times while they are cooking.

To serve: Put chicken pieces, potatoes, and sauce into a bowl and serve with hot *chapatis*, *parathas*, or *pooris*. Serve green beans or peas with it and at least one kind of relish (a yogurt relish might be a good idea).

Chicken with sliced lemon and fried onions

Serves 4–6

Cooked with lemon slices, sugar, and fried onions, this chicken dish is unusual and quite delicious. You could use a whole bird, cut into small sections, or you could buy just legs and breasts, dividing the legs into drumstick and thigh and quartering the breast.

N.B. This dish should be cooked in a stainless steel pot or a pot lined with porcelain, enamel or teflon.

3–3½ lbs chicken sections
3 medium-sized onions
a piece of fresh ginger, about
   1-inch cube, peeled and
   coarsely chopped
4 cloves garlic, peeled and
   coarsely chopped
8 tbs vegetable oil
1 tbs ground coriander
1 tsp ground cumin

½ tsp ground turmeric
2 tbs plain yogurt
1 tbs tomato purée
1 tsp salt
¼ tsp ground cinnamon
¼ tsp ground cloves
⅛ tsp cayenne pepper
1 whole lemon
1 tbs sugar
⅛ tsp freshly ground pepper

Skin all the chicken pieces and pat them dry.

Peel the onions. Chop two of them coarsely and put them into the container of an electric blender. Cut the third one in half lengthwise, then slice it into thin half-rounds and set aside.

Add 6 tablespoons of water, the ginger, and the garlic to the onions in the blender and blend at high speed until you have a smooth paste.

Heat 6 tablespoons of the oil in a 10–12-inch pot over medium-high flame. When hot, put in the sliced onions and fry them, stirring, until they are darkish brown and crisp, though not burned. Remove onions with a slotted spoon and leave them to drain on paper towels.

In the same oil, brown the chicken pieces on all sides until they are golden. (Do this speedily over high flame so chicken browns but does not cook through. You will need to do it in at least two batches.) Remove chicken with slotted spoon to a bowl or plate.

Add the remaining 2 tablespoons of oil to the pot. Pour in the paste from the blender. (Keep face averted.) Stirring, fry on medium-high heat for about 10 minutes or until paste turns a nice golden-brown. Now put in the coriander, cumin, and turmeric and fry, stirring continuously; after another 2 minutes add yogurt, a teaspoon at a time; after 2 or 3 minutes, the tomato purée, a little at a time, continuing to stir and fry. Finally, add salt, cinnamon, cloves, cayenne pepper, and ¾ pint of water. Bring to the boil, cover, lower heat, and simmer gently for 10 minutes.

Cut the lemon into 4 or 5 slices, discarding the end pieces, and remove the seeds. Add lemon slices along with the chicken pieces, fried onions, sugar, and freshly ground pepper to the sauce, stir, and bring to the boil. Cover, lower heat, and simmer gently for 20 to 25 minutes or until chicken is tender, turning the pieces every now and then. If chicken sticks to bottom of pot, add a little more water. You should end up with a very thick sauce.

To serve: Empty contents of pot into shallow serving bowl. Arrange the cooked lemon slices on top of the chicken pieces. Serve with any rice dish or with *pooris* or *chapatis*. Yogurt with Tiny Dumplings goes well with it. For vegetables you could serve Carrots and Peas with Ginger and green coriander or cauliflower or any other vegetable you like. Almost any kind of *dal* would also complement the dish.

Chicken with tomato sauce and butter

Serves 6

The original version of this dish is to be had at the Moti Mahal restaurant in Delhi. There, the *Tandoori* Chicken (page 179) is cut into small serving sections and put into a rich sauce of creamed tomatoes, butter, and spices.

My very inventive sister, Kamal, has worked out her own version, slightly different, but equally good. The Indian chicken being as tough as it is, what she does is to combine all ingredients — tomatoes, onions, ginger, garlic, butter, whole spices, and chicken sections — in a covered pot and cook them until the chicken is three-quarters done. By this time the meat has absorbed all the necessary flavours. Then she lifts off the cover and over a high flame stirs and fries the chicken and sauce until almost all the water evaporates and the chicken and paste-like sauce are a dark reddish-brown.

This is very hard to do in Britain, because, as I mentioned earlier, the chicken is very tender and cooks too fast to allow all the flavours to be absorbed and the final frying to be accomplished without disintegration. So I have worked out a third version! Here it is.

4 chicken legs
2 chicken breasts
2 medium-sized onions,
  peeled and coarsely
  chopped
5 cloves garlic, peeled and
  coarsely chopped
a piece of fresh ginger, about
  2 inches long and 1 inch
  wide, peeled and coarsely
  chopped
1 stick of cinnamon, 2½–3
  inches, broken up
seeds from 6 cardamom pods

8 whole cloves
1 tsp whole black pepper-
  corns
2 bay leaves, crumbled
1 hot dried red pepper (or
  more, as and if desired),
  crumbled
6 tbs vegetable oil
8 medium-sized tomatoes
  (tinned or fresh), peeled
  and finely chopped
1 tsp salt
4 tbs lightly salted butter

125

Remove skin from all chicken pieces. Divide legs into drum-stick and thigh, and quarter the breasts. Pat dry and put aside.

In the container of an electric blender, combine the onions, garlic, ginger, cinnamon, cardamom seeds, cloves, pepper-corns, bay leaves, red pepper, and 3 tablespoons water. Blend until you have a smooth paste.

Heat the oil in a 10–12-inch casserole-type pot over a high flame. When hot, put in the chicken pieces, 4 or 5 at a time, and brown them quickly (about a minute on each side). Re-move with a slotted spoon. You will need to brown the chicken in several batches.

Turn heat to medium and pour in the paste from the blender. (Keep face averted.) Stir and fry the paste for 5 minutes, scrap-ing the bottom of the pot well as you do so. Now add the chopped tomatoes, ¼ pint water, and the salt. Bring to the boil and cover. Turn heat to very low and simmer gently for 30 minutes, stirring every 6 or 7 minutes.

Add the chicken pieces to the pot, as well as any juices that may have collected. Bring to the boil, cover, and simmer over low heat for 25 to 30 minutes. Stir gently every 5 or 6 minutes to avoid sticking and burning. Be careful not to break the chicken pieces as you stir. Lift cover, turn up heat and burn off most of the liquid.

Cut the butter into 4 pats. Take the chicken off the heat. Drop in the pats of butter and stir them in gently. Serve immediately.

To serve: Place contents of pot in a warm dish and serve with Rice with Black-eyed Peas or *naan*. For vegetables, you could have Aubergine *Bharta* or Fresh Peas with Ginger and Green Coriander. You could, if you like, also serve Onions Pickled in Vinegar as they do at the Moti Mahal Restaurant in Delhi.

Chicken cutlets

Serves 2

Breaded chops and cutlets were brought to India by its last conquerors, the French and the British. They passed along the delicacy to the Indian upper classes, who were only too eager to ape and copy. But while these upper classes ate chops and cutlets as a status symbol, they were secretly very bored by the blandness of these foods. So they began to spice them up. Soon a whole new class of cooks developed. Under the distinguished titles of *khansama* ('lord of the pot') and *babarchi*, they cooked for the rich and specialized in Westernized foods adapted to the Indian palate, or, very often, Indian foods adapted to the Western palate. They could cook a treacle pudding just as easily as they could a roast duck stuffed with Indian herbs and spices, and a jam tart just as easily as a delicate *pullao*.

It is from this line of cooks that we get the recipe for chicken cutlets. Our family cook had not only inherited the recipe for an Indianized version of the cutlet, but he had also been taught a different name for it. As he said it, it sounded more like 'cutliss' than anything else. So every Friday, which was the day off for all Muslim butchers (and most butchers were Muslim), we had either fish or chicken. And when it was chicken, it was frequently 'chicken cutliss'. The 'cutliss' were very often served with boiled beans and potatoes as a first course for dinner. Then, as a second course, we had *chapatis* with the usual Indian lentils and vegetables. For dessert, we switched again to a sponge roll or lemon tarts, both of which were very popular. These sudden changes of cuisine at the same meal struck no one as peculiar.

I use chicken breasts for the cutlets. One breast (two cutlets) serves one person generously, two people skimpily. If you are having cutlets as a first course, you could serve four people easily with two breasts. The chicken breasts are boned and skinned (your butcher will do this on request, but it is easy to do yourself), and marinated overnight in a paste of onions, garlic, ginger, green coriander, lemon juice, salt, and pepper. They are then dipped in a beaten egg, breaded, and fried. Very simple, and very mild.

2 whole chicken breasts, boned, skin removed, and each breast split into 2 sections (about 1 lb of meat)

3 cloves garlic, peeled and coarsely chopped

a piece of ginger, 1 inch long and 1 inch wide, peeled and coarsely chopped

½ medium-sized onion, peeled and coarsely chopped

1 fresh hot green chili, finely sliced (this will make your chicken only very mildly hot; use 2 or 3 if you want it hotter)

2 tbs chopped fresh green coriander or Italian parsley, as a second-best substitute

3 tbs lemon juice

¾ tsp salt

⅛ tsp freshly ground pepper

1 egg

bread crumbs (homemade bread crumbs are best: leave 6 slices of white bread exposed for 24 hours, or until they harden; then crush with rolling pin or spin in the blender)

vegetable oil, enough for at least ¼ inch in frying-pan

Garnish

lemon juice and wedges
salt and freshly ground pepper

a few sprigs fresh green coriander

Four to 24 hours before cooking, marinate chicken. Place the garlic, ginger, onion, green chili, fresh green coriander, lemon juice, salt, and pepper in the container of an electric blender. Add a tablespoon of water and blend at high speed until you have a smooth paste. (You may need to stop the blender and scrape down the paste a few times.)

Place the 4 boned and skinned chicken pieces in a bowl. Prick all over with a fork. Pour the marinade paste over chicken and rub into the pieces. Cover, and leave refrigerated 4 to 24 hours.

(It will taste better if you can marinate it 24 hours.)

30 minutes before serving: Beat the egg in a bowl.

Spread out the bread crumbs on a flat plate.

Lift out chicken pieces, one at a time, leaving marinade sticking to them. Dip first in beaten egg and then in bread crumbs. Coat both sides generously with bread crumbs and set aside. Prepare all chicken pieces this way, and let them sit, breaded, for 10 minutes.

15 minutes before serving: Heat oil in a 10–12-inch frying pan over medium-low flame. When the oil is hot, place chicken cutlets in the frying-pan and fry 6 to 7 minutes on each side. (Adjust heat carefully so chicken pieces turn a rich golden-brown in the given time.) Remove gently with a spatula.

To serve: Place cutlets on a warm platter. Sprinkle with salt, freshly ground pepper, and lemon juice. Serve garnished with lemon wedges and fresh green coriander. With cutlets serve Rice with Peas or Rice with Potatoes and Cumin Seed and a green salad. If you like, you could serve boiled potatoes and peas. Almost all vegetables go with this dish.

Marinated grilled chicken

Serves 4–6

This is a simple recipe in which the marinade, a mixture of onions, ginger, garlic, cumin, coriander, vinegar, and oil, is made in the electric blender. The chicken is marinated, then grilled. It could also be barbecued over charcoal.

**3–3½ lbs chicken, preferably
legs, thighs, and breasts,
or a whole chicken, cut
into serving pieces**

Marinade

2 medium-sized onions,
   peeled and coarsely
   chopped
4 cloves garlic, peeled and
   coarsely chopped
a piece of fresh ginger, about
   1 inch long and 1 inch
   wide, peeled and coarsely
   chopped

2–3 fresh hot green chilies,
   or $\frac{1}{4}$–$\frac{1}{2}$ tsp cayenne pepper
   (optional)
1 tsp whole cumin seeds
1 tbs ground coriander
$\frac{1}{4}$ pint wine vinegar
$\frac{1}{4}$ pint olive or vegetable oil
2 tsp salt
$\frac{1}{8}$ tsp freshly ground pepper

Garnish

fresh green coriander,
   chopped

Combine all the ingredients for the marinade in the container of an electric blender. Blend at high speed until you have a smooth paste.

Pull off and discard the skin from chicken pieces. Prick chicken all over with a fork and place in a bowl. Pour marinade over chicken. Cover and refrigerate 2 to 3 hours (24 hours would be best).

Fifty minutes before serving, heat your grill. Remove chicken pieces from bowl and, with as much marinade clinging to them as possible, place on baking sheet lined with aluminium foil. Grill 15 minutes on each side or until chicken gets well browned. (Adjust distance from grill so it does not brown too fast.)

To serve: Place chicken on a warm platter and sprinkle green coriander over it. Serve with a rice dish, a green vegetable, and a *dal*.

Grilled chicken strips

Serves 6–8

Chicken breasts are boned, cut into narrow strips, and then mixed with a paste consisting of oil, vinegar, onion, ginger, garlic, and fennel seed, and the 'hot' (*garam*) spices: cardamom, cloves, cinnamon, black peppercorns, etc. The chicken sits in the marinade 4 to 5 hours. It is then grilled and served. This dish is very easy to prepare, since most of the work is done by the electric blender. Its taste is heavenly, lightly but definitely spiced. It is very versatile—I have successfully served it as an hors d'œuvre with toothpicks, at lunches with salad, at big dinners along with a meat dish, and at picnics, having made it the night before. It tastes as good cold as it does hot.

Get your butcher to bone and skin the chicken breasts for you. Many supermarkets sell already boned and skinned chicken breast 'cutlets' which could be used, or you could do the skinning and boning yourself without undue exertion.

3 lbs chicken breasts, boned and skinned (weight after boning and skinning)

Marinade

5 tbs olive or vegetable oil
4 tbs red wine vinegar
1 medium-sized onion, peeled and chopped
1 whole head of garlic (each clove peeled and chopped)
a piece of fresh ginger, about 1-inch cube, peeled and chopped
2 tbs whole fennel seeds
2 tbs ground cumin

2 tsp ground coriander
seeds from 8 cardamom pods
1 tsp ground cinnamon
8 whole cloves
20 black peppercorns
$\frac{1}{2}$–$\frac{3}{4}$ tsp cayenne pepper (use as desired; these measures are for a mildly hot dish)
2 tsp salt
1 tbs tomato purée

Combine all ingredients needed for the marinade in the container of an electric blender. Blend at high speed until you have a smooth paste.

Wipe all the chicken pieces thoroughly dry. Divide breasts in 2 sections and then cut each section into strips that are $1\frac{1}{2}$ or 2 inches long and about $\frac{1}{2}$ inch wide.

In a bowl combine the chicken and the marinade, and mix well. I use my hands to rub the marinade into the chicken pieces. Cover and refrigerate 4 to 5 hours.

Preheat the grill (45 minutes before serving if you are going to eat it hot). Line a baking tray with aluminium foil. Spread the chicken (most of the marinade will cling to it) thinly on the tray. (You will need to do two batches unless you have an extra large grill.)

When the grill is well heated, put in the tray with the chicken. Grill for 10 minutes, turn the pieces over, and grill another 10 minutes, or until the chicken is lightly browned. Remove chicken pieces with a spatula and place in warm serving dish. Cover and keep in warm place. Do the second batch the same way. (I usually put the second batch in to grill and serve the first batch. As soon as people are ready for seconds, the next batch is almost ready.) Remember, this chicken will *not* have a uniformly dark-brown colour; it should be dark only in spots.

To serve: Place on warm platter and serve with a rice dish, a lamb dish if you are entertaining, a yogurt dish, and at least one vegetable. Serve as an appetizer with toothpicks. Eat it cold at picnics, also with the aid of toothpicks.

Roast chicken stuffed with spiced rice

Serves 4

If you are tired of your usual chicken roast, try this one. With the expenditure of just a wee bit more time and energy, you can create a sensational dish—spicy without being hot, simple without being dull!

I use precooked (usually left-over!) rice for the stuffing. Adjust the salt for the stuffing according to the saltiness of the precooked rice.

1 roasting chicken, 4 lbs (at room temperature)

Marinade

2 tbs olive oil (or vegetable oil
1 tbs lemon juice
¼ tsp salt

⅛ tsp freshly ground pepper
½ tsp ground cumin
¼ tsp ground garam masala

Stuffing

1 medium-sized onion, peeled and coarsely chopped
2 cloves garlic, peeled and coarsely chopped
a piece of fresh ginger, about 1-inch cube, peeled and coarsely chopped
3 tomatoes (tinned or fresh), peeled and chopped

1 tsp ground coriander
1 tsp ground cumin
4 tbs vegetable oil
¼ tsp whole black mustard seeds
¼ tsp whole cumin seeds
2 teacups (well-packed) cooked rice
½ tsp salt (or as needed)

Mix all the ingredients for the marinade. Wipe chicken well with a cloth or paper towel so it is as dry as possible. Brush three-fourths of the marinade all over the chicken, inside and out. Let the chicken sit, unrefrigerated, for about 2 hours. Save rest of marinade.

Preheat oven to 450°F., Mark 8.

Place the onions, garlic, ginger, tomatoes, coriander, and cumin in the container of an electric blender. Blend at high speed until you have a smooth paste.

Heat the 4 tablespoons of oil in a 10–12-inch frying-pan over medium-high flame. When very hot, drop in the mustard and cumin seeds. When the mustard seeds begin to rise and pop (15 to 30 seconds), add the paste from the blender, keeping face averted, as the mixture will bubble rapidly and splatter. Stirring, fry the paste on medium-high heat until it is browned. The oil should separate from the paste (this will take about 10 minutes). You will need to stir more frequently as the moisture evaporates.

Add the cooked rice, and the salt as and if you need it. Turn heat to low and mix the browned paste with the rice. Loosely stuff the chicken with the rice and truss it. Place it in an ovenproof baking dish, breast up, and put it in the preheated oven.

Let the chicken brown for about 20 minutes, basting it with the remaining marinade mixture every 5 minutes. Turn down the heat to 350°F., Mark 4. Cook another hour or until the leg moves easily when pushed up and down at its socket. Baste every 10 minutes with the juices that will come out of the chicken.

To serve: Lift chicken gently and put on a warm platter. Let it sit for 15 minutes so juices will not flow out when carved. Serve simply with a green salad or, if you like, with any green beans, peas, or cauliflower dish. Sweet Tomato Chutney also tastes good with this roast.

Murgh mussallam
(whole chicken with spices)

Serves 4

In this royal dish, a whole chicken is first marinated in a paste consisting of garlic, ginger, turmeric, hot green chilies, *garam masala*, yogurt, and salt for about 2 hours. It is then browned and simmered with a second paste made up of fried onions and garlic, ginger, almonds, lemon juice, and an array of spices like cardamom, cinnamon, nutmeg, mace, etc. Hard-boiled eggs are put into the sauce about 10 minutes before the chicken is done and then arranged around the chicken.

1 whole chicken, about 3½ lbs
1 tsp loosely packed leaf
  saffron

4 hard-boiled eggs

Marinade

6 cloves of garlic, peeled and
  coarsely chopped
a piece of fresh ginger, about
  2 inches long and 1 inch
  wide, peeled and coarsely
  chopped
1½ tsp salt

½ tsp garam masala
½ tsp ground turmeric
4 tbs plain yogurt
2 fresh hot green chilies,
  sliced, or ¼–½ tsp cayenne
  pepper (optional)

Cooking paste

8 tbs vegetable oil
4 medium-sized onions,
  peeled and coarsely
  chopped
4 cloves garlic, peeled and
  coarsely chopped
a piece of fresh ginger, about
  1 inch long and 1 inch
  wide, peeled and coarsely
  chopped
1 tbs blanched almonds,
  slivered
1 tbs ground coriander
1 tsp ground cumin

seeds from 4 large black or
  8 small green cardamom
  pods
$\frac{1}{4}$ tsp ground cloves
$\frac{1}{2}$ tsp ground cinnamon
$\frac{1}{4}$ tsp ground nutmeg
$\frac{1}{4}$ tsp ground mace
$1\frac{1}{2}$ tsp salt
$\frac{1}{4}$ tsp freshly ground black
  pepper
$\frac{1}{2}$ tsp cayenne pepper
  (optional)
3 tbs lemon juice

Garnish

2 tbs finely chopped fresh green coriander

First make your marinade.

Put the ingredients for the marinade into the electric blender. Blend at high speed until you have a smooth paste.

Peel the skin off the whole chicken. Where it is hard to peel, as on the wing tips, you can leave it on. Prick the chicken all over with a fork, place in a bowl, and pour marinade over it. Rub the chicken well with the marinade, both inside and out, and leave, unrefrigerated, for about 2 hours.

Rinse out your blender container. You will need it again.

Soak the saffron in 2 tablespoons of hot water.

Now make the paste to cook the chicken in. Heat 6 tablespoons of the vegetable oil in a 10–12-inch heavy-bottomed pot over a medium-high flame. When hot, put in the chopped onions, garlic, and ginger. Stir and fry for 8 to 10 minutes or until the onions are brown at the edges but still soft. With a slotted spoon, remove onions, garlic, and ginger and place them in the blender container. Reserve the cooking oil.

Place a small iron or aluminium frying-pan over a medium flame. When it is hot, put the blanched almonds in it. Stir them around until they turn golden, then add them to the blender container. In the same small frying-pan put the ground coriander and cumin. Stir, watching, until the spices turn a few shades darker (do *not* let them burn). They will smoke quite a bit, but don't worry—it is to be expected. Then put them in the blender along with the cardamom seeds, cloves, cinnamon, nutmeg, mace, salt, black pepper, cayenne, lemon juice, and ¼ pint of water. Blend all to a smooth paste, pausing, if necessary, to push the mixture down with a rubber spatula a few times.

When the chicken has marinated for 2 hours, heat the reserved oil and add 2 more tablespoons of oil to it. Do this over medium-high flame. Lift the chicken out of the bowl along with any clinging marinade and place in the oil. Brown it as well as you can on all sides. You will not be able to do this too evenly, but it does not matter.

When the chicken has browned, turn heat down to low. Take the paste from the blender and, using a rubber spatula, spread it all over the chicken. Add ½ pint of water to the pot and bring to the boil. Cover tightly. Turn heat to low and simmer gently for about 40 minutes or until chicken is tender. Turn chicken 2 or 3 times during the first 15 minutes of this cooking time. After that, leave it breast up and baste it every 5 to 7 minutes with the sauce.

Peel the hard-boiled eggs, and 10 minutes before the chicken is fully cooked put them in the pot, spooning some sauce over them as well. Pour saffron and saffron water over chicken. Cover and continue simmering until chicken is tender.

To serve: Lift chicken carefully out of pot and place it on warmed platter. Arrange eggs around it. If you like, skim the oil off the sauce before pouring it over chicken and eggs. Sprinkle with chopped green coriander. Serve with a fish *pullao* or Rice with Peas. You could also serve any vegetable you like: Fried Aubergines with Sour Green Chutney, or a cauliflower or bean dish might be nice. A yogurt relish is almost a must with *Murgh Mussallam*. I often serve Yogurt with Spinach.

Duck—stuffed and roasted

Serves 2

The duck here is stuffed with rice, spices, raisins, and nuts to make a superbly festive meal. I find that a 4–4½-lb duck really serves only two people well. It has a large cavity inside and rather small legs. Most of the meat is around the breast area, and that is not too much.

1 duck, 4–4½ lbs, at room temperature—liver, gizzard, and heart included

2 tbs vegetable oil

½ tsp whole cumin seeds

½ tsp whole fennel seeds

15 fenugreek seeds

1 medium-sized onion, finely chopped

a piece of fresh ginger, 1 inch long and ½ inch wide, grated or minced

1 hot green chili, cut into thin rounds, or ⅛–¼ tsp cayenne pepper (optional)

1 tbs tomato purée mixed with 2 tbs water

3 tbs minced fresh green coriander

2 teacups cooked rice

2 tbs golden raisins

1 tbs dried apricots, chopped to the size of raisins

3 tbs pine nuts or slivered blanched almonds

½ tsp salt (more if the rice is unsalted)

⅛ tsp freshly ground black pepper

1½ tsp lemon juice

1½ tsp sugar

additional salt, pepper

If the duck was frozen, defrost completely well ahead of time. It must be at room temperature before you cook it. Pat it dry (otherwise it will not brown well). Prick the skin with a fork to allow the lining of fat to ooze out as it melts. Mince the liver, gizzard, and heart.

Preheat oven to 450°F., Mark 8.

Heat the oil in a 10–12-inch frying-pan over medium-high flame, and add the cumin, fennel, and fenugreek seeds. Stir. When the cumin seeds begin to darken (this will take 10 to 20 seconds) add the onions, ginger, and green chili if you wish to use it. Fry, stirring, for about 2 minutes or until onions turn a little brown. Now add at intervals, continuing to stir and fry, the minced liver, gizzard, and heart; after a minute or two, the tomato purée and minced green coriander; in another 2 minutes, the cooked rice, turning heat to low; and finally, the raisins, apricots, and pine nuts or almonds, mixing everything well. Stir and fry another 5 minutes.

Season with salt, cayenne pepper (if you wish to use it instead of the green chili), black pepper, lemon juice, and sugar.

Stuff the duck loosely with the mixture in the frying-pan, truss, place it in roasting pan breast up, and set in the preheated oven.

Let duck brown for 20 to 25 minutes. There is no need to baste. Remove fat with a bulb baster as it accumulates in roasting pan.

Turn heat to 350°F., Mark 4, and let duck cook another 1½ hours, or until the juices of the bird run a clear yellow when it is pricked

To serve: Place duck on a warm serving platter. Sprinkle skin with a little salt and freshly ground pepper. Serve with green beans or peas, or with a simple green salad if you like.

Khitcherie unda
(scrambled eggs, Indian style)

Serves 2–3

3 tbs butter
½ medium-sized onion,
    finely chopped
1 small tomato, chopped
1 tbs chopped fresh green
    coriander

½–1 hot green chili, finely
    sliced
4 medium–large eggs, well
    beaten
salt and pepper to taste

Melt the butter in a 10-inch frying-pan over medium heat. Add onions and sauté them for a minute or until they begin to turn translucent.

Add diced tomato, green coriander, and sliced green chili. Stir and cook for 3 to 4 minutes or until tomatoes soften a bit.

Pour in the beaten eggs. Sprinkle on salt and pepper lightly. Stir and move eggs around with a fork. Indians like their scrambled eggs rather hard (cooked about 3 minutes), but you can stop whenever the desired consistency has been achieved.

To serve: While some Indians eat their scrambled eggs with toast, others eat them with hot *parathas*, *chapatis*, or *pooris*.

Chicken Moghlai

Serves 6

This rich, elaborate, saffron-flavoured dish justifies the time taken in preparing it by its exquisite taste and appearance. It has a burnt-red colour and smells of cardamom, cloves, and cinnamon. It tastes even better if you cook it a night before serving it, thus allowing the sauce to act as a marinade for the chicken.

I use legs, thighs, and breasts of chicken for this recipe, but you could buy a whole 2½–3-lb chicken and have it cut into smallish serving portions. It may, then, feed only 4 people. You could also use 6 whole quail, skinned, or 6 whole partridges, skinned.

2½–3 lbs chicken legs, thighs, and breasts

4 medium-sized onions, 2 peeled and chopped and 2 cut into half lengthwise, then sliced into thin half-rings

a piece of fresh ginger, about 1½ inches long and 1 inch wide, peeled and chopped

8 cloves garlic, peeled and chopped

10 tbs vegetable oil

2 cinnamon sticks, 2½–3 inches long

2 bay leaves

10 cardamom pods, slightly crushed

10 whole cloves

1 tsp whole cumin seed

1½ tbs ground coriander } *Dry-roasted together, following instructions for roasting ground coriander, page 40.*

½ tbs ground cumin

½ tsp ground turmeric

¼–½ tsp cayenne pepper

3 tbs yogurt

1 medium-sized tomato (tinned or fresh), peeled and finely chopped

1–1½ tsp salt

1 well-packed tsp leaf saffron, roasted and crumbled (see page 44)

1 tbs warm milk

Skin the chicken pieces. Quarter the breasts and divide the legs into drumstick and thigh. Pat chicken dry and set aside.

Put the chopped onions, ginger, and garlic in the container of an electric blender along with 4 tablespoons of water. Blend at high speed until you have a smooth paste.

In a 10-inch, heavy-bottomed pot, heat 8 tablespoons of the oil. Put in the sliced onions and fry, stirring, over a medium-high flame for 10 to 12 minutes or until onions are dark brown and crisp but not black and burned. Remove them with a slotted spoon and set aside in bowl or plate.

Raise heat to high and put the chicken pieces in the same oil a few at a time. Without letting chicken cook too much, brown to as dark a colour as possible. Remove each batch to a platter.

Turn heat down to medium high. Add remaining 2 table-spoons of oil to the pot, and put in the cinnamon sticks, the bay leaves, the cardamom pods, the cloves, and the cumin seed. Stir and turn the spices once. Now put in the paste from the blender, and fry, stirring, for 10 minutes. Turn heat down to medium and add the dry-roasted coriander and cumin powder, the turmeric, and the cayenne pepper. Stir and mix for 1 minute.

Add at intervals, constantly stirring and frying, the yogurt, a little bit at a time, the chopped tomato, and after another minute, the chicken pieces and salt, and finally, after another 2 minutes, ¼ pint water. Mix well, bring to the boil, cover, lower heat, and simmer gently for 30 minutes, turning chicken pieces gently every 8 to 10 minutes.

While the chicken is cooking, soak saffron in warm milk for 20 to 30 minutes.

When chicken is cooked, add the browned onions and the saffron-milk. Mix, cover, and simmer gently another 5 minutes.

To serve: This royal dish can be served very simply with *pooris* and a relish, or it can be a part of a banquet along with a *pullao*, a baked stuffed fish, and *Kheer* for dessert.

Eggs Moghlai

Serves 6

Follow preceding recipe for Chicken *Moghlai*, but substitute 12 hard-boiled eggs for the chicken.

Omit the step in which chicken is browned, and cook hard-boiled eggs in the sauce for only about 20 minutes. Put browned onions and saffron-milk over eggs and cook gently another 5 minutes.

To serve: See preceding recipe.

Fish &
Shellfish

Marinated prawns with whole spices
Prawns with crushed mustard seeds
Prawns with peas and green coriander
Prawns with sweet Italian peppers
Prawns in bread crumbs, Indian style
Prawns with brown sauce
Prawns with dill and ginger
Prawn, crab, or lobster, Kerala style
Baked sea bass with yellow rice
Sea bass in green chutney
Codfish steaks in yogurt
Stuffed flounder
Mackerel with onions

SEE ALSO

Barbecued Pacific king prawns (page 181)
Barbecued salmon steaks (page 183)
Prawn pullao (page 251)
Halibut or cod pullao (page 252)

ROUND the age of seven, while I was still fishing with a bent pin for a hook and a piece of cane for a float, my greatest heroes were my brothers. A decade separated us in age—but it was more than the age difference that elicited my respect. They were 'proper' fishermen. When *they* went fishing it was not just to the Jumna River. The Jumna was, after all, just across the street from us, and therefore quite ordinary. With their tapering fishing rods and their complex array of reels, hooks, bait, jars, and nets, they set out to catch *rahu* at the Okhla dam and trout in the cold streams of Kashmir.

They were always accompanied, on these trips, by *their* hero, a mysterious, magnificent man called Munnia. I never knew his second name. I never really understood exactly who he was. Munnia was then about forty, tall and silent with shining dark brown skin and thick black wavy hair. He knew *everything* about fish. He knew where the fish were biting, and when. He knew which bait was most effective on which day. I once saw him clad in a white loincloth, leaping on the slippery rocks that formed stepping stones across a shallow stream of water at the Okhla dam. Suddenly he stopped and jerked his head to one side. Silently he bent over. He held that pose patiently for fifteen minutes. Then he straightened up, triumphantly holding a *singhara* that he had 'tickled' and caught. Once the fish for the day had been caught, Munnia would open his knapsack, pull out a pot and some spices, light a fire with twigs, and produce an instant feast for his entire party. Often he would rub the fish with salt, turmeric, and hot red pepper and then fry it. Munnia's world was, of course, limited to fresh-water fish. I doubt if he ever saw an ocean or a fish from the sea.

With improved refrigeration some seafood is now available

in all the major cities of India. While availability of molluscs remains limited to the coast, prawns of varying sizes, lobster, and pomfret can be found even in Delhi. And pomfret is, in my family, easily the most popular fish. It is a flat salt-water fish, on an average about 8 to 9 inches long, with its skeletal structure so obligingly designed as to make filleting a pleasure and eating a bone-free ecstasy. Its flesh is tender but firm, flaking delicately when cooked. The pomfret can be fried, baked, grilled, or cooked in banana leaves or green chutney. It is served at lunches, dinners, and official banquets.

Unfortunately, neither the pomfret nor the *rahu* and *singhara* mentioned earlier are available in Britain. What I will do in this chapter is to give you Indian recipes adapted for fish normally found in British fish markets. The recipes for prawns and lobsters remain basically unchanged, but I have modified some of the pomfret recipes and used them for the sea bass, mackerel, and the flounder. Instead of *rahu*, I have used cod. You could also use carp.

Coconut palms fringe most of the India's coast from Bombay down to Cape Comorin and up again to Calcutta. Quite naturally, therefore, the fish caught along there are often cooked with grated coconut or with the 'milk' obtained from soaking freshly grated coconut in water. In Bengal, where the populace has rioted when fish was temporarily unavailable, a paste made out of ground black mustard seeds is often added to fish to give it a very special nose-tingling pungency. Moghul recipes from North India call for neither mustard seeds nor coconuts, but often for northern spices like saffron.

I need hardly stress that fish must be bought fresh—the eyes must look bright and the gills very red. It must also smell fresh. Cook it until just done. Overcooking will make it disintegrate or—in the case of prawns and lobster—become hard and leathery.

How to peel and devein prawns

This is really not as tiresome as it sounds. The secret is to make yourself entirely comfortable as you go about the task. Spread a double layer of newspaper at a table. Bring a clean plate, a sharp pointed knife, and a bag of prawns to the table.

Cut off the head of each prawn. Then pull off the legs that dangle on the belly side. Next, peel the shell from the body. It will come off in wide rings. Pull off the tail separately. To devein, make a shallow incision along the length of the prawn, right where the backbone would be if the prawn had one—all the way from head to tail. Here you will see a threadlike tube, often filled with black or green or yellow substance. Pull this out. If you don't find it, do not discard the prawn. It is still quite edible. Place all peeled and deveined prawns on a clean plate. Next, wash prawns thoroughly in cold running water and pat dry.

Marinated prawns with whole spices

Serves 6–8

Prawns are marinated in a paste of garlic, ginger, hot green chilies (or use cayenne pepper as a substitute), lemon juice, salt, and pepper. They are then fried with a bay leaf, cinnamon, cardamom, cloves, and peppercorns. The actual cooking time is less than 10 minutes. The prawns should be fried *just* before serving.

3 lbs prawns (large prawns are particularly good for this recipe)

10 cloves of garlic, peeled and coarsely chopped

a piece of fresh ginger, 2 inches long and $1\frac{1}{2}$ inches wide, peeled and coarsely chopped

2 fresh hot green chilies, sliced (or use $\frac{1}{4}$–$\frac{1}{2}$ tsp cayenne pepper as substitute)

3 tbs lemon juice

1 tsp salt (more for sprinkling later if necessary)

$\frac{1}{8}$ tsp freshly ground black pepper

6 tbs olive oil (or vegetable oil)

1 cinnamon stick, $2\frac{1}{2}$–3 inches long

5 cardamom pods

6 whole cloves

10 whole peppercorns

1 bay leaf

$\frac{1}{4}$ tsp ground turmeric

Garnish

2 spring onions

Peel and devein prawns (see page 147). Wash under cold running water. Drain and pat dry as thoroughly as you can.

In the container of an electric blender, combine the garlic, ginger, green chilies, lemon juice, salt, and freshly ground pepper. Blend at high speed until you have a smooth paste.

In a bowl, combine the prawns and the paste from the blender. Mix well. Cover. Leave, unrefrigerated, for an hour. If you wish to leave it longer (2 to 4 hours is fine), put bowl in the refrigerator.

Ten minutes before serving, heat the oil in a 10–12-inch frying-pan over a high flame. Add the cinnamon, cardamom, cloves, peppercorns, and bay leaf. Stir for 10 seconds or until bay leaf darkens. Then put in the prawns and marinade and let this mixture bubble and cook, stirring constantly, only until the prawns turn pink and opaque all over. Remove them (and any whole spices that cling to them) with a slotted spoon and place them in a bowl. Add turmeric to contents of frying-pan. Keep cooking the marinade mixture over high flame, stirring all the time, until it becomes thick and paste-like. This will take just a few minutes. Now put the prawns back into the frying-pan. Stir around until the prawns are well coated; there should be no sauce left in the frying-pan. Check the salt. You may need to sprinkle on a bit more. Turn off heat.

To serve: Place the prawns on a warm platter. Wash the spring onions and slice into fine rounds, including at least an inch of the green part as well, and sprinkle them over the prawns. Serve with a rice dish, some kind of lentils, a vegetable, and a yogurt dish. Warn people not to bite into the whole spices.

Prawns with crushed mustard seeds

Serves 3–4

1 lb prawns
1 tsp black mustard seeds, crushed (use heavy mortar and pestle, coffee-grinder or grinding stone)
$\frac{1}{8}$ tsp ground turmeric
2 tsp tomato purée
4 tsp mustard oil (or any other vegetable oil)

2 cloves of garlic, peeled
2 slices of fresh ginger, 1 inch long, 1 inch wide, and $\frac{1}{16}$ inch thick, peeled
1 hot dried red pepper
$\frac{3}{4}$ tsp salt
$\frac{1}{8}$ tsp freshly ground pepper
1 tbs lemon juice

149

Peel and devein the prawns (see page 147). Wash under cold running water. Pat dry as thoroughly as you can.

In a cup, combine the crushed mustard seeds, turmeric, tomato purée, and 3 tablespoons of water. Set aside.

Heat the oil in a 10–12-inch frying-pan over a medium-high flame. When hot, put in the cloves of garlic, the ginger slices, and the hot red pepper. Stir and turn around. In a few seconds, as soon as contents begin to darken, add the prawns. Keep stirring until the prawns turn pink and opaque. Now put in the mustard seed paste. Turn heat to a moderate low. Keep stirring. Add the salt, pepper, and lemon juice. Stir and fry another 2 minutes. Turn off heat.

To serve: Place on heated platter and serve with a rice dish or with hot *pooris*. Serve one or two vegetables with it, perhaps cabbage and peas, as well as a yogurt relish.

Prawns with peas and green coriander

Serves 3–4

1 lb prawns
1 tbs lemon juice
salt
freshly ground pepper
5 cloves garlic, peeled and coarsely chopped
a piece of fresh ginger, 1 inch long and 1 inch wide, peeled and coarsely chopped
4 tbs olive oil (or vegetable oil)

$\frac{1}{4}$ tsp ground turmeric
3 tbs tomato purée
5 tbs minced fresh green coriander
1 small (or $\frac{1}{2}$ large) sweet green pepper, cut in $\frac{1}{4}$-inch squares
$\frac{1}{2}$ teacup freshly shelled peas
$\frac{1}{8}$–$\frac{1}{4}$ tsp cayenne pepper (optional)

Peel and devein the prawns (see page 147). Wash under cold running water. Pat dry. Sprinkle lightly with salt and pepper.

Place the garlic and ginger in the container of an electric blender, along with 3 tablespoons of water. Blend at high speed until you have a smooth paste.

Heat the oil in a 10–12-inch frying-pan over a medium-high flame. When hot, put in the prawns. Fry and stir the prawns until they barely turn pink and opaque all over. Remove them to a bowl with a slotted spoon.

Into the same frying-pan pour the paste from the blender. Add the turmeric and fry, stirring, over medium heat for about 2 minutes.

Lower the heat and add tomato purée, coriander, green pepper, peas, lemon juice, salt and pepper to taste, cayenne pepper, and 3 tablespoons of water. Bring to the boil, cover, and simmer gently for about 5 minutes or until peas are just cooked.

Remove the cover from the frying-pan, raise heat, and boil away most of the liquid. When a thick paste-like sauce remains, put the prawns back in. Stir and cook until the prawns are well coated (there should be almost no sauce left in the pan). Taste, and add more salt if necessary. Turn off heat.

To serve: Place in a warm dish and serve with hot *pooris*, *chapatis*, or *parathas*, or with any kind of rice dish. You could also have a sauced potato dish, e.g., Potatoes with Asafetida and Cumin or, if you like, Mushrooms with Cumin and Asafetida.

Prawns with sweet Italian peppers

Serves 3–4

Even though green peppers are normally used for this dish, I often substitute the Italian peppers because of their sweeter taste. Try to pick them so they are about the same length — about 3 inches long. This dish has a wonderful sauce made up of onions, garlic, coriander, cinnamon, cardamom, bay leaf, tomato purée, and lemon juice.

1 lb prawns	5 whole cardamom pods
¾ tsp salt	1 bay leaf
¼ tsp ground turmeric	1 cinnamon stick, 2½–3
6 medium-sized Italian	inches long
peppers	2 tbs tomato purée
5–6 tbs olive or vegetable oil	1 tsp ground coriander
1 medium-sized onion,	¼ tsp cayenne pepper
peeled and very finely	(optional)
minced	1 tbs lemon juice
4 cloves garlic, peeled and	1 tsp brown sugar
very finely minced	

Peel and devein the prawns (see page 147). Wash thoroughly under cold running water, drain, and then pat dry.

Place the prawns in a bowl. Sprinkle them with ¼ teaspoon of the salt and the turmeric. Mix well with your hands, rubbing the salt and turmeric into the flesh.

Cut the caps off the green peppers. Slice each in half lengthwise, then each half into 3 or 4 long strips. Remove seeds.

Heat 4 tablespoons of the oil in a 10–12-inch frying-pan over a medium-high flame, and fry the slices of pepper, stirring, for about 5 minutes or until they brown a bit and turn slightly limp. Remove them with a slotted spoon to a plate.

In the same frying-pan, adding a little more oil if necessary, stir and fry the prawns for 2 to 3 minutes or until they become pink and opaque on the outside. Remove with a slotted spoon to a bowl.

Turn heat to low. Add a tablespoon of oil to the frying-pan, and put in the minced onions and garlic, cardamom, bay leaf, and cinnamon. Sauté for 4 to 5 minutes or until onions get a bit soft. Now add the tomato purée, coriander, cayenne pepper, lemon juice, brown sugar, the remaining ½ teaspoon of salt, the fried green pepper slices, and ¼ pint of water. Bring to the boil. Cover and simmer very gently for 10 minutes.

Remove the cover and add the prawns along with any juice that may have accumulated in bowl. Turn heat to medium high. Stir the prawns to coat them with the sauce, and continue cooking and stirring 4 to 5 minutes while the sauce thickens. You should be left with only a little sauce at the bottom of the frying-pan.

To serve: Place in a shallow bowl and serve with rice and some kind of *dal*. Plain boiled rice and *karhi* together with Cucumber and Tomato with Lemon Juice would make a very nice meal.

Prawns in bread crumbs, Indian style

Serves 3–4

Follow recipe for Chicken Cutlets, page 127. Substitute 1 lb of large prawns for the chicken breasts. To prepare prawns, peel and devein them first, leaving the tails on. As you slit their backs for deveining, cut almost all the way through the prawns but not quite—leave a bit of flesh intact so the prawn can open up like a butterfly. Flatten each prawn by hitting it with the broad side of a cleaver so it lies open (otherwise it will curl up).

You do not need to prick prawns with a fork or to marinate them for 4 hours—2 hours in the refrigerator will do.

Directions for breading and frying prawns are the same as for the chicken. You will, of course, be able to fry more prawns in the frying-pan at one time.

Prawns with brown sauce

Serves 6–8

3 lbs prawns (medium or
large size)

2 medium-sized onions,
peeled and coarsely
chopped

8 cloves garlic, peeled and
coarsely chopped

a piece of fresh ginger, about
1-inch cube, peeled and
coarsely chopped

3 tbs vinegar (white or red)

5 tbs vegetable oil

$\frac{1}{4}$ tsp whole fennel seeds

$\frac{1}{4}$ tsp whole cumin seeds

12 whole fenugreek seeds

1 tsp ground coriander

1 tsp ground cumin

$\frac{1}{2}$ tsp ground turmeric

2 medium-sized tomatoes
(tinned or fresh), peeled
and finely chopped

5 tbs tamarind paste (see
page 44)

2 tsp salt

$\frac{1}{8}$ tsp freshly ground pepper

$\frac{1}{2}$ tsp cayenne pepper
(optional—use as desired)

1 tbs brown sugar

$\frac{1}{4}$ tsp ground cinnamon

$\frac{1}{4}$ tsp ground cloves

$\frac{1}{4}$ tsp ground mace

3 tbs finely chopped fresh
green coriander

Peel and devein prawns (see page 147). Wash, drain, and dry thoroughly. Cover and set aside.

Place the onions, garlic, ginger, and vinegar in the container of an electric blender. Blend at high speed until you have a smooth paste.

Heat the oil in a wide, heavy-bottomed, 3-quart pot over a medium-high flame. Drop in the whole fennel, cumin, and fenugreek seeds, and as soon as they begin to darken pour in the blender paste, using a rubber spatula to get it out quickly. Stir and fry the paste for 10 to 12 minutes or until it is a golden brown.

Add the coriander, cumin, and turmeric to the fried paste, lower the heat, and continue to stir and fry for 2 minutes. Pour in the chopped tomatoes, raise the heat to medium, and stir and fry another 5 minutes. Finally, add the tamarind paste, salt, pepper, cayenne, brown sugar, cinnamon, cloves, mace, green coriander, and ½ pint of water. Mix well, bring to the boil, cover, lower heat, and simmer gently for 30 minutes. (This much of the recipe can be made ahead of time if necessary.)

Ten minutes before serving, wipe the prawns again. Bring the brown sauce to the boil and drop in the prawns. Stir and mix well; continue cooking and stirring at high temperature from 5 to 10 minutes, until the prawns turn opaque.

To serve: Spoon into warm serving bowl and serve with a rich dish. Rice with Peas might be nice, as well as a vegetable, a *dal*, and a few relishes.

Prawns with dill and ginger

Serves 4–6

a piece of fresh ginger, about 1-inch cube, peeled and coarsely chopped
4 tbs vegetable oil
½ tsp whole black mustard seeds
1 fresh hot green chili, finely sliced (use more or less as desired)
1 tsp ground coriander
1 tsp ground cumin
1 tsp garam masala
1 tsp salt
1 tsp lemon juice
2 teacups fresh dill, washed and trimmed
2 lbs medium-sized prawns, peeled and deveined (see page 147)

Place the ginger in the container of electric blender along with 3 tablespoons water. Blend until smooth.

Heat the oil in a 10–12-inch frying-pan over medium flame. When hot, put in mustard seeds. As soon as they begin to pop (10 to 15 seconds), add the following at intervals, continuing to stir and fry over medium heat: first, the paste from blender; after a minute, the green chili, adding a teaspoon of water if the mixture sticks; then the coriander, cumin, *garam masala*, salt, lemon juice; and after another 2 minutes, the dill and ¼ pint of water. Bring to the boil. Cover, lower heat, and simmer 10 minutes.

Pat the prawns dry and add to frying-pan. Turn heat to high, stir well and cook until prawns turn opaque, about 5 minutes.

To serve: Serve with Buttered Saffron Rice and a salad. A relish with tomato or onion in it would also go well with it.

Prawns, crab, or lobster, Kerala style

Serves 4–6

This dish comes from Kerala, a state along India's southwestern coast. Roasted coconut is added to the seafood to give it a thick, dark sauce. It is quite delicious.

3 tbs vegetable oil

2 medium-sized onions, peeled and finely chopped

a piece of fresh ginger, about ¼-inch cube, peeled

4 cloves garlic, peeled and chopped

½ teacup grated and roasted fresh coconut (see page 40)

½ tsp ground turmeric

1 tbs ground coriander, roasted (see page 40)

¼ tsp cayenne pepper

3 tbs tamarind paste (see page 44)

3 medium-sized tomatoes (tinned or fresh), peeled and chopped

½–¾ tsp salt

2 lbs medium-sized prawns, peeled and deveined (see page 147), or 2 lbs uncooked lobstermeat, cut into 1-inch pieces, or 2 lbs uncooked crabmeat, cut into bite-sized sections

Heat oil either in deep 10-inch frying-pan or in 10-inch heavy-bottomed pot over a medium-high flame. Put in the chopped onions and fry, stirring, for 7 to 8 minutes or until the onions are slightly browned, but soft. Turn off heat.

In a blender container combine the ginger, garlic, tomatoes, and grated roasted coconut. Blend at high speed until you have a paste. Add contents of blender container to frying-pan or pot. Also add the turmeric, coriander, cayenne, tamarind paste, salt, and $\frac{1}{4}$ pint water. Bring to the boil. Cover, lower heat, and simmer gently for 5 minutes.

(This much of the recipe can be made up to a day in advance. Keep covered and refrigerated until ready for use.)

Seven to 8 minutes before serving, bring the sauce to the boil. Add the prawns or lobstermeat or crabmeat, fold in, and cook at high temperature, stirring continuously, until the meat turns opaque (about 5 minutes). The sauce should be very thick and cling to the meat, but if you desire a thinner sauce, add a bit more water.

To serve: Place in warm bowl and serve with a rice dish and some kind of *dal*. *Masoor Dal* with Vegetables would be good on this menu.

Baked sea bass with yellow rice

Serves 4–6

Pomfret is normally used in this recipe. It also seems to work very well with sea bass. A paste of onion, ginger, garlic, and turmeric is first browned in oil. The fish is covered with it and then baked. The yellow rice is served on the side.

1 sea bass, 3½–4 lbs, cleaned thoroughly, with head and tail still on

1 medium-sized onion, peeled and coarsely chopped

a piece of fresh ginger, 2 inches long and 1 inch wide, peeled and coarsely chopped

6 cloves garlic, peeled and coarsely chopped

½ tsp ground turmeric

4 tbs olive or vegetable oil

¼ tsp whole cumin seeds

¼ pint tomato sauce (see page 225)

3 tbs chopped fresh green coriander; reserve a bit for garnishing (as substitute, use regular parsley or fresh dill)

¾ tsp salt

⅛ tsp freshly ground pepper

⅛–½ tsp cayenne pepper (optional)

¼ tsp ground cloves

2 tbs lemon juice

157

Preheat oven to 400°F., Mark 6.

Wash the fish thoroughly in cold running water and pat dry, inside and out.

Place the onion, ginger, garlic, turmeric, and 4 tablespoons of water in the container of an electric blender. Blend at high speed until you have a smooth paste.

Heat oil in 8–10-inch frying-pan over medium flame, put in the whole cumin seeds, and as soon as they darken add the paste from the blender. Fry, stirring, for 5 or 6 minutes. Now add the tomato sauce and green coriander. Cook, stirring, another 2 to 3 minutes. Remove frying-pan from heat. Add salt, pepper, cayenne, cloves, and lemon juice, stir, and leave to cool slightly. (Check the salt in the paste. Remember it has to be enough to season *all* of the fish.)

Cut 4 diagonal slits, at the same angle as the gills, on each side of the fish. Distribute paste inside fish, over fish, and inside the slits. Place fish on baking platter or on baking tray covered with aluminium foil, and bake 40 to 50 minutes, basting every 8 to 10 minutes. Meanwhile, prepare the Yellow Rice.

1 tbs vegetable oil	**½ tsp ground turmeric**
½ tsp whole cumin seeds	**1 tsp salt**
12 oz long-grain rice	

Heat oil in a 2-quart heavy-bottomed pot over medium heat. When hot, add cumin seeds. Stir a few seconds or until cumin seeds begin to darken. Add rice and turmeric. Mix and stir, fry for a minute, lower heat a bit if necessary. Add 1¼ pint water and salt. Bring to the boil, cover, turn heat down very low, and cook, without lifting lid, for 30 minutes.

To serve: It is much easier if your baking dish is also your serving platter. This way there is less danger of breaking the fish. If you do need to move it, however, be very, very careful during the transfer. You can arrange the rice around the fish if the platter is large enough. If not, serve the rice separately and garnish your fish with freshly chopped green coriander. Serve with a green salad and sweet tomato chutney.

Sea bass in green chutney

Serves 2

Here is my version of a very popular dish in which the pomfret is smothered in green chutney and then cooked in banana leaves. Having no banana leaves handy, I use the prosaic but serviceable kitchen-aid — aluminium foil. It seems to work.

1 sea bass, 1½–2 lbs (with head and tail on, but otherwise cleaned)

a piece of fresh ginger, 1 inch long and 1 inch wide, peeled and coarsely chopped

5 cloves garlic, peeled and coarsely chopped

2 tbs olive or vegetable oil

½ tsp whole black mustard seeds

2 whole hot dried red peppers (optional)

½ tsp ground turmeric

1 teacup chopped fresh green coriander

2 tbs lemon juice

½ tsp salt

Clean and wash fish thoroughly under cold running water. Pat dry, inside and out.

Preheat oven to 400°F., Mark 6.

Place the ginger and garlic in the container of an electric blender, along with 3 tablespoons of water. Blend at a high speed until you have a smooth paste.

Heat oil in 8–10-inch frying-pan over medium-high flame, and add the mustard seeds. Within a few seconds, they will begin to expand and pop. Add the red peppers, and stir them once. Pour in the paste from the blender, add the turmeric, and fry, stirring, for about 2 minutes.

Pour contents of frying-pan into the blender. Add the green coriander, lemon juice, and salt. Blend at high speed until you again have a smooth paste, adding up to 2 tablespoons of water if necessary.

Line a large baking dish with a sheet of aluminium foil, large enough to fold over the fish. Cover the fish with the green paste, inside and out. Fold the foil over so the fish is completely enclosed in it. Place in the oven and bake 30 minutes.

To serve: Remove fish carefully, place on warm platter, and serve with Plain *Basmati* Rice. A tomato or onion relish would also go well with it.

Codfish steaks in yogurt

Serves 2

This easy-to-make dish is absolutely scrumptious. My Bengali sister-in-law, Maya, makes it with cut-up chunks of *rahu*, a very popular fresh-water fish. Not finding any *rahu* around, I've turned to cod. (You could also use fresh-water carp.) Cod flakes rather easily, so handle it very gently as it cooks. I leave the codfish in steaks (instead of cutting it into smaller sections) to avoid disintegration. In India, sliced hot green chilies are added to the fish 2 or 3 minutes before the cooking time ends. I have used cayenne pepper instead.

2 codfish steaks, $\frac{3}{4}$ inch thick (about 1 lb of fish)
$\frac{1}{4}$ tsp ground turmeric
$\frac{3}{4}$ tsp salt
3 medium-sized onions
6–8 cloves garlic
$\frac{1}{4}$ pint plain yogurt
freshly ground black pepper

$\frac{1}{4}$ tsp cayenne pepper (optional)
$\frac{1}{8}$ tsp sugar
6–8 tbs vegetable oil
6 whole cardamom pods
2 cinnamon sticks, 2–2$\frac{1}{2}$ inches long

Wash the codfish steaks. See that no scales adhere to skin. Pat them as dry as possible. Sprinkle steaks on both sides with the turmeric and ¼ teaspoon of the salt, rubbing the seasonings gently in.

Peel the 3 onions. Chop 2 of them very finely and set aside. Chop the third one coarsely and place in the container of an electric blender.

Peel and chop the cloves of garlic. Put them in the blender container along with the yogurt, remaining ½ teaspoon salt, black pepper, cayenne, and sugar. Blend at high speed until you have a smooth, thin paste.

Heat 5 tablespoons of the oil in a 12-inch frying-pan over a medium flame. Put in the 2 steaks and sauté them lightly, about 3 minutes on each side, turning them over gently and carefully. (They should not get brown or crisp.) Remove with a spatula to a plate. Pour the oil from the frying-pan into a small bowl, leaving behind any sediment or pieces of fish.

Wash and dry the frying-pan. Measure the oil in the bowl and put it back in the clean frying-pan. Add more oil to make up 5 tablespoons. Turn heat to medium, and when the oil is hot, put in the 2 finely chopped onions, the cardamom, and the cinnamon. Fry the onions lightly, stirring, until they turn a light, golden-brown, about 5 minutes. Turn the heat down to low and pour in liquid from blender. Simmer (do not boil) on low heat for 10 minutes, stirring now and then.

Remove half of the sauce to a small bowl. Spread out the sauce in the frying-pan evenly, place codfish steaks on top, then pour the reserved sauce over them, spreading it evenly on top of the steaks. Cover and keep simmering at low temperature for about 10 minutes or until fish is cooked through.

To serve: I like to serve these steaks with plain boiled rice and a green salad with an oil and vinegar dressing, but you could choose any other rice dish and green beans, cauliflower, peas, or okra.

Stuffed flounder

Serves 2

Get your fishmonger to slit the whole flounder from its stomach down to its tail on the underside, and to remove its backbone. (You could do this yourself with a little patience and a very sharp knife, taking care not to destroy the outside appearance of the fish.) Make sure all the scales are removed and that the fish is washed out thoroughly. In this recipe, again borrowed from one for pomfret, the whole fish is stuffed with a mixture of potatoes, fried onions, ginger, and fennel, and then grilled. It is quite delicious. You can easily double or triple the recipe if you are feeding more people.

$3\frac{1}{2}$ tbs oil, preferably olive or mustard oil
1 tbs whole fennel seeds
4 medium-sized onions, finely minced
a piece of fresh ginger, 1 inch long and 1 inch wide, grated
1 large potato, boiled and roughly mashed
salt

freshly ground black pepper
$\frac{1}{8}$–$\frac{1}{4}$ tsp cayenne pepper (optional)
$\frac{1}{2}$ tsp garam masala
$1\frac{1}{2}$ tbs lemon juice
1 flounder, about 2 lbs, with head and tail on, cleaned, with scales and backbone removed
2 tbs butter

Garnish

fresh green coriander

Preheat the grill.

Heat 3 tablespoons of oil in an 8–10-inch frying-pan over a medium flame, put in the fennel seeds, and fry, stirring, for about 5 seconds. Add onions and ginger, and continue to cook, stirring, for 5 to 8 minutes, or until onions are a darkish golden-brown. Turn off heat. Add the mashed potato, $\frac{1}{2}$ teaspoon salt, $\frac{1}{8}$ teaspoon black pepper, cayenne, *garam masala*, and 1 tablespoon of lemon juice. Mix well.

Line a baking tray with aluminium foil. Rub a little oil on it. Stuff fish with the potato stuffing and either close opening with skewers or sew it with a needle and thread. Place fish on aluminium foil. Sprinkle the upper side with salt, pepper, half the remaining lemon juice. Cut the butter into 6 pats and lay 3 of them over the fish. Place under grill. Grill slowly, basting with the butter. When one side is a golden-brown, turn the fish over carefully, sprinkle this side with salt, pepper, and remaining lemon juice, lay the remaining pats of butter on it, and grill it also to a golden-brown, basting with the butter. Remove carefully.

To serve: Place on warm platter, decorate with coriander, and serve with either a green salad with an oil and vinegar dressing or some Indian vegetable dishes, such as green beans or carrots or peas.

Mackerel with onions

Serves 2

5 tbs vegetable oil
4 medium-sized onions, peeled and chopped
5 cloves garlic, peeled and minced
3 tbs (loosely packed) grated fresh ginger
½ tsp ground cinnamon
¼ tsp freshly ground black pepper
½ tsp ground fennel or crushed fennel seeds

5 cardamom seeds, crushed
½ tsp ground cloves
½ tsp cayenne pepper (optional—use more or less as desired)
1 tsp salt
4 tbs tamarind paste (see page 44)
2 mackerels, 1–1½ lbs each, cleaned, with head and tail removed if desired

163

Garnish

**4 tbs chopped fresh green   extra salt and pepper
   coriander**

**(To double the recipe, use 6–7 tbs cooking oil and double all
   other ingredients.)**

Preheat oven to 350°F., Mark 4.

In 10–12-inch frying-pan, heat oil over medium-high heat.
When hot, put in the chopped onions, the minced garlic, and
the grated ginger. Fry, stirring, for 7 to 8 minutes or until the
onions are lightly browned and translucent. Turn heat to low
and add cinnamon, black pepper, fennel, cardamom, cloves,
cayenne, salt, and tamarind paste. Stir and mix. Cook on low
heat for 2 to 3 minutes until well mixed. Turn off heat.

Wash fish well and pat dry. Sprinkle inside and out lightly
with salt and pepper. Make 3 or 4 diagonal slashes on either
side of each fish. Place fish in oval baking dish. Put onion
mixture inside, under, and over fish, stuffing some in the slashes.
Pour any oil or juice left in frying-pan over fish. Cover fish
with waxed paper cut about the same size as the oval dish.
Place dish in oven and bake about 30 minutes or until fish is
cooked through.

To serve: Place fish on a large warm platter and sprinkle with
green coriander, salt, and pepper. Serve with a rice dish and a
simple green salad. I also like to serve it with grilled tomato
halves, sprinkled with salt, pepper, cayenne, and lemon juice.

Summer Cooking &
Barbecued Foods

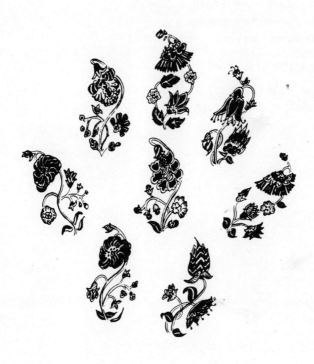

'Butterflied' leg of lamb, marinated and barbecued
Cubed leg of lamb, barbecued
Boti kabab (cubed lamb kabab)
Kidney kabab
Seekh kabab
Marinated pork chops
Tandoori chicken — my version
Barbecued Pacific king prawns
Barbecued salmon steaks

SEE ALSO

Cold yogurt soup (page 57)
Seekh kabab, flat style (page 60)

THERE are several kinds of Indian cooking that are done out of doors over a charcoal grill. Many of these dishes can make welcome additions to English summer menus.

Chicken, fish, beef, lamb, and pork are rubbed with a well-spiced marinade (slits are often made in the meat to absorb the spices) and then grilled over hot coals. An indoor grill could of course be used for all the recipes in this chapter, but the taste will never equal that achieved by the outdoor grill. I find these recipes are particularly good for the summer months. If you wish to spend a day at the beach, you can marinate the meat in the morning, leave it refrigerated, and then come back just in time to light the grill and barbecue it.

Tandoori cooking

The most popular school of outdoor cooking in India is the one from the former north-west frontier. (This was the north-west frontier of India until 1947, and is now the north-west frontier of Pakistan.) In Delhi, this style of cooking was totally unknown before the partition of the Indian subcontinent. Shortly after 1947, as waves of refugees crossed the border from both sides, a tiny restaurant opened in a lower-middle-class section of town. A family of refugees, with little more than a determination to start again, owned it. Called Moti Mahal (Pearl Palace), it was right on the main thoroughfare; it didn't look exactly hygienic; and it specialized in chicken, meats, fish, and bread cooked in a *tandoor* (a clay oven with a charcoal or wood fire). Within a few months, the cars of the rich began rolling up to its rather humble front doors to buy the very red-looking *tandoori* chicken and the long, flat bread, *naan*. Now, almost two decades later, it is considered a Delhi landmark which no tourist is allowed to miss, frequented by ambassadors, princes, and movie stars (as well as the lower middle class for whom it was intended!). It now offers a choice of air-conditioned indoor seating or canopied outdoor seating accompanied by recitals of *qavvalis*, poems set to a specific style of music. The tables, chairs, cutlery, plates, and waiters all have a very rough and ready look, but that is part of the attraction. *Tandoori* chicken (chicken being a great delicacy in India) is now famous throughout the country and is served in all major restaurants. The chicken (or meat, fish, or bread) is placed in a clay oven, open at the top, with a blazing fire inside. The foods get deliciously roasted and are served with small onions pickled in vinegar. All the meats are marinated in yogurt and spices before being cooked. In India, they are also tenderized with crushed green papaya and given a bright orange appearance with a vegetable colouring, rather like the Spanish *bijol*.

Muslim cooking

Another style of outdoor cooking which, for want of a better word, I'll call the 'Muslim' school, includes the *seekh kabab* and *boti kabab*. It consists of putting minced or cubed meat (kidney, liver, and udders can be used as well) on skewers and grilling it over live coals. The meats are either marinated first or, as in the case of chopped meat, ground to a paste with yogurt and then patted around a thick skewer. As they are turned and roasted, they are basted with *ghee*.

In Delhi, the best sampling of this Muslim school can be had around Jama Masjid, one of the largest and most beautiful mosques in Asia, built in the seventeenth century by the emperor who built the Taj Mahal, Shah Jahan. Under the shadows of its massive walls, surrounding it on all sides, are hundreds of tiny stalls. They sell everything—pots, pans, bedcovers, saris, lungis (a kind of male 'sarong'), and of course all the different *kababs*. On hot days, huge buckets of *thandai*—a cool drink made with milk, almonds, and cardamom—are prepared and sold to thirsty passers-by.

The recipes in this chapter are not Moti Mahal's, nor are they acquired directly from a Jama Masjid cook. They are mine—and are adaptations of the *tandoori* and Muslim styles to the kinds of meat available here. When marinating meats, I tend to use olive or peanut oil in the marinade. Indians never use olive oil, but I like its taste and use it frequently.

Vegetables for outdoor meals

In the introduction to the chapter on vegetables I discuss corn on the cob, grilled outdoors and served with lemon juice, salt, and pepper. In India this kind of corn usually is not served *with* a meal, but only as a snack or with tea; still, you may like to try it with some of the meat dishes in this chapter. Traditionally, the vegetables, rice, and potatoes are cooked indoors and then served with the barbecued foods, but when the days are too hot or I am at the beach too long, I serve lots of salads and raw vegetables, all good accompaniments to Indian barbecued food.

I also serve at least one kind of *raita* or yogurt dish; this is very easy to make and very refreshing. For good cold dishes, yogurt can be combined with boiled potatoes, with cucumber, with tomatoes and onion, with dumplings, with cooked or raw spinach, and best of all, with a combination of roasted aubergine (which you can do on the charcoal grill), raw onions, and finely minced fresh mint (see Aubergine *Bharta*, page 206).

For dessert I generally serve just fruit, but when confronted with guests who have a sweet tooth, I often prepare *Kulfi*, a rich Indian ice cream made with nuts and milk, or *Kheer*, a kind of cold custard made with milk and rice.

'Butterflied' leg of lamb, marinated and barbecued

Serves 10–12

This is, quite easily, one of my favourite meat dishes. I ask the butcher to 'butterfly' a 8–9 lb. leg of lamb for me. The 'butterflying' process involves boning the leg in such a manner that the whole piece of meat lies flat, rather like a large, uneven steak. I then marinate it for 24 hours in olive oil, lemon juice, and a paste of onions, garlic, ginger, coriander, cumin, turmeric, mace, nutmeg, cloves, cinnamon, black pepper, cayenne pepper, *garam masala*, salt, and an orange food colouring which gives it the orange look that traditional *tandoori* meats have. After it is well marinated, it is best grilled outdoors on charcoal, though you could do it in your indoor grill—with less spectacular results! It is excellent to take along on cook-out picnics (pack the meat in a couple of plastic bags and the marinade in a tight jar—take along a pastry brush for brushing on the thick marinade paste), and refrigerated left-overs taste superb the next day. It is difficult to describe what 'style' this meat is cooked in. It is perhaps a combination of the *tandoori* school, my sister Kamal's lamb chops, and our Indian cook's roast mutton.

Note: You can always freeze half a butterflied leg of lamb and cook the rest. Halve all the ingredients in the marinade and cook the same way.

1 leg of lamb, 8–9 lbs,
butterflied

2 medium-sized onions (1
coarsely chopped, 1 for
garnishing)

a piece of fresh ginger, 3
inches long and 1 inch
wide, peeled and coarsely
chopped

5–7 cloves garlic (depending
on preference—I use 7),
peeled and coarsely
chopped

6 fl. oz lemon juice

1 tbs ground coriander

1 tsp ground cumin

1 tsp garam masala

1 tsp ground turmeric

$\frac{1}{4}$ tsp ground mace

$\frac{1}{4}$ tsp ground nutmeg

$\frac{1}{4}$ tsp ground cinnamon

$\frac{1}{4}$ tsp ground cloves

8 fl. oz olive oil

$2\frac{1}{2}$ tsp salt

$\frac{1}{4}$ tsp freshly ground pepper

$\frac{1}{2}$–1 tsp cayenne pepper
(optional—use less if you
like, or none)

2 tsp orange food colouring
(Spanish bijol, or Indian
food colouring obtainable
in powdered form, or
Bush's orange-red powder)

Garnish

12 radishes

Put the chopped onion, ginger, garlic, and 4 tablespoons of the lemon juice in the container of the electric blender, and blend at high speed to get a smooth paste (about 1 minute).

In a bowl or a pot with non-metallic lining large enough to hold the meat, put the paste from the blender and all the other ingredients except the meat and the onion and radishes to be used for garnishing later. Mix well.

Carefully cut off all fat and tissue from the meat, and with the point of a knife make lots of jabs in it on both sides. Put the meat in the marinade paste. Fold the meat over, or cut it into 2 pieces, if there is not room. Make a few more jabs with the knife, and be sure the paste gets rubbed into the meat and goes way inside the gashes. Cover the container and leave refrigerated for 24 hours. Turn the meat over at least 3 or 4 times during this period.

The meat is now ready for grilling. But before you start, get your garnishes ready.

Peel the second onion and slice it into *very* fine rounds (paper-thin if possible). Separate the rounds into rings and put them into a bowl of ice water, cover, and refrigerate.

Cut off the stems, leaves, and tips from the radishes and then cut them into flowers. (Starting from the tip end, start cutting into halves, but stop short as you reach the stem end. Next, cut into quarters and eighths the same way.) Put into a small bowl of ice water, cover, and refrigerate. It will look prettier if you use unblemished radishes of approximately the same size for this.

Now light your fire. If it takes 20 to 30 minutes to get red hot, start about 1 hour and 15 minutes before you intend to eat. When hot, place the metal grill at the lowest notch.

Lift meat from bowl (leaving marinade) and place on grill. Sear 5 to 8 minutes (depending on your stove) on either side. Now raise the grill to its topmost notch and cook about 20 minutes on each side. Brush frequently with the marinade until it is all used up. If you don't have a grill that moves up and down, just remember that the meat needs to cook about 50 minutes and it should be very dark on the outside and pinkish inside. Most Indians like their meat well done; you may prefer it a bit rare, but don't cook it too rare, as the spices inside won't get a chance to cook through.

To serve: Warm a large platter. Meanwhile place the meat on a carving board and cut it into thin slices. Use a very sharp knife, and do this as fast as you can, as you don't want the meat to cool off too much. Now slide the meat pieces onto the warm platter, leaving the slices in roughly the same shape as the piece of meat. Drain off the water from the radishes and onion rings. Arrange radishes around meat and lay raw onion rings on top of meat. Serve immediately.

This meat can be served with many kinds of foods. At a picnic, you could have it with a green salad and roasted corn. If you are cooking it at home, you could serve it with *Sookhe Aloo* ('Dry' Potatoes) and Green Beans with Onion Paste.

Cubed leg of lamb, barbecued

Serves 10–12

Here the leg of lamb is cut into 1-inch cubes, marinated as above, skewered, cooked, and served pretty much the same way as the butterflied leg of lamb.

Read the preceding recipe.

Just remember to remove all the fat and tissue from the meat cubes. After they have marinated overnight, push 6 or 7 cubes on each skewer and first sear on all four sides (5 to 8 minutes on each side). Now raise grill and cook on each side for about 10 minutes, basting frequently.

Garnish and serve as above.

Boti kabab
(cubed lamb kabab)

Serves 6

In this recipe, cubed lamb pieces are marinated overnight in a blend of yogurt, tomato purée, dry mustard, oil, lemon juice, garlic, ginger, turmeric, and a host of other spices. The next day, they are skewered and grilled over charcoal. The meat must cook slowly, as it needs to cook through. Also, nothing tastes worse than uncooked turmeric! (You could make this same recipe in a gas or electric grill.) Keep the meat about 4 inches from heat and cook 7 to 10 minutes on each side or until each side is well browned, depending on the heat of the grill. It should not be too rare inside or the spices will taste uncooked.

3 level tbs tomato purée
6 level tbs plain yogurt
2 tsp dry English mustard
2 tsp salt
¼ pint olive oil (or vegetable oil)
4 tbs lemon juice
1 tbs ground coriander
1 tbs ground cumin
1 tbs ground turmeric
1 tbs garam masala
½ tsp ground cloves

½ tsp ground mace
½ tsp ground nutmeg
½ tsp ground cinnamon
10 cloves garlic, peeled and coarsely chopped
a piece of ginger, 1 inch square, peeled and coarsely chopped
¼–1 tsp cayenne pepper (optional, or use as desired)
2½ lbs meat from leg of lamb, cut into 1-inch cubes

Garnish

1 medium-sized onion

In the container of an electric blender, place the tomato purée, yogurt, mustard, salt, 2 fl. oz. of the olive oil, lemon juice, coriander, cumin, turmeric, *garam masala*, cloves, mace, nutmeg, cinnamon, garlic, ginger, and cayenne. Blend marinade paste at high speed until all the spices are well mixed and the ginger and garlic have puréed (about 1 minute).

Remove all the fat from the meat pieces. Stab pieces with the point of a sharp knife, then place them in a glass or ceramic bowl. Pour the marinade over the meat. Mix well, cover, and refrigerate at least 4 hours but preferably overnight.

The meat will take 30 to 40 minutes to cook, so light your charcoal fire or preheat your grill accordingly. String the meat cubes loosely on several skewers. If you crowd them too tightly, adjacent sides of the cubes will not brown. Arrange the grill so that it is not too close to the flame (4–5-inches away). Place skewers on grill and cook each side 7 to 10 minutes or until it is nicely browned. Baste frequently with remaining olive oil. When all sides are browned, remove meat from skewers and place on warm platter.

To serve: Peel the onion and slice into *very* fine rings, paper-thin if possible. Separate the rings and place them on top of meat. Serve simply with green salad and boiled potatoes. (A good idea is to boil the potatoes ahead of time and then, when you begin your grilling, peel the potatoes, rub them with oil and some of the marinade paste, and grill them along with the meat for about 20 minutes, turning them as they brown.) This meat could also be served with Rice with Spinach or Rice with Peas. At a banquet, if you wish to serve a 'sauced' meat and a 'dry' meat, serve *Koftas* and *Boti Kabab*.

Kidney kabab

Serves 6

Follow the preceding recipe. Substitute $2\frac{1}{2}$ lbs of lamb kidney for the cubed leg of lamb.

Seekh kabab

Serves 6

This delicious recipe involves grinding the meat to a paste before wrapping it around the skewers. This fine paste is a little difficult to handle, but patience and perseverance will take care of *that* problem.

2 slices white bread

2 lbs minced lamb meat or
minced beef (put twice
through the mincer)

5 cloves garlic, peeled and
coarsely chopped

a piece of fresh ginger, 1
inch square, peeled and
coarsely chopped

½ teacup chopped fresh
green coriander, or fresh
mint, or ¼ teacup each
green coriander and fresh
mint

1 tsp ground cloves

1 tsp ground cinnamon

1 tsp ground cumin

1 tsp ground nutmeg

1 tbs ground coriander

¼ tsp freshly ground pepper

2 tsp salt

1 tbs garam masala

½–1 tsp cayenne pepper
(optional), or 1–2 hot
green chilies, finely
chopped (optional)

1 egg

8 tbs melted butter

Garnish

1 medium-sized onion
2 lemons

extra lemon juice

Soak the bread in just enough water to dampen it; squeeze out any excess. Set aside.

If your butcher has not put the meat twice through the mincer, do it yourself.

In a large non-metallic bowl, combine the meat, bread, chopped garlic, ginger, green coriander and/or mint, cloves, cinnamon, cumin, nutmeg, coriander, pepper, salt, *garam masala*, and cayenne or green chili. Mix well. Put this mixture through the fine blade of a mincer once. Taste (if you are up to it), and add more salt if needed.

(This much can be done the night before. The meat can then be tightly covered and refrigerated. The *seekhs* can be grilled in the afternoon, covered in aluminium foil, and set aside. In the evening they can be reheated, covered, in a 300°F., Mark 2 oven, and served.)

The meat should be covered and refrigerated for at least 2 hours.

Light the charcoal fire. (This dish can also be made in an

indoor grill.) While the grill is heating, peel the onion for the garnish and slice it paper-thin. Separate the rings and set them in a bowl of ice water, cover, and refrigerate.

When the fire is almost ready, begin to prepare your first batch of *seekhs* for grilling. (The number of batches will depend on the size of your stove and the number of skewers you possess.) Break the egg into the bowl with the meat mixture. Mix well. Using your palm and fingers, wrap meat around the skewers, making sausage shapes about 6 inches long and 1 inch in diameter. You have to work fast, as the meat is very fine and tends to fall off; if it is too difficult to handle, add more dampened bread. As each skewer is done, place it on the grill, which should be about 5 inches away from the fire. You may need to put your palm under the meat as you carry each skewer to the fire.

In a small bowl, mix melted butter with 4 tablespoons warm water, and baste meat frequently with this combination. When one side is browned, slide a long spatula or cleaver under the meat and gently turn it over. Cook slowly until all sides are lightly browned and cooked through. Each batch of *seekhs* will take you 15 to 20 minutes. As they are done, lift the skewers gently, putting a plate underneath in case of accidents, slide *seekhs* off skewer, and place on warmed platter. Keep platter covered with aluminium foil and in a warm place. Prepare the remaining *seekhs* in the same way.

To serve: Cut the lemons into wedges. Drain the onion rings and pat them dry on paper towels. Arrange the lemon wedges around the platter and lay the onion rings on top of the *seekh kababs*. Squeeze lemon juice over *seekhs* before eating. Serve with *naans* or *parathas* or *pooris* and a vegetable — perhaps Cauliflower with Ginger and Green Coriander — or if you like, with Rice with Spinach and Yogurt with Tiny Dumplings.

Marinated pork chops

Serves 4

In this recipe the pork chops should marinate for at least 6 hours.

1 medium-sized onion, peeled and coarsely chopped

a piece of fresh ginger, 1 inch square, peeled and coarsely chopped

4 cloves garlic, peeled and coarsely chopped

2 tbs tomato purée

3 tsp ground coriander

½ tsp ground cumin

½ tsp ground turmeric

¼ tsp ground mace

¼ tsp ground cloves

1 tsp salt

⅛ tsp freshly ground pepper

2 tbs olive or peanut oil

2 tbs lemon juice

¼–½ tsp cayenne pepper (optional) or to taste

8 rib or loin pork chops

Put the chopped onions, ginger, and garlic in blender along with 4 tablespoons of water and blend to a smooth paste about 1 minute at high speed).

Combine paste with remaining ingredients except the pork chops and mix well.

With a fork, prod holes in the chops and put them in the marinade. Rub them well with the marinade, cover, and leave refrigerated for at least 6 hours.

Light the charcoal. When the fire is really hot, put the grill on its lowest notch. Lift the pork chops out and place them on the grill. Reserve any marinade. Sear for about 8 minutes on each side. Now put the grill in its highest notch and cook for about 20 minutes on each side. Brush with the marinade before you turn chops over each time.

To serve: If you want a very simple meal, these chops could be served with plain boiled potatoes and a salad of spinach, radishes and onion rings. Or if you like, you could serve it with Sweet Rice with Carrots and Raisins.

Tandoori chicken—my version

Serves 6–8

I have already discussed *tandoori* chicken at the beginning of this chapter. There are, however, two things that I need to point out here. The chickens used for the *tandoor* in India are usually spring chickens, weighing 2–2½ lbs each. They are cooked whole, with only wings and neck removed, on all sides at once. I find it more convenient to marinate and cook the chicken cut in pieces (it is also easier to serve and to eat this way). I buy the legs and breasts of grilling or frying chickens. (You may have an odd member of the family who just loves wings, and who will need to be placated some other way at some other time.) Also, I should point out again that Indians seem to dislike the chicken skin and always remove it before cooking.

The chicken in this recipe should be marinated for about 24 hours. Assuming that most people like both dark and light meat, I am allocating one whole leg and half a breast for each of 6 people.

1 medium-sized onion,
  peeled and coarsely
  chopped
6 whole cloves garlic,
  peeled and coarsely
  chopped
a piece of fresh ginger, about
  2 inches long and 1 inch
  wide, peeled and coarsely
  chopped
3 tbs lemon juice
8 oz plain yogurt
1 tbs ground coriander
1 tsp ground cumin
1 tsp ground turmeric
1 tsp garam masala
$\frac{1}{4}$ tsp ground mace
$\frac{1}{4}$ tsp ground nutmeg

$\frac{1}{4}$ tsp ground cloves
$\frac{1}{4}$ tsp ground cinnamon
4 tbs olive oil (or vegetable
  oil)
2 tsp salt
$\frac{1}{4}$ tsp freshly ground black
  pepper
$\frac{1}{4}$–$\frac{1}{2}$ tsp cayenne pepper
  (optional, or use as desired)
$\frac{1}{2}$–1 tsp orange food colouring
  (use the Spanish bijol, or
  Indian powdered food
  colouring, or Bush's
  orange-red powder; its use
  is optional)
6 chicken legs
3 chicken breasts, halved

Garnish

1 medium-sized onion
2 lemons

extra lemon juice (optional)

Make the marinade first. Put the chopped onions, garlic, ginger, and lemon juice in an electric blender, and blend to a smooth paste, about 1 minute at high speed. Place this in a bowl large enough to accommodate the chicken. Add the yogurt, coriander, cumin, turmeric, *garam masala*, mace, nutmeg, cloves, cinnamon, olive oil, salt, black pepper, cayenne, and food colouring. Mix thoroughly.

Skin the chicken legs and breasts. With a sharp knife make 3 diagonal slashes on each breast section, going halfway down to the bone. Make 2 diagonal slashes on each thigh, also going halfway down to the bone. With the point of a sharp knife, make 4 or 5 jabs on each drumstick.

Put the chicken in the marinade and rub the marinade into the slashes with your finger. Cover and leave refrigerated for 24 hours. Turn 4 or 5 times while the chicken is marinating.

About $1\frac{1}{2}$ hours before serving, light your charcoal. It should take 20 to 30 minutes to get red hot. Place the grill on its lowest notch.

Peel the onion for garnishing and slice it paper-thin. Separate the rings and set in a small bowl of ice water, cover, and refrigerate.

When the fire is hot, lift out the chicken pieces and place on the grill. Cook about 7 or 8 minutes on each side, then raise the grill a few notches to cook more slowly for another 15 to 20 minutes on each side. Baste with marinade as you cook.

To serve: Warm a large platter. Place the chicken pieces on it. Drain the water from the onion rings and lay them on top of the chicken. Quarter the lemons lengthwise and place them around the chicken. The chicken tastes very good with extra lemon juice squeezed on it.

This chicken is considered a delicacy and can be served at a banquet with *Pullao, naans*, a few vegetable dishes, and onions pickled in vinegar.

Try it also with Rice with Spinach and Yogurt with Potatoes.

Barbecued Pacific king prawns

Serves 6

This dish tastes best when the prawns are fresh. If, however, you wish to use the peeled frozen prawns available in most supermarkets, allow them to thaw completely first. Then squeeze out all the water by pressing between your palms, and marinate after that.

3 lbs fresh Pacific king
  prawns
¼ pint olive oil (or vegetable
  oil)
3 tbs lemon juice
1 medium-sized onion,
  peeled and coarsely
  chopped
1 whole head of garlic,
  peeled and coarsely
  chopped

a piece of fresh ginger, about
  1 inch square, peeled and
  coarsely chopped
1–3 fresh hot green chilies
  (if desired), sliced, or
  ¼–1 tsp cayenne pepper
  (if desired)
salt
freshly ground pepper

Garnish

2 lemons cut into wedges

fresh green coriander sprigs
  or fresh dill

Peel the prawns and devein them. As you devein them, slit their backs three-quarters of the way through and then spread the prawns out, butterfly fashion. When all the prawns are done, wash them and leave aside to drain.

In the container of an electric blender, put 2 tablespoons of the olive oil, lemon juice, chopped onion, garlic, ginger, chilies or cayenne, 1½ teaspoons salt, and ½ teaspoon pepper, and blend at high speed until you have a smooth paste (20 seconds).

(*Note:* If you are unsure of your ability to gauge how 'hot' it will turn out to be, first blend in half a green chili, then the other half, then a whole, and so on. Taste a drop each time. Remember, though, that once the mixture is spread over the prawns, it will taste only about half as hot.)

Place the marinade in a non-metallic bowl. Pat the prawns dry and marinate. Mix well, cover, and refrigerate for an hour.

Light your charcoal, keeping grill at a medium distance from the fire, about 5 inches. Next to the stove place salt, pepper, the remaining olive oil, and a pastry brush for basting.

When the fire is ready, brush the underside of prawns with oil and place them on the grill, leaving as much marinade on them as clings naturally. Sprinkle salt and pepper on the upper side and baste with oil. Let the prawns cook until they brown slightly, 5 to 10 minutes, depending on your stove. Then turn over with a pair of tongs, season again, and baste with oil. Cook another 5 to 10 minutes.

To serve: Place prawns on warmed platter. Garnish with lemon wedges and sprigs of parsley or dill. For a simple meal, serve with Rice with Peas and a green salad. At a more elaborate dinner, serve with meat and chicken dishes.

Barbecued salmon steaks

Serves 6

I barbecue salmon steaks very much the way I do prawns, and it tastes delicious. The marinade is almost the same as for prawns, except for the addition of a teaspoon of ground turmeric. It is, of course, best to use fresh salmon steaks.

6 salmon steaks, $\frac{3}{4}$–1 inch thick

4 fl. oz olive oil (or vegetable oil)

3 fl. oz lemon juice

1 medium-sized onion, peeled and coarsely chopped

1 whole head of garlic, peeled and coarsely chopped

a piece of fresh ginger, about 1 inch square, peeled and coarsely chopped

1–3 fresh hot green chilies (if desired), sliced, or $\frac{1}{4}$–1 tsp cayenne pepper (if desired)

salt

1 tsp ground turmeric

freshly ground pepper

Garnish

2 lemons cut into wedges

6 sprigs fresh green coriander

In the container of an electric blender, place 2 tablespoons of the olive oil, the lemon juice, and the chopped onion, garlic, ginger, green chilies or cayenne, 1½ teaspoons salt, turmeric, and ½ teaspoon pepper, and blend at high speed until you have a smooth paste (20 seconds).

(*Note:* If you are unsure of your ability to gauge how 'hot' it will turn out to be, first blend in half a green chili, then the other half, then a whole, and so on. Taste a drop each time. Remember, though, that once the mixture is spread over the fish, it will taste only about half as hot.)

Place the marinade in a non-metallic bowl. Wash and pat dry the pieces of fish and place in marinade. Mix well, cover, and refrigerate at least 2 hours. (Longer won't hurt.)

Heat the charcoal, keeping grill about 2–3 inches from fire. Next to stove place salt, pepper, the remaining olive oil, and a pastry brush for basting.

When the fire is ready, brush the salmon steaks with oil and place on grill. Sprinkle the top with a little salt and pepper. Baste with oil. Let them grill until one side gets little brown patches (about 5 to 6 minutes). Turn over with a spatula and grill on the other side. Sprinkle top with salt and pepper. Baste again with oil. Cook another 6 minutes or until this side is also lightly browned. Remove.

To serve: Place on warmed platter and garnish with lemon wedges and green coriander. Serve with Rice with Spinach, Carrots and Peas with Ginger and Green Coriander, and Tomato and Cucumber with Lemon Juice. You could also serve it very simply with boiled parslied potatoes and a green salad.

Vegetables

Green beans with onion paste
Green beans with ginger
Green beans with mustard
Cabbage with onions
Cabbage leaves stuffed with potatoes
Carrots and peas with ginger and green coriander
Cauliflower with ginger and green coriander
Cauliflower with onion and tomato
Fried aubergines with sour green chutney
Fried aubergines
Fried aubergines with tomato chutney
Aubergine bharta (smoked aubergine)
Mushrooms with cumin and asafetida
Crisp fried okra
Okra with onions
Stuffed whole okra
Whole pea pods with cumin
Fresh peas with ginger and green coriander
Sookhe aloo ('dry' potatoes)
Pyazwale sookhe aloo ('dry' potatoes with onions)
Potatoes with asafetida and cumin
New potatoes cooked in their jackets
Maya's potatoes
Maya's potatoes with yogurt
Potatoes in thick sauce
Potato patties (aloo-ki-tikiya)
Tomato sauce

SEE ALSO

Kheema used as stuffing (for peppers, tomatoes, and aubergines)(pages 80–82)
Recipes in the Rice chapter for rice cooked with various vegetables
  (pages 238–50)
Recipes in the Dals chapter for dals cooked with various vegetables
  (pages 270–73, 281)
Recipes in the Chutneys, pickles, and other relishes chapter (pages 290–306)

NDIAN vegetable markets are an absolute delight to the eye and a source of great anticipatory glee to the palate. The wily shopkeepers have been tutored by centuries of salesmanship and by fierce competition. They call to you as you walk by, offering you samples to handle. What better enticement can you have than a couple of small, firm, shiny aubergines placed on the palm of your hand, or a ripe Alphonso mango waved under your nose? Or they will entice you with: 'These fresh fenugreek greens just came in from the fields—at least take a look!' Another of their tricks is to begin peeling a fruit just as you think you have succeeded in resisting them. A bunch of fresh red leechees is hard enough to pass up, but when they start peeling them and the fragrant fruit juice drips to the ground, you need no further urging to pull out your wallet.

India produces most of the kinds of fruit and vegetables found in Britain and many, many more. But, of course, everything is seasonal. You can expect corn only in August, September, and October, mangoes only in the summer, cauliflower only in the winter, and fresh mushrooms only during the humid monsoons. So a change of seasons for us is more than just a change of weather. Our menu changes considerably, and for most Indians who are vegetarians it changes drastically. If you eat carrot 'water pickles' in the winter, you eat watermelon-rind pickles in the summer, and if you eat tangerines, guavas, and apples in the winter, you can have melons, loquats and *cheekoos* (a kind of round, all-brown persimmon) in the summer. There are no frozen vegetables or fruit to be had all year round, and no large-scale hot-houses raising out-of-season vegetables. India does, now, produce varieties of dried vegetables, but they are used rather rarely. Winter is our good vegetable season, and summer brings the most luscious varieties of fruit.

When an Indian housewife goes shopping and buys about 50 pence worth of vegetables, the shopkeeper, if he is friendly, will throw in a handful of green chilies and a bunch of fresh green coriander free. These two items are, as you may have already noted in many recipes, essential to a lot of our cooking, and there is a detailed note on them at the beginning of the book (pages 43 and 40). The Indian housewife will also stock up on ginger (the rhizome or 'root', see page 42), considering herself very lucky indeed if she manages to find the young, tender ginger. This has many advantages. Its skin can be lightly scraped instead of peeled; the tough fibres have not yet developed so it can be used for an instant relish which combines ginger slices, lime juice, and salt; it can also be cut, chopped, grated, or minced with much greater ease. This young ginger looks slightly pink, and if you ever happen to see it in some store, do buy it.

Onions are another important vegetable. Raw, they are used for relishes and garnishing. Ground, they are used to make the paste in which some vegetables and meats are cooked. They can be sautéed or fried and then cooked along with cauliflower or aubergine or used as stuffing for okra pods.

India grows many varieties of mushrooms, the most delicious (and expensive) of which is one that grows in Kashmir and resembles a heart-shaped black sponge! Since I have been unable to find the small, slim mushroom commonly seen in North India, my recipes are adapted to the commercial variety found in most English grocery stores.

Indians eat a lot of greens—fenugreek greens, mustard greens, white radish greens, gram (or chickpea) greens, and, of course, spinach. Each is seasonal, and each area has traditional ways of cooking its greens. In northern India, where I come from, fenugreek greens, being very strong-flavoured, are nearly always cooked with tiny new potatoes in their jackets, or with carrots. The Punjab, in north-western India, is famous for its creamed mustard greens, which both the poorest and the richest

Punjabi serves with flat corn bread and a glass of butter-milk. A very popular dish in Bengal is *chorchuri* in which various greens are first sautéed and then allowed to simmer gently with fried fish-heads. When cooking white radishes, we tend to use both the radish and its leaves. Chickpea, or gram, greens, which I used to eat raw with salt and pepper, are not to be found in this country. Spinach, which is popular throughout India, is often creamed, or dipped in batter and fried, or cooked with meat.

Corn, in India, is available only during the late summer months. The fresh cobs, peeled and roasted, are sold on street corners, rather like chestnuts. The corn seller carries a light, portable charcoal stove on which he roasts his corn, and he sells it sprinkled with salt, red pepper, black pepper, and lime juice. I have tried roasting the hybrid 'sweet corn' available in most English shops, but it is too tender, and very often it just shrivels up. The only times I have been successful have been with what the English would call the 'tougher' ears of corn. If you ever do manage to find some 'tougher' ears which won't 'melt in your mouth', peel them and roast them over charcoal. They can be superb. And don't, for heaven's sake, put butter on them. Eat them either plain or sprinkled with salt, freshly ground pepper, and a little lime or lemon juice.

Fresh okra is not always easy to find, and when it is available be sure to buy it as you would green beans. Pick a pod up and snap it, and if it is young and crisp, you buy. Otherwise, walk on. If you are lucky enough to find good fresh okra, you can slit and stuff the pods with fried onions and spices (page 211); you can slice them very fine, deep-fry them until they are crunchy (page 209) and serve them with an omelet; you can also slice them and cook them with onions, garlic, ginger, and tomatoes.

Potatoes are a popular staple throughout North India. Not only are they cooked in combination with meats, other vegetables, rice, and *dals*, but they are also cooked with every imaginable permutation of spices. A young child may want his potatoes boiled and then fried with cumin seeds; at a picnic one might have 'dry' potatoes cooked with red peppers, fenugreek, fennel, cumin, and mustard seeds; at a banquet one might be served potatoes cooked with yogurt and the *garam masalas*, cinnamon, cloves, cardamom, bay leaves, etc.; and of course, there is my favourite, potatoes cooked with asafetida and cumin, a 'wet' dish best enjoyed with *pooris*.

A vegetable that was once basically ignored in Britain and that is now evoking the first stirrings of interest, is the aubergine. Still, it seems confined to the occasional parmigiana, moussaka, or ratatouille. It deserves better. Stuffed, baked, and covered with sauce, it makes a glorious main course. Its roasted pulp, when mixed with yogurt and fresh mint, makes a refreshing summer 'salad'. Deep-fried in slices and smothered in one of many sour chutneys, it can serve as an appetizer or an accompanying vegetable dish.

I can't really begin to list all the Indian vegetables and fruit. We have a 'pickling' carrot that is dark red, like a beetroot; during late winter, Indians buy green chickpeas, or *chholas*, which can be cooked or eaten raw; our sweet potato has the consistency of a crumbly baking potato; we eat lotus stems and water chestnuts; we have *jamuns* and *falsas* and *bair* and *kaseru* and *parval*—fruits and vegetables which don't even have any English names. And this list could go on and on.

The recipes in this chapter are mostly for vegetables that can be found in supermarkets—beans, carrots, cauliflower, cabbage, aubergines, peas, potatoes, etc. I do have some recipes for okra which should be cooked only when fresh pods are available.

Green beans with onion paste

Serves 4–6

Green beans can be cooked in many ways. In India we tend to overcook them — at least according to the best Chinese and French standards. But as I have explained earlier, it is mainly to kill germs and because we love spices. We like our spices to permeate a vegetable, and this cannot happen unless a vegetable is allowed to become fairly tender. When you finish preparing this recipe, your beans will not look bright green, nor will they be very crisp. They will be a brownish dark-green, smothered in spices, and utterly delicious.

1½ lbs fresh green beans
1 medium-sized onion, peeled and coarsely chopped
3 cloves garlic, peeled and coarsely chopped
a piece of fresh ginger, about 1 inch square, coarsely chopped
1 medium-sized tinned or fresh tomato, peeled and coarsely chopped
½ tsp ground turmeric
10 tbs vegetable oil

2 tsp ground coriander
1 tsp ground cumin
½ tsp whole cumin seeds
½ tsp whole black mustard seeds
1 or 2 whole dried red peppers (optional), or ½ hot fresh green chili, sliced in half (optional), or ¼ tsp cayenne pepper (optional)
1 tsp salt (or to taste)
2 tsp lemon juice (or to taste)

Garnish

1 tbs finely chopped fresh green coriander

Wash the beans. Trim the ends. Slice them into fine rounds about ⅛ to ¼ inch thick. (This takes a while, so it is best to sit down somewhere with chopping board and sharp knife and do about 8 beans at a time.)

Put the onion, garlic, ginger, tomato, and turmeric in a blender and blend to a smooth paste.

Put 6 tablespoons of the vegetable oil in an 8-inch frying-pan or heavy-bottomed pan, and heat it on medium. Pour in mixture from blender and fry for about 5 minutes, stirring all the time, adding a teaspoon of warm water if and when it starts to stick at the bottom. Now put in the coriander and cumin and continue frying another 5 minutes, again adding a teaspoon of warm water if necessary to prevent sticking. Turn off heat.

In a 10-inch frying-pan, heat the remaining tablespoons of oil over medium flame. When very hot, put in the whole cumin and mustard seeds. After 10 seconds, add the whole red peppers if you are using them. Stir once, and as the peppers darken and the mustard seeds begin to pop, put in the sliced green beans and the sliced green chili if you are using it. Now scrape up all the mixture from the first frying-pan and add it to the beans. Fry the beans on medium flame for 5 minutes, stirring all the time. Turn heat to low, add the salt and lemon juice, and let the beans cook covered, stirring now and then, until they are tender (about 35 minutes). If you are using cayenne pepper, stir it in 5 minutes before end of cooking time. If the beans stick to the frying-pan, add 1 tablespoon of water, stir, and keep cooking.

To serve: These beans can be cooked in advance and reheated over a low flame. Serve them in a warm dish and, if you like, sprinkle finely chopped green coriander over them. They are good with *Koftas* and plain rice, go well with nearly all meats, and especially well with *parathas*, *pooris*, and *chapatis*.

Green beans with ginger

Serves 4–6

This dish is simple to make and has a very fresh, gingery taste.

1½ lbs fresh green beans
a piece of fresh ginger, about
   2 inches long and 1 inch
   wide, peeled and coarsely
   chopped
6 tbs vegetable oil
¼ tsp ground turmeric
½ fresh hot green chili
   (optional), washed and
   sliced very fine

3 tbs chopped fresh green
   coriander
1 tsp ground cumin
2 tsp ground coriander
1¼ tsp garam masala
2 tsp lemon juice (or to
   taste)
1 tsp salt (or to taste)

Wash the green beans and trim the ends. Slice into fine rounds, ⅛ to ¼ inch thick. When all the beans are chopped. set aside in a bowl.

Put the ginger in the blender with 3 tablespoons of water and blend at high speed until it is a smooth paste.

Heat the oil in a 10-inch frying-pan over medium heat. While it is heating, pour in paste from blender and add turmeric. Fry, stirring constantly, for 2 minutes, then add the sliced green chilies and the green coriander, and after another minute, put in the green beans and continue cooking and stirring for about a minute. Add the cumin, coriander, 1 teaspoon of the *garam masala*, lemon juice, salt, and 3 tablespoons of warm water. Cover frying-pan, turn flame very low, and let beans cook slowly for about 40 minutes, stirring every 10 minutes or so.

To serve: These beans can easily be cooked in advance and reheated. Serve them in a warm dish, with ¼ teaspoon *garam masala* sprinkled on top.

They go well with nearly all meat and chicken dishes. They can be eaten with plain boiled rice and *Moong Dal*, or served with hot *pooris* or *parathas* or *chapatis*.

Green beans with mustard

Serves 4–6

Here is another easy recipe for beans, in which they are slightly sweet.

1½ lbs fresh green beans
3 level tbs plain yogurt
½ hot fresh green chili, sliced very thinly, or ¼ tsp cayenne pepper (optional)
3 tbs finely chopped fresh green coriander
1 tsp salt

1 tsp sugar
¾ tsp dry English mustard
¾ tsp ground cumin
2 tsp lemon juice
5 tbs vegetable oil
5 whole fenugreek seeds
¼ tsp whole cumin seeds
¼ tsp garam masala

Wash green beans and trim ends. Slice finely into rounds of about ¼ inch.

In a cup or small bowl, mix the yogurt with the green chili or cayenne, parsley, salt, sugar, dry mustard, cumin, and lemon juice. Add 3 tablespoons water and mix well.

Heat the oil in a frying-pan over medium heat. When hot, add the whole fenugreek and cumin seeds. When the fenugreek seeds begin to change colour (about 20 seconds) put in the beans. Fry, stirring, for about 5 minutes.

Beat the yogurt mixture once again and stir into the beans. When the frying-pan begins to make bubbling noises, cover, reduce heat to very low, and allow to cook slowly for 40 minutes. Stir every 10 minutes or so.

To serve: Place in warm serving dish and sprinkle with with *garam masala*. Serve with Rice with Cauliflower and Cumin Seed, *Masoor Dal*, and Chicken with Tomatoes and Butter. Or serve with *Kheema*, plain boiled rice, and *Moong Dal*. Or serve with *parathas*. If you are having many vegetables, then serve these beans with Cauliflower with Ginger and Green Coriander, *Sookhe Aloo, Khare Masale Ka Gosht*, and hot *chapatis* or *pooris* — an excellent meal.

Cabbage with onions

Serves 4–6

There are many ways of cooking cabbage in India. It can be cooked by itself or with peas or potatoes. It can be cooked with prawns and with meat. Here are some of these recipes. Just remember that when you start cooking the cabbage, it looks like a lot. But it reduces. So make sure you cook enough to feed all the people you are planning for. I find that one medium-sized head of cabbage will feed 4 people easily. It can be stretched to 6 if there are many other dishes. As with most of our vegetables, we tend to overcook cabbage, but the end result tastes very good, so who cares!

1 medium-sized head of cabbage

2½ medium-sized onions

9 tbs vegetable oil

6 whole fenugreek seeds

½ tsp whole cumin seeds

½ tsp whole black mustard seeds

½ tsp whole fennel seeds

2 cloves garlic, peeled and coarsely chopped

a piece of fresh ginger, 1 inch by 1½ inches, peeled and coarsely chopped

1 medium-sized tomato (tinned or fresh), peeled

½ tsp ground turmeric

½–1 hot green chili, thinly sliced (optional)

¾–1 tsp salt

1 tsp garam masala

1 tbs lemon juice

Trim away the outer damaged leaves of the cabbage, wash it, and cut it in quarters. Remove the stem and hard core and shred cabbage lengthwise as finely as you can.

Peel 2 of the onions and cut them each into half, lengthwise. Now slice finely into half-circles.

Heat 6 tablespoons of the oil in a 10-inch heavy-bottomed pot over medium heat, and add the fenugreek, cumin, mustard, and fennel seeds. As the seeds start sizzling and changing colour (about 10 seconds), put in the sliced onions. Fry them over medium heat for about 3 minutes. Add the shredded cabbage, stir a few times, put the lid on, lower flame, and cook for 15 minutes.

Uncover and cook over fairly low heat for 30 minutes, stirring occasionally to prevent burning.

Meanwhile, peel and coarsely chop the remaining ½ onion and put it with the garlic, ginger, and peeled tomato in electric blender. Blend to a paste.

In a frying-pan heat the 3 remaining tablespoons of oil. Add the paste from the blender, the turmeric, and the green chili. Fry, stirring all the time, for 8 to 10 minutes (adding, if necessary, 1 teaspoon of warm water at a time to prevent sticking). When the cabbage has cooked for 30 minutes, add this fried paste mixture, along with the salt, *garam masala*, and lemon juice. Stir and let it cook for another 5 minutes.

To serve: Serve with *parathas*, *pooris*, or *chapatis*. If serving with rice, serve *karhi* or *dal* and a chicken or meat dish like Chicken Cooked with Yogurt or Lamb *Korma* or *Koftas*. Plain yogurt or Yogurt with Potatoes would also go well with it.

Cabbage leaves stuffed with potatoes

Serves 6–8

Cabbage leaves can be stuffed with meat or potatoes. Here is my mother's recipe for the latter.

5 medium-sized potatoes	3½ tsp salt
7 medium-sized onions	¼ tsp cayenne pepper
10 tbs vegetable oil	(optional)
2 tsp whole fennel seeds	1 tbs lemon juice
1 tsp whole cumin seeds	1 medium-sized head of
1 tsp garam masala	cabbage

The stuffing: Boil the potatoes, then peel and dice them into ¼-inch pieces.

Peel the onions, cut them in half lengthwise, and slice them into fine half-circles.

In a frying-pan, heat 6 tablespoons of the oil over medium heat. Add the onions, frying, stirring, and separating the rings until the onions are brownish, about 7 or 8 minutes; they should not get crisp.

Add the fennel and cumin seeds and fry another 7 or 8 minutes on lower flame. The onions should look a rich reddish-brown now.

Add the diced boiled potatoes to the onion mixture and continue frying. As you fry, mash the potatoes with the back of a slotted spoon or potato masher.

To the potato and onion mixture add the *garam masala*, 2½ teaspoons salt, cayenne pepper if desired, and lemon juice. Mix it all up and set aside, uncovered, to cool slightly.

The cabbage: Cut off the hard stem of the cabbage, remove the hard, damaged outer leaves, and wash it. In a pot large enough to hold the whole cabbage, bring to the boil water to which 1 teaspoon salt has been added. Drop the cabbage in (the water should cover at least three-quarters of it), cover, and allow to boil for 5 minutes. Lift cabbage out of boiling water, run under cold water, and carefully remove each leaf, taking care not to break it. Dry. If the inner leaves are still crisp, drop them again in the boiling water until they go limp. Remove and cool under cold water.

Spread out one leaf at a time. Snip out the hard core of the outer leaves with a sharp knife or a pair of kitchen shears. You can snip to about an inch into the leaf, removing a kind of narrow V. Now place a tablespoon of the stuffing in the centre of the leaf and fold the edges over. Put the stuffed leaf on your left palm and with your right palm gently squeeze out any extra moisture. This also helps to keep the stuffed cabbage leaves tightly closed.

In a 10-inch frying-pan, heat the remaining 4 tablespoons of oil over medium heat. Squeeze each stuffed cabbage leaf again between paper towels and put in frying-pan. Fry, a few pieces at a time, until each piece is browned on all sides. Take care not to let the leaves open. Remove them to a plate. When all the pieces are done, lower the heat, arrange the stuffed cabbage pieces in the frying-pan in tight layers, add 2 tablespoons water, cover, and cook on very low flame for 10 to 15 minutes.

To serve: Remove very carefully and serve on large, warm platter. Serve with Cubed Lamb with Onions and Raisins and Rice with Peas or with *Karhi, Koftas,* and plain boiled rice. This dish is also very good served with hot *parathas*.

Carrots and peas with ginger and green coriander

Serves 4–6

a piece of fresh ginger, 2 inches by 1 inch, peeled and coarsely chopped
1½ lbs young, slim carrots
6 tbs vegetable oil
¼ tsp whole black mustard seeds
5 whole fenugreek seeds
¼ tsp ground turmeric
1 packed teacup coarsely chopped fresh green coriander

1 fresh hot green chili, washed and finely sliced (optional, or substitute ¼ tsp cayenne pepper)
1 lb fresh peas, shelled
1 tsp ground coriander
1 tsp ground cumin
1 tsp garam masala
1 tsp salt

Put the ginger in blender with 3 tablespoons of water and blend until smooth (about one minute).

Peel the carrots and slice them into rounds about ⅛ inch thick.

Heat the oil in a 10–12-inch frying-pan over medium heat. When very hot, add the mustard and fenugreek seeds. When mustard seeds begin to pop (10 to 20 seconds), put in the ginger paste and turmeric, keeping your face averted. Fry for about 2 minutes, stirring frequently. Add chopped green coriander and green chili or cayenne, and cook, stirring, another 2 minutes. Add carrots and peas and cook 5 minutes more, stirring frequently.

Now put in the coriander, cumin, *garam masala*, salt, and 3 tablespoons of warm water. Stir for a minute, cover, lower heat, and cook slowly 30 minutes. Stir gently every 10 minutes or so.

To serve: Lift gently out of frying-pan and place on serving dish. Serve with hot *pooris* or *parathas*. This dish goes well with any sauced meat dish—Lamb with Onions and Mushrooms, etc. It is also good with Shrimp with Dill and Ginger, plain *Moong Dal*, and Rice with Potatoes and Cumin Seed.

Cauliflower with ginger and green coriander

Serves 6–8

a piece of fresh ginger, about
    2½ inches by 1 inch,
    peeled and coarsely
    chopped
1 large head fresh cauliflower,
    or 2 small ones
8 tbs vegetable oil
½ tsp ground turmeric
1 fresh hot green chili, finely
    sliced, or ¼ tsp cayenne
    pepper (optional)

1 packed teacup coarsely
    chopped fresh green
    coriander (coriander
    greens or cilantro)
1 tsp ground cumin
2 tsp ground coriander
1 tsp garam masala
1 tbs lemon juice
2 tsp salt

Put the ginger into a blender jar with 4 tablespoons of water, and blend until it becomes smooth (about 1 minute).

Cut off the thick, coarse stem of the cauliflower and remove all leaves. First break the cauliflower into large flowerets, using your hands if it is a loosely packed head and a sharp knife if it is too tightly packed. Since you want to end up with *small* flowerets, not longer than 1 to 1½ inches and not wider at the head than ½ to 1 inch, I find that the best way is to take each large floweret and begin by slicing the stems crosswise into fairly thin rounds. Keep these, as they are quite edible. When you reach the upper end of the stem, start breaking off the small flowerets. Slice the stem into rounds whenever it seems too long, and keep the rounds. Wash the flowerets and the stem rounds in a colander and leave to drain.

Heat oil in 10–12-inch frying-pan over medium heat. Add the ginger paste and turmeric. Fry, stirring constantly; after about 2 minutes, add green chili or cayenne and green coriander; after another 2 minutes, put in the cauliflower, continuing to cook and stir for 5 minutes. (If necessary, add 1 teaspoon warm water at a time to prevent sticking.) Now add the cumin, coriander, *garam masala*, lemon juice, salt, and 3 tablespoons warm water, cook and stir for about 5 minutes, then cover, lower flame, and let cook slowly for 35 to 45 minutes (the tightly packed cauliflower takes longer to cook), stirring gently every 10 minutes. The cauliflower is done when it is tender with just a faint trace of crispness along its inner spine.

To serve: Lift out gently and place in serving dish—a low, wide bowl would be best. Serve with hot *chapatis*, *pooris*, or *parathas*, or serve with any kind of lentils and plain boiled rice. It is particularly good with Lamb *Pullao* and Cucumber *Raita*.

Cauliflower with onion and tomato

Serves 6–8

1 medium-sized onion, peeled and coarsely chopped

4 cloves garlic, peeled and coarsely chopped

a piece of fresh ginger, 2 inches long and 1 inch wide, peeled and coarsely chopped

1 large head fresh cauliflower, or 2 small ones

8 tbs vegetable oil

½ tsp ground turmeric

1 medium-sized fresh or tinned tomato, peeled and chopped

1 tbs chopped fresh green coriander

1 fresh hot green chili, washed and finely sliced, or ¼ tsp cayenne pepper (optional)

2 tsp ground coriander

1 tsp ground cumin

1 tsp garam masala

2 tsp salt

1 tbs lemon juice

Put chopped onion, garlic, and ginger in blender with 4 tablespoons of water and blend to a paste.

Break off cauliflower into small flowerets (see preceding recipe), not longer than 1 to 1½ inches, and not wider at the head than ½ to 1 inch. Wash in colander and leave to drain.

Heat the oil in a heavy-bottomed 10–12-inch pot over medium flame, pour in the paste from the blender, and add the turmeric. Fry, stirring, for 5 minutes.

Add the chopped tomato, green coriander, and green chili or cayenne, and fry 5 minutes. If necessary, add 1 teaspoon of warm water at a time and stir to prevent sticking. Now put in the cauliflower, coriander, cumin, *garam masala*, salt, and lemon juice. Stir for a minute. Add 4 tablespoons warm water, stir, cover, lower flame, and allow to cook slowly 35 to 45 minutes (the tightly packed cauliflower heads take longer to cook). Stir gently every 10 minutes or so. The cauliflower is done when each floweret is tender with just a faint trace of crispness along its inner spine.

To serve: Follow suggestions of previous recipe.

Fried aubergines with sour green chutney

Serves 6

1 packed teacup chopped
    fresh green coriander
1 fresh hot green chili,
    washed and finely sliced,
    or ¼ tsp cayenne pepper
    (optional)
8 oz plain yogurt
½ tsp salt (a little more if you
    need it; sometimes yogurt
    is more sour than at other
    times)
½ tsp roasted, ground cumin
    seeds (see page 41)
1 tbs lemon juice
vegetable oil for deep frying

6 small, oval aubergines or
    1 large one (aubergines
    come in so many sizes
    that after reading this
    recipe, I'm afraid you have
    to be your own judge
    about how many you need)
8 fenugreek seeds
½ tsp fennel seeds
½ tsp black onion seeds
    (kalonji), if available
¼ tsp cumin seeds
salt
freshly ground black pepper

For the chutney: Put green coriander and chili in blender with 3 tablespoons water and blend until smooth paste (about 1 minute). You may need to push coriander down a couple of times.

In a bowl, combine yogurt, salt, roasted ground cumin seeds, lemon juice, and the paste from blender. Cover and refrigerate green chutney until ready for use.

Cooking the aubergines: Ten minutes before eating time, heat oil at a depth of 1½ to 2 inches in frying-pan, wok, or *karhai* over medium heat. While heating, wash and dry aubergines. If you have the small, oval ones, quarter them lengthwise, preserving the stem and the sepals. If you have a very large one, quarter it lengthwise and slice each quarter into ½-inch thick pieces.

When oil is very hot, add the fenugreek, fennel, onion, and cumin seeds. After 10 or 20 seconds, drop in as many aubergine pieces as the container will hold in one layer. Deep-fry each batch until golden-brown. Drain on paper towels, sprinkle each batch with salt and freshly ground pepper, and place in a warm dish. When the aubergines have fried, spoon one-quarter of the cold chutney over them and serve immediately. Serve the rest of the chutney on the side.

To serve: While the aubergine fries, I usually put all the rest of my dinner into serving dishes and bring them to the table. I bring the aubergine dish out last. This dish is usually served at meals along with other vegetables. It is very rarely the only vegetable at the table. Try it at a Sunday lunch along with Prawn with Dill and Ginger, Rice with Black-eyed Peas, and green beans.

You can also cut the aubergine fairly small, insert toothpicks, and serve it with drinks.

Fried aubergines

Serves 4

This dish is made best with the small young aubergines that are only 3 or 4 inches long. It is very simple, but *cannot* be prepared in advance. Ten minutes before you are to eat, excuse yourself and go and cook the aubergines. Serve them crisp and piping hot. (You can take the rest of the food to the table while the aubergines fry.)

vegetable oil for deep frying
8 whole fenugreek seeds
½ tsp whole fennel seeds
¼ tsp whole cumin seeds
½ tsp black onion seeds
   (kalonji), if available

4 small oval aubergines, 3–4
   inches long
salt and freshly ground
   black pepper
dash of cayenne pepper, if
   desired
1 tbs lemon juice

Put 1½ to 2 inches of oil in a wok, *karhai*, or frying-pan and heat on medium heat.

Measure out fenugreek, fennel, cumin, and onion seeds and keep handy. Wash and wipe the aubergines (leave them unpeeled), and slice lengthwise into flat, ⅛-⅙-inch slices.

When the oil is heated, put in all the seeds. When they change colour or begin to pop (5 to 10 seconds), put in the sliced aubergine pieces—only as many as your utensil will hold in one layer. Fry to a golden-brown on both sides. Drain on paper towels and sprinkle with salt, black pepper, cayenne, and lemon juice.

To serve: Serve each batch hot, as soon as it is seasoned. The aubergine should be slightly crunchy. This is really a side dish which should never be the only vegetable at a meal. Serve it along with Carrots and Peas with Ginger and Green Coriander or cauliflower as an accompaniment to any meat, chicken, or fish. You can also use it as a garnish for baked fish or a chicken roast by arranging the slices, petal-like, around a platter.

Fried aubergines with tomato chutney

Serves 6

To make this recipe, first prepare the tomato chutney, and 10 minutes before serving, fry the aubergines according to directions in preceding recipe. They will be served with the hot chutney spooned over them.

Tomato chutney

lump of tamarind size of large walnut

½ tsp whole cumin seeds
½ pint tomato sauce (page 225)

1 medium-sized onion, peeled and coarsely chopped

4 cloves garlic, peeled and coarsely chopped

4 tbs vegetable oil

$\frac{1}{8}$ tsp ground asafetida, or $\frac{1}{8}$-inch lump asafetida

4 whole cardamoms

4 whole cloves

1 tsp whole mustard seeds

1 tsp salt (or more to taste)

$\frac{1}{8}$–$\frac{1}{4}$ tsp cayenne pepper (optional)

1 tsp garam masala

$\frac{1}{8}$ tsp ground cinnamon

1 tsp sugar

$\frac{1}{8}$ tsp freshly ground black pepper

4 tbs finely chopped fresh green coriander

Soak the lump of tamarind in 6 fl. oz. hot water. Leave at least 4 hours or overnight. Make paste (about 4 fl. oz.), following directions on page 44.

Put onion and garlic in electric blender with 3 tablespoons of water. Blend at high speed to a smooth paste (1 minute).

Heat olive oil in 2-quart pot, preferably with non-metallic lining, over medium heat. Put in the asafetida, then add the cardamoms and cloves, and finally the mustard and cumin seeds. When the seeds pop, expand, and change colour (10 to 20 seconds), add the paste from the blender, keeping face averted. Fry paste, stirring, for 4 to 5 minutes, sprinkling a teaspoon of warm water in it if it sticks.

Now add the tamarind paste, tomato sauce, salt, cayenne (if desired), *garam masala*, cinnamon, sugar, and black pepper. Bring to the boil. Cover and allow to simmer gently for 15 minutes.

While chutney is simmering, prepare aubergines according to preceding recipe.

Taste the chutney, and check the salt and sugar. You may want to put in more of one or the other. At this stage, I pick out the cardamoms and the cloves from the chutney and discard them. Mix the green coriander with the chutney.

To serve: Arrange the fried aubergines on a platter. Pour some of the hot chutney over them and serve the rest on the side. See preceding recipe for suggested accompaniments.

Aubergine bharta (smoked aubergine)

Serves 4–6

Until the advent of gas, most cooking in India was done on wood or coal, and one of the waste products of wood and coal is, of course, ash. Not wishing to waste even a waste product, we geared our cuisine so that while some foods were cooking on top of the flame, others were being roasted in the ashes. (Later, the ash was used like Brillo pads to scour the pots and pans.) As a child, I remember begging the cook to put some onions in the ashes, just for me. He would pick out a tiny onion from the vegetable basket and bury it deep in the ashes with his iron tongs. Then, about an hour later, he would whisper to me that it was ready. I would pick off the burned outside, scorching my hands as I did so, and gobble up the succulent inside.

Another vegetable that was roasted was the aubergine. Once roasted, it was peeled and the inside was either mixed with chopped raw onion, fresh mint, and yogurt (page 303) or cooked further with onions and tomatoes — which is the recipe I'm going to give you now.

Lacking ashes in my 'modern' kitchen, I roast the aubergine right on top of the stove over an open flame. This is a bit messy, so I would advise you to insert an aluminium burner liner before you start.

1 large aubergine, preferably with a stem

1 medium-sized onion, peeled and coarsely chopped

a piece of fresh ginger, about 1 inch square, peeled and coarsely chopped

½ fresh hot green chili, finely sliced (optional)

1 tbs chopped fresh green coriander; reserve a little for garnishing

2 medium-sized tomatoes (tinned or fresh), peeled and coarsely chopped

2 cloves garlic, peeled and
  coarsely chopped
5 tbs vegetable oil
½ tsp ground turmeric

¾–1 tsp salt (according to
  size of aubergine)
1 tsp lemon juice
1 tsp garam masala

Line your gas burner with aluminium foil. (If you have an electric stove, place the aubergine under a preheated grill, and turn it around until it is blackened on all sides, although it will never taste quite as smoky as when done over a flame.) Stand your aubergine, stalk up, directly over a medium-low flame. Leave it there until the bottom has burned black and looks completely scorched. Now lay it on its side. As soon as the area nearest the flame darkens and turns soft, turn the aubergine slightly. Use the stem of the aubergine to turn with. Keep turning until the whole aubergine is done. (You could use tongs, but take care not to burst the aubergine or you will have a big mess.) As more and more of the aubergine is 'scorched' it will turn softer and be more difficult to handle. Don't give up. This whole process will take 20 to 25 minutes.

Once the aubergine is 'smoked', put it on a plate and carry it to the sink. Put it under cold running water and peel the blackened outer skin under the running water. Drain, shaking off as much water as you can.

Put the peeled inside of the aubergine on a chopping board and chop it coarsely. Set aside in a plate or bowl.

Put the onion, ginger, and garlic in a blender with 3 tablespoons of water and blend to a paste at high speed.

Heat the oil in a frying-pan over medium heat. While heating, pour in the paste from the blender and add the turmeric. Fry this mixture, stirring frequently; after about 5 minutes, when it begins to turn brown, add the green chili and the green coriander; then after about 1 minute, the chopped tomatoes. Lower the flame and cook for 10 minutes, stirring occasionally. Finally, add the chopped aubergine, raise the flame to medium low, and fry, stirring, for 10 to 15 minutes, seasoning with the salt, lemon juice, and *garam masala*.

To serve: Remove the *bharta* to a warm dish and serve sprinkled with green coriander. It is best when eaten with *pooris* or hot *chapatis*. Serve *Khare Masale Ka Gosht* with it and *Sookhe Aloo* ('Dry' Potatoes).

Mushrooms with cumin and asafetida

Serves 4–6

1½ lbs fresh mushrooms
2 tbs vegetable oil
a generous pinch ground
   asafetida, or ⅛-inch lump
   asafetida
½ tsp whole cumin seeds

2 whole hot dried red peppers
¼ tsp ground turmeric
½ pint tomato sauce (see
   page 225)
1 tsp salt

Clean mushrooms. Chop off the coarse stem ends.

Heat oil in 2–3-quart pot over medium heat, and put in the asafetida. It will sizzle and expand within 5 seconds. Now add the cumin seeds, and as soon as they darken (5 to 10 seconds), the red peppers. Stir once and add the turmeric and the mushrooms. Stir mushrooms for ½ minute and add the tomato sauce, 1 pint of water, and the salt. Cover, lower heat, and simmer gently 15 to 20 minutes.

Remove from heat. The mushrooms can be eaten now, but it is better to let them sit 1 to 2 hours to absorb the taste of the broth-like sauce and then reheat.

To serve: Serve in little individual bowls. The thin, delicious sauce can be eaten with a spoon or with hot *chapatis* or *pooris*. You can easily build a meal around the mushrooms. *Sindhi Gosht*, Yogurt with Tiny Dumplings, and a *dal* would complete the meal nicely.

Crisp fried okra

Serves 4

I have discussed okra earlier (see page 189). Buy it only when it is young, fresh, and crisp. Serve this crisp-fried okra to people who think they dislike okra—they will hardly recognize it. Another advantage of this dish is that it cooks easily and quickly. It can take less than 15 minutes from the time you begin washing the okra until you serve it.

1 lb fresh young okra	**⅛ tsp cayenne pepper**
oil for deep frying	**(optional)**
salt	**½ tsp garam masala**
freshly ground black pepper	**(optional)**

Wash the okra. Wipe it with paper towels. Remove head and tail and slice the pods in rounds of ⅛-inch thickness. You can slice 2 or 3 at the same time.

Heat 1 inch of oil in a 10-inch frying-pan over medium-low flame. Check heat by dropping in one slice of okra; if it sizzles immediately, the fat is ready. Put in as much okra as will fit in one layer. You will need to do at least three batches. Fry each batch 4 to 5 minutes, until the okra turns crisp and a bit brown.

Remove from frying-pan with a slotted spoon and place on paper towels to drain. Sprinkle each batch with salt, pepper, cayenne, and *garam masala*. Serve immediately.

To serve: Fried okra is delicious with a mushroom omelet for lunch or with a variety of other vegetables at dinner. Okra goes particularly well with *Urad Dal* and with *Koftas*. Or you could use it as an unusual garnish for a lamb roast, frying about 2 lbs of okra and surrounding the leg of lamb with it.

Okra with onions

Serves 4–6

This is the way okra is generally cooked in most parts of Delhi. The success of this dish depends upon the onion paste's being cooked to the right consistency before the okra is added.

4 medium-sized onions, peeled and coarsely chopped

5 cloves of garlic, peeled and coarsely chopped

a piece of fresh ginger, about 2 inches long, 1 inch thick, and 1 inch wide, peeled and coarsely chopped

6 tbs vegetable oil

1 tsp whole cumin seeds

2 tsp whole fennel seeds

1 tsp ground turmeric

1 tbs ground coriander

1 tbs tomato purée

1 lb fresh young okra

1 tsp salt

2 tsp garam masala

2 tbs lemon juice

¼ tsp cayenne pepper (optional)

Put onion, garlic, and ginger in electric blender, add ¼ cup warm water, and blend to a paste.

Heat oil in a 10–12-inch frying-pan over medium heat. Add the cumin and fennel seeds. When the fennel begins to change colour (20 seconds or so), add the paste from the blender and the turmeric.

Cook this paste over medium heat for about 20 minutes, stirring frequently and scraping the bottom. The paste will reduce and turn a lovely brown colour.

Add the coriander and fry, stirring; after a minute, add the tomato purée and cook, stirring, for about 1 minute. Turn off the heat under the frying-pan.

Wash the okra and wipe it with a paper towel. Slice a few pods at a time into ¼-inch rounds.

Turn the heat to medium again under the frying-pan with the onion paste. Add the okra, salt, *garam masala*, lemon juice, and 4 fl. oz. of warm water. When the onion paste starts bubbling, cover, turn heat very low, and allow to cook slowly for 35 minutes, or until tender. Stir every 10 minutes or so to prevent sticking.

To serve: Serve like stuffed okra, the next recipe.

Stuffed whole okra

Serves 4–6

This recipe, which comes from my maternal grandmother, is perhaps *the* most delicious way to cook okra. Fresh young okra pods are slit and stuffed with a mixture of fried onions, fennel, cumin, and fenugreek. Then they are lightly fried and allowed to simmer until cooked. Stuffing the slim okra requires a little patience, but don't let that stop you. The most confirmed okra hater will be converted and the ooooh's and aaaah's of your guests will be ample reward for your trouble.

8 medium-sized onions, peeled and finely chopped
8 cloves garlic, peeled and minced
a piece of fresh ginger, about 2 inches by 1½ inches by 1 inch, peeled and grated
2 tsp whole cumin seeds
4 tsp whole fennel seeds
20 whole fenugreek seeds
10 tbs vegetable oil
1 tsp ground turmeric
salt
4 tsp garam masala
2 tbs lemon juice
1 lb fresh young okra

The stuffing: Since this dish is to be cooked in two 10-inch frying-pans to accommodate all the okra, divide the onions, garlic, and ginger into two equal piles. Make two separate equal piles of the cumin, fennel, and fenugreek seeds.

Heat 5 tablespoons of oil in each frying-pan over medium heat, and when hot, put in the cumin, fennel, and fenugreek seeds. As they begin to pop and change colour (5 to 10 seconds), put half the onion, garlic, and ginger and ½ teaspoon turmeric into each frying-pan. Stir and fry over medium heat for about 10–12 minutes until the onions look a rich brown. Stir frequently.

Add ½ teaspoon salt and 1 teaspoon *garam masala* to each frying-pan and stir. Turn off heat under both frying-pans. Using a slotted spoon, remove onion mixture from frying-pans, leaving as much of the cooking fat behind as possible. You will need it later. Collect the onion mixture from both frying-pans in a bowl, add 2 more teaspoons *garam masala* and the lemon juice, mix, and set aside to cool.

The okra: Wash the okra and pat it dry with paper towels. Trim off the head and the lower tip.

Since the stuffing of the okra takes a little time, place the okra, the bowl of stuffing, a clean platter, and a small sharp knife on a table, and settle yourself on a chair. Pick up one okra pod at a time. Make a slit along its length, being sure that you do *not* go through the opposite side and that you leave about ⅛ inch at the top and bottom unslit.

Assuming you are right-handed, slip your left thumb into the pod to keep the slit open. With your right thumb and fingers, pick up a little stuffing at a time and push it into the slit. You will need from ¼ to 1 teaspoon of stuffing for each pod, depending on its size. As each pod is stuffed, set it aside on the platter.

Turn on the flame under both frying-pans and keep on medium-low heat. Divide the okra between the two frying-pans and lay them slit side up in the pans in a single layer if possible (a few overlapping won't matter). Cook for 5 minutes, shake salt (about ¼ teaspoon to each pan) over okra, add 2 table-spoons warm water to each pan, cover, lower flames to very, very low, and cook gently for 30 minutes or until the okra is tender.

To serve: Lift out gently and arrange on warm platter. Serve with Lamb *Pullao* or Rice with Peas, Pork Chops à la Jaffrey, and Potatoes with Asafetida and Cumin. It also goes very well with all Indian breads.

Whole pea pods with cumin

Serves 4

This is an unusual dish which I have eaten only in my own family. The peas are not shelled, but cooked whole, and are eaten rather like artichokes. Each pea pod is picked up by its stem, placed in the mouth between the teeth, and then pulled; you are eating not just the peas but the fleshy part of the pod as well. All that you leave is the stem and the inner tough lining of the pea pod. Needless to say, the peas that you buy must be very fresh and tender and not too long or you might just gag! The peas must also look very green and undamaged.

1½ lbs fresh peas	1 tbs lemon juice
2 tbs vegetable oil	½–1 tsp garam masala
⅛-inch lump asafetida, or	1 tsp salt
⅛ tsp ground asafetida	⅛ tsp freshly ground pepper
½ tsp whole cumin seeds	

Wash the pea pods, discarding any old ones.

Heat the oil in a wide 10–12-inch casserole-type pot over medium heat. When hot, add the asafetida and cumin seeds. In 10 or 20 seconds the cumin seeds will begin to change colour. Put in the pea pods immediately and stir for a minute. Now add the lemon juice, ½ teaspoon *garam masala*, salt, and pepper. Stir, put in 2 tablespoons of warm water, cover, turn heat to very low, and allow to cook gently for 20 to 30 minutes, until tender. Stir once or twice while cooking, but do it gently.

To serve: Lift pea pods out very carefully (some may have split, but that is quite normal). Serve in a warm dish, sprinkled with ½ teaspoon *garam masala*, if desired.

This dish may be served at a lunch, with an Indian 'tea', or as an appetizer at dinner.

Fresh peas with ginger and green coriander

Serves 4–6

Follow the recipe for Carrots and Peas with Ginger and Green Coriander on page 198. Substitute for the carrots and peas 3 pounds of fresh peas. Shell them and then proceed according to the recipe. Cook till peas are tender, about 10 minutes.

Serve with fresh *parathas*, Potatoes with Asafetida and Cumin, and *Koftas*. Instead of *parathas*, you could substitute Rice with Potatoes and Cumin Seed, *Moong Dal*, and Cucumber *Raita*.

For a Western meal, try serving it with a loin of pork or roast leg of lamb.

Sookhe aloo
('dry' potatoes)

Serves 6–8

Here is a very simple potato dish which can even be made with left-over boiled potatoes. In fact, it is best if the potatoes are boiled at least 4 hours in advance of the final cooking.

7 medium-sized potatoes, boiled in their jackets and cooled	1 tsp whole black mustard seeds
10 tbs vegetable oil	12 whole fenugreek seeds
⅛ tsp ground asafetida, or ¼-inch lump asafetida	3 whole dried hot red peppers
1 tsp whole fennel seeds	½ tsp ground turmeric
1 tsp whole cumin seeds	1½ tsp salt (or to taste)
	1 tbs lemon juice

Peel the boiled potatoes and dice them into pieces about 1 inch by ½ inch.

In a wok, *karhai*, or 10–12-inch pot, heat the oil over medium flame. When very hot, put in first the asafetida, 5 seconds later the fennel and cumin seeds, then the mustard seeds and fenugreek seeds in quick succession. As they begin to change colour and pop (about 10 seconds), add the red peppers. As soon as the red peppers swell and darken, add the diced potatoes, turmeric, and salt. Keep on medium heat and fry, turning gently so as not to break the potatoes. Fry for 15 to 20 minutes, until the potatoes are browned unevenly. Squeeze lemon juice over potatoes, and check the salt.

To serve: Lift out carefully with a slotted spoon and serve in a shallow dish. Warn guests not to bite on red peppers unless they mean to. This dish goes very well with most Indian meals. (I used to take *sookhe aloo*, *parathas*, and mango pickles to school as my lunch.) It can be taken on picnics, where it can be heated in aluminium foil and served with *parathas* or *pooris*, or it can be served with a lamb or pork roast as a 'different' kind of starch. Try it also with my marinated charcoal-grilled 'Butter-flied' Leg of Lamb.

Pyazwale sookhe aloo
('dry' potatoes with onions)

Serves 6–8

Here is another simple potato dish that can be served as a vegetable with *pooris* or as an appetizer, on top of savoury biscuits.

6 medium-sized potatoes	1 medium-sized onion,
5 tbs vegetable oil	peeled and coarsely
⅛ tsp ground asafetida, or	chopped
⅛-inch lump asafetida	½ tsp ground turmeric
½ tsp whole cumin seeds	1¼ tsp salt
2½ tsp whole black mustard	1 tsp garam masala
seeds	2 tbs lemon juice
1–3 whole dried red peppers	
(optional—1 red pepper	
will make it mildly hot;	
3 very hot)	

Boil the potatoes in their jackets. Peel them and mash them coarsely with a fork or hand masher.

Heat the oil in a 10–12-inch frying-pan over medium heat. When hot, first put in it the asafetida; after it has sizzled for a few seconds, add the cumin and mustard seeds; then in 10 seconds or so, the red pepper (or peppers). When pepper changes colour (1 to 5 seconds), put in the chopped onions and turmeric. After the onions have cooked 3 to 5 minutes and turned brown at the edges, put in the mashed potatoes, salt, *garam masala*, and lemon juice. Fry, stirring and mixing, for 5 to 7 minutes.

To serve: Place in a warmed dish and serve with *chapatis*, *pooris*, or *parathas*. This is a good dish to take on picnics, too. Serve as an appetizer on top of Melba toast or savoury biscuits. (Remove whole red peppers before placing on any kind of toast.)

Potatoes with asafetida and cumin

Serves 4–5

This was one of the most popular potato dishes in our family. It is a 'wet' dish and needs to be served in small individual bowls. It is very good—and easy to make.

4–5 medium-sized potatoes
2 tbs vegetable oil
$\frac{1}{8}$ tsp ground asafetida, or
   $\frac{1}{8}$-inch lump asafetida
$\frac{1}{2}$ tsp whole cumin seeds
1–2 dried hot red peppers
   (optional)

$\frac{1}{2}$ tsp turmeric
12 fl. oz tomato sauce
   (see page 225)
1 tsp salt

Wash, peel, and quarter potatoes. Put them in bowl with cold water to cover.

In 2–3-quart pot, heat oil over medium heat. As it heats, put potatoes in colander to drain. When the fat is hot, put in the asafetida; after it sizzles (5 seconds), add the cumin seeds; when they sizzle and change colour (5 to 10 seconds), add the red peppers, which will begin to change colour in a couple of seconds. Now put in the drained potatoes and the turmeric. Fry the potatoes for about 2 minutes, stirring them now and then.

Now put in $\frac{3}{4}$ pint water, tomato sauce, and salt. Bring to the boil. Cover and allow to simmer very gently for about $1\frac{1}{2}$ hours.

To serve: Take to the table in a deep dish. Give each person a little bowl to serve himself the potatoes as well as the sauce. These potatoes are best served with *pooris*, *chapatis*, or *parathas*, but they are also good with plain boiled rice and Lamb with Onions and Mushrooms. Left-overs can be put in the blender or mashed to make an excellent soup.

New potatoes cooked in their jackets

Serves 4–6

In India we get tiny new potatoes which are about ¾ inch in diameter. They have soft skins and are satiny inside. We cook them in many ways, one of my favourites being a dish in which they are cooked whole with fenugreek greens. Use fenugreek greens if available. If not, I have worked out a substitute dish with green coriander. Also, if you cannot find the very tiny potato I just use the regular 'new potato' and dice it.

6–8 medium-sized new potatoes (depending on size) or 1 lb tiny new potatoes
a piece of fresh ginger, about 1½ inches square, peeled and coarsely chopped
½ tsp ground turmeric
5 tbs vegetable oil
¼ tsp whole cumin seeds

½ fresh hot green chili, finely sliced (optional), or ¼ tsp cayenne pepper
2 teacups chopped fresh green coriander or fresh fenugreek greens
1¼ tsp salt
1 tsp garam masala
1 tbs ground coriander
2 tbs lemon juice

Wash the potatoes well, but do not peel. Leave whole if small. If not, quarter them lengthwise, then dice them. Set aside in a bowl of cold water.

Put the ginger in the electric blender with the turmeric and 3 tablespoons water. Blend at high speed until smooth.

Heat the oil in a 10–12-inch heavy-bottomed pot over medium heat. Add the whole cumin seeds, and after about 10 or 20 seconds, when they change colour, add the paste from the blender and cook for about 1 minute. Put in the sliced green chili if you are using it, and cook another 30 seconds.

Drain the potatoes and add them to the pot. Fry them, stirring, for about 5 minutes. Scrape the bottom of the pan as you stir. Put in the green coriander or fenugreek greens, lower heat a bit, and fry another 5 minutes, stirring gently. Add the salt, *garam masala*, coriander, lemon juice, cayenne pepper if you are using it, and 3 tablespoons warm water. Stir, scrape bottom gently, and cover. Reduce flame to very low and let the potatoes cook about 25 minutes, until done. Stir very gently every 10 minutes or so.

To serve: Lift out carefully and serve in warm shallow dish or platter. Try these potatoes with roast pork or lamb. They are very versatile in an Indian meal and can be served in an all vegetarian lunch with cabbage, Whole Pea Pods with Cumin, *Pappadum*, *Karhi*, and rice—or they can be served with almost any meat or poultry dish. They are very good with hot *chapatis* and Tomato and Onion with Lemon Juice.

Maya's potatoes

Serves 6–8

My sister-in-law makes this dish, so I've named it after her. In India, we take it with us on picnics, heat it on a portable charcoal stove, and eat it with 'stale' *pooris* and hot mango pickle.

8 medium-sized potatoes
oil for deep frying
1 onion, peeled and coarsely
    chopped
4 garlic cloves, peeled and
    coarsely chopped
6 tbs oil (or re-use 6 tbs
    strained deep-frying fat)
asafetida (optional), ⅛-inch-
    square piece or 1 large
    pinch ground
7 fenugreek seeds
½ tsp fennel seeds

¼ tsp black onion seeds
    (kalonji), if available
¼ tsp black mustard seeds
1 bay leaf
3 dried hot red peppers
    (optional, or use less)
½ tsp ground turmeric
2 medium-sized tomatoes
    (tinned or fresh), peeled
    and chopped
1 pinch sugar
1½ tsp salt

Boil potatoes, preferably 2 hours ahead, and leave to cool. Just before you begin cooking, peel the potatoes and halve them; quarter them if they are large.

Heat over medium flame 1 to 2 inches of oil in 10–12-inch frying-pan, wok, or *karhai*, and fry the potatoes in two or three batches until golden-brown on all sides. (If you prefer, you can fry the potatoes in much shallower fat. Just make sure you get them lightly browned on all sides.) Drain and set aside.

Put the chopped onion and garlic into blender with 3 tablespoons water and blend to a paste.

Heat 6 tablespoons of oil in a heavy-bottomed 10–12-inch pot. Keep heat on medium. When very hot, add asafetida, fenugreek seeds, fennel seeds, onion seeds, mustard seeds, bay leaf, and red peppers in this order and in quick succession. Fry 10 to 20 seconds, until bay leaf and peppers begin to turn dark. Add paste from blender and turmeric, and fry, stirring, for 5 minutes; then add chopped tomatoes and sugar and cook another 5 minutes. Stir in gently 1 pint water, salt, and fried potatoes, and bring to boil. Cover, lower flame, and simmer 10 minutes. Raise cover, gently lift each potato and turn it over, cover, and simmer another 10 minutes.

To serve: Place potatoes gently in a shallow serving dish. Pour the sauce over them and serve with *pooris* or *parathas*. For a simple meal try Kheema with Fried Onions, *chapatis*, and this potato dish. It would also go well with a lamb roast and Aubergine *Bharta*, or you could serve it with Prawn *Pullao* and plain yogurt.

Maya's potatoes with yogurt

Serves 6–8

This is a mild variation on the preceding recipe and is quite delicious.

5 oz plain yogurt   **½ tsp salt**

Prepare preceding recipe. While it cooks, empty yogurt into a small bowl, add ¼ pint cold water and salt, and stir to a smooth paste. Strain it and set aside. When potatoes are done, take them off heat and leave 10 minutes to cool a bit.

Five minutes before serving, pour the yogurt over the potatoes, making sure to distribute it evenly. Stir and mix it in very gently. (The potatoes tend to break a little as you do this, but don't worry!) Now heat the dish. Don't let it boil, or the yogurt will curdle. When heated through, turn flame off.

To serve: Place potatoes gently in serving bowl and pour sauce over them. Serve with *pooris* or *parathas*, a 'dry' meat like *Khare Masale Ka Gosht*, or grilled chicken pieces. You could also have it with *Pullao* and a cauliflower dish.

Potatoes in thick sauce

Serves 6

My mother's family in Delhi still lives a stone's throw from Parathe-wali-gulley, the 'gulley' or lane where *parathas* (special Indian breads) are cooked. This narrow lane is flanked on right and left by stalls which have been famous for their *parathas* for more than a century. Each *paratha* costs less than 5 pence. And with it you can have as many vegetables and pickles as you like — free! This potato recipe is one of the dishes served there.

5 medium-sized boiling
  potatoes
1 piece of fresh ginger, 2
  inches long, 1 inch thick,
  and 1 inch wide, peeled
  and coarsely chopped
1 tbs ground coriander
1 tsp ground cumin
2 medium-sized tomatoes
  (tinned or fresh), peeled
  and chopped

6 tbs vegetable oil
1 tsp whole fennel seed
10 fenugreek seeds, whole
½ tsp black onion seeds
  (kalonji), if available
½ tsp black mustard seeds
1–3 whole dried hot red
  peppers (optional)
1½ tsp salt
1½ tsp lemon juice
1 tsp garam masala

Boil the potatoes in their jackets at least 2 hours ahead. Leave to cool.

Put ginger in electric blender along with the coriander, cumin, tomatoes and 3 tablespoons warm water. Blend to a paste at high speed.

Peel the cooled potatoes. The charm of this dish is that the potatoes are not cut with a knife; they are broken by hand. Break each potato in half, then in half again, and the larger pieces once again. Each potato should be broken up into about 6 to 8 pieces, depending on its size.

Heat the oil in a 10-inch heavy-bottomed frying-pan over medium heat. When hot, add the fennel, fenugreek, onion, and mustard seeds. When the mustard seeds begin to pop (20 seconds or so), put in the red peppers. As they darken, put in the paste from the blender. Fry for about 5 minutes, stirring frequently. Now put in the pieces of potato and fry another 3 to 5 minutes, stirring constantly. Add ¾ pint hot water, salt, and lemon juice. Bring to the boil. Cover, lower flame, and allow to simmer gently for 15 to 20 minutes. The sauce should now be fairly thick.

To serve: Sprinkle with the *garam masala*, stir, and serve in a warm bowl or dish. This tastes best eaten with most Indian breads—*pooris* and *parathas* in particular—but it is also good with plain boiled rice, *Moong Dal*, and *Kheema*.

Potato patties
(aloo-ki-tikiya)

12 patties

These delicious patties are sold on street corners in India pretty much the way chestnuts are sold here. Eaten as snacks or with meals, they consist of mashed potatoes stuffed with lentils and spices.

6 medium-sized potatoes
3 tbs yellow split peas (the kind available in super-markets), soaked overnight in ½ pint cold water and ½ tsp salt
3 tsp salt

2 tbs vegetable oil plus oil for frying patties
5 fenugreek seeds
2 tbs chopped onion
3 tbs trimmed, chopped fresh green coriander
½–1 fresh hot green chili, finely sliced (optional)

Two hours before dinner, boil the potatoes in their jackets.

While potatoes are boiling, drain split peas. Then boil them in a 1–2-quart pot with 1 pint cold water and ½ teaspoon salt for 15 minutes. Remove from heat and drain in a colander or strainer, shaking it to get out as much water as you can, and invert peas in bowl. Cover the bowl.

In a frying-pan heat 2 tablespoons oil over a medium flame. When very hot, add the fenugreek seeds, and when they begin to change colour (5 to 10 seconds), put in the onions, continuing to fry about 2 minutes until the onions begin to turn brown at the edges. Add the green coriander and green chili, and stir another 2 to 3 minutes. Next, put in the drained split peas and ½ teaspoon salt. Keep stirring and cook for about 5 minutes, until all the water has evaporated and the mixture in the frying-pan seems to become one lump. Cover and set aside.

Peel and mash potatoes with a fork or hand masher. (Do not use a whipping gadget or an electric mixer. Don't add butter.)

A few lumps will remain, but don't worry—just get the potatoes as smooth as you can. Add 2 teaspoons salt and mix thoroughly.

To form patties: Divide the mashed potatoes into 12 balls. Divide the split pea mixture into 12 portions. Flatten each potato ball on the palm of your hand, put a portion of the split pea stuffing in the centre of it, and cover the stuffing with the mashed potato by bringing the outer circumference to the centre. Make a ball again. Flatten it gently to have a patty about 3 inches in diameter. Make all the patties this way, keeping them covered on a platter if you are not going to be eating soon. (You can prepare this much of the recipe from a few hours to a day ahead.)

Cooking these patties is an art in itself. In India they are cooked on a *tava*, a large, slightly curved iron plate. If you have a *tava*, it is really the ideal utensil to use. If you don't, use a heavy-bottomed frying-pan, but remember to cook only two or three patties at a time. If you crowd them it becomes difficult to lift and turn them.

Since these patties are cooked like pancakes with very little oil, use only enough to coat the bottom of your frying-pan or *tava*, and heat over medium-low flame. Put in a few potato patties and cook them slowly—about 8 to 10 minutes on each side. When one side turns a golden-red, carefully work your spatula under it without breaking the hard crust and drop it over on its unfried side. Add another teaspoon of oil, swirling it around. Fry this side for 8 to 10 minutes also, until it has formed a red-brown crust. If the patties brown too quickly, lower the heat.

Note: Since these have to be served hot, and since you may not be able to make many at a time in a frying-pan, you could use two frying-pans.

To serve: Place on a heated platter and serve hot. These patties are marvellous for snacks. They are usually served with Tomato Tamarind Chutney, or Fresh Green Chutney with Coriander Leaves and Yogurt.

Or you could serve them as part of any meal. I once cooked a rather pleasant lunch of chicken breasts grilled with just butter, salt, pepper, and lemon. I also made a simple green salad and we had these potato patties. It was wonderful!

Tomato sauce

Tomato sauce is used in some of my recipes. This is how you can make it:

Take 1 lb tin of tomatoes and pour the contents into a stainless steel pot or a pot lined with a non-metallic substance. Add ¼ teaspoon salt and ¼ teaspoon sugar. Bring to the boil. Cook on medium heat, stirring frequently and breaking up the tomatoes, until you reduce contents of pot by half. Pour these contents into an electric blender and blend until you have a smooth paste. A 1 lb tin of tomatoes should yield 8 to 10 fl. oz of sauce. The sauce can be frozen or kept covered in the refrigerator for at least a week.

Rice

Plain boiled rice
Plain baked rice
Plain basmati rice
Buttered saffron rice
Basmati rice with spices and saffron
Sweet rice
Sweet rice with carrots and raisins
Sweet rice with carrots and raisins cooked in aromatic broth
Rice with whole spices
Rice with peas
Rice with peas and whole spices
Rice with potatoes and cumin seed
Rice with cauliflower and cumin seed
Rice with spinach
Rice with spinach cooked in aromatic broth
Rice with black-eyed peas
Rice with yellow split peas
Left-over rice with mushrooms
Prawn pullao
Halibut or cod pullao
Chicken biryani
Pullao (rice with lamb)
Fried onion rings for garnishing

SEE ALSO

Roast chicken stuffed with spiced rice (page 133)
Duck—stuffed and roasted (page 138)
Baked sea bass with yellow rice (page 157)

THE statistics astonish me. They say an average Indian eats one-half to two-thirds of a pound of rice per day whereas the Englishman eats, on an average, about four pounds of rice per year! You may think that the poor Indians eat so much rice because they have nothing better to fill themselves up with. Recently, there was a great shortage of rice in an area of South India, and famine conditions were beginning to prevail. The government offered the people a flour rich with soybean and fish protein as a substitute. The people refused it. They wanted rice. They *liked* rice. The English, on the whole, have really not discovered rice. They dismiss rice as a 'starch' and as a poor relative of the more popular 'starches' — potatoes and pasta. Potatoes can be baked, fried, mashed, boiled, 'duchessed', varied ad infinitum, and there are so many different kinds of pasta ... But rice? What can you do with rice? So even when it *is* served here, more often than not it is cooked unimaginatively and amateurishly. I have seen the English eat mushy rice without any complaints. I have watched some of the better cooks using precooked and partially cooked rices in recipes. While most of the English are aware of what good roast beef should taste like, few indeed are even conscious of what good rice *is*.

Let us start at the very beginning. What kind of rice should you buy? Looking at the varieties available in the average supermarket, I can more easily tell you what not to buy. Don't buy quick-cooking or 'instant' rice. Don't buy parboiled or partially cooked rice. Neither of them really tastes like rice. Also, don't buy prepackaged mixes with herbs and spices. There is no 'mix' that you cannot manage better on your own. Once you understand and master the different methods of cooking rice, there is no limit to the number of recipes you can invent.

Buy a long-grain uncooked rice. Patna rice is good and easily available. If you are lucky enough to be near a delicatessen carrying *basmati* rice do buy it. This rice is grown in the foothills of the Himalayas. It has a narrow, long grain and a very special flavour and smell. The best *basmati* is aged before it is cooked—and it is cooked only by the rich because it is also very expensive. In the last few years, India, being short of foreign exchange, has been exporting so much of its *basmati* rice that it is often easier to buy it in London than it is in New Delhi! But keep the *basmati* for special occasions.

For most of the recipes in this book, I have used long-grain rice. If you use some other variety, you may have to experiment with the amount of water needed and the cooking time. All uncooked rices are not the same. Where I have used Indian *basmati* rice, I have indicated how it should be cooked.

Even though India consumes a lot of rice, not all Indians are rice eaters. In fact, the Indians can be divided into the rice eaters and the wheat eaters. While most of South India and Bengal are considered rice-eating areas, Delhi, Punjab, Uttar Pradesh, and Madhya Pradesh are generally conceded to be the wheat-eating areas. During times of grain rationing, each Indian has to declare himself a wheat eater *or* a rice eater and have a big 'W' or 'R' stamped on his ration card. This entitles him to get the major portion of his weekly ration in the grain of his choice.

To confuse matters further, there are those Indians, too, who eat both rice *and* wheat. Even though I come from a wheat-eating area, our family in India ate both rice and wheat bread for lunch, and wheat bread (*chapatis*) for dinner. With the rice and the *chapatis*, we ate our meat, vegetables, and lentils (*dals*). When rice and wheat breads (*chapatis*, *pooris*, *parathas*, etc.) are served at the same meal, one is usually served before the other. In our family rice was always served first, but I have eaten in homes where the *chapatis* were served first.

Most Indians eat rice with their hands. It is mixed with the lentils or meat and vegetables and eaten with the tips of the fingers. Not all the rice is mixed with the rest of the food at once. You serve yourself each dish on a separate part of your plate. The only things you may put on top of your rice are the lentils and other soup-like and semi-liquid dishes.

Rice can be cooked with almost any meat, vegetable, or fish and served as a main dish. It can be cooked with whole or powdered spices; it can be boiled, steamed, or baked; it can be cooked in water or in aromatic broths. It can be the side dish as in plain boiled rice, or it can be the main course as in *pullao* and *biryani*. It can be pounded or ground to make desserts like *kheer* and *phirni*. The visiting physician prescribes it when he leaves with the injunction, 'Give her *khitcherie* and chicken soup'. (*Khitcherie*, which means 'hodge-podge', consists, in this case, of a porridge made of rice and lentils.) The wary tourist with stomach tremors is advised, 'Eat nothing but boiled rice and yogurt for a few days!' Every festival, the rice-growing villagers get drunk on their local variety of rice wine — 'wine' being a polite word for the rotgut they generally produce.

For important occasions, rice is tinted a bright yellow with turmeric or vegetable colouring or, best of all, with saffron, which gives it not just a yellowish-orange saffron colour but a delicious fragrance as well. I'll never forget my first introduction to saffron. I was in my early teens and on my first visit to Kashmir. We were riding past a hill and valley that were completely purple from all the crocuses growing there. I remarked on their beauty to my Kashmiri companions, who in turn told me that the flowers meant something more than just beauty to them. 'This is *zaafraan*,' they said. *Zaafraan*? I thought. I wondered vaguely why, if this was the saffron flower, it was not saffron-coloured. One of the young Kashmiri boys got off his horse, plucked a flower, and brought it to me. He pulled its petals apart, showing me the stigma, which is dried and called saffron, and he told me that thousands of stigmas were needed to get a tablespoon of saffron.

Rice is not used merely for eating, though. It has its place in all the Hindu religious ceremonies; it is thrown into the fire at weddings because it is the great symbol of fertility. My family priest explained it to me this way: 'A young girl is like a rice plant. The rice is planted in one field, but it cannot bear fruit until it is transplanted into another field. So it is with the girl. She is born in her father's house, but she cannot bear children until she is transplanted into her husband's house.'

There are several methods of cooking rice so that each grain comes out firm and separate, as you will see in the recipes that follow. Rice will always stay warm, left covered, for about 20 minutes after the burner has been turned off.

Plain boiled rice

Serves 4–6

12 oz long-grain rice   **1 tbs butter**
1¼ pints water   **1 tsp salt**

Combine all the ingredients in a 2–3-quart heavy-bottomed pot with tight-fitting lid. Bring to the boil, cover, and turn flame as low as it will go. Leave for 25 to 30 minutes. Lift cover and quickly check to see if rice is cooked through. Turn off heat, and leave lid on until ready to serve.

(When cooking plain boiled rice, I always cook more than I need because there are such wonderful ways of dressing up cooked rice. I cover and refrigerate the left-overs, and cook them for breakfast, lunch, or dinner.)

Plain baked rice

Serves 6

12 oz long-grain rice   **4 tbs butter**
1 tbs salt

Preheat oven to 300°F., Mark 2.

Fill a 3-quart pot with about 5 pints of water, add the salt, and set over a high flame.

Meanwhile, wash and drain the rice in a colander.

When the water is boiling, put the rice in it. Bring to a second boil, and boil rapidly for exactly 5 minutes.

Drain the rice by pouring it through a colander.

Put the rice in an ovenproof dish. Cut the butter into 4 patties and place over the rice. Now cut a piece of aluminium foil 2 inches larger than the rim of the dish, cover the dish, and then put the lid on top of the foil. Crinkle foil around the edges to seal as thoroughly as possible. The rice has to cook in its own steam, so that steam must not be allowed to escape.

Place dish in oven for 45 to 50 minutes (check after 45 minutes to see whether rice is done).

Plain basmati rice

Serves 6

I love the taste of a plain *basmati* rice eaten with *moong dal*. When I was a child, these two items were always on our luncheon menu — but today, with most of the *basmati* supply controlled by exporters or black marketeers, even the thought seems extravagant! *Basmati* is, however, available in English delicatessens, so do buy it and cook it when you can. This method of cooking rice can also be used for any long-grain fine-quality rice.

12 oz basmati rice   **1 tbs butter**
1¼ tsp salt

Wash the rice well in cold water. Soak it in a bowl with 2 pints of water and ½ teaspoon salt for 30 minutes. Then drain.

Melt the butter in a heavy-bottomed pot over medium flame. Pour in the drained rice and stir for a minute. Add 18 fl. oz water and ¾ teaspoon salt. Bring to the boil, cover, lower heat to *very* low, and cook for 20 minutes.

Lift lid. Mix rice gently with fork. Cover again and cook another 10 minutes, or until rice is tender.

Serve with almost any dish you like. I love it with *Moong Dal, Pyazwala Khare Masale Ka Gosht*, lime wedges, and a cucumber relish of some kind.

Buttered Saffron rice

Serves 6

**2 tsp leaf saffron, loosely
  packed, roasted and
  crumbled according to
  directions on page 44**

**2 tbs warm milk
1 tbs salt
12 oz long-grain rice
4 tbs butter**

Preheat oven to 300°F., Mark 2.

Soak saffron in warm milk. (I just leave the milk to heat on top of the pilot light area of my stove. You could heat it slightly in a small pot if you like.)

Fill a 3-quart pot with about 5 pints water. Add the salt and bring to the boil.

Meanwhile, wash and drain the rice in a colander.

When the water is boiling, put the rice in it and bring to a second boil. Boil rapidly for exactly 5 minutes.

Drain the rice in a colander.

Put the rice in an ovenproof dish. Pour the saffron milk over it in streaks. Cut the butter into 4 patties and place over the rice. Now cut a piece of aluminium foil 2 inches larger than the rim of the dish. Place foil on top of the dish and put the lid on top of the foil. Crinkle foil around edges to seal.

Place dish in oven for 45 to 50 minutes, checking after 45 minutes to see if the rice is done.

To serve: The rice, when ready to serve, will have saffron-coloured streaks in it. Spoon it out onto a large warm platter and serve with any Indian meal. It goes particularly well with Lamb with Spinach, Lamb *Korma*, and Chicken with Tomato sauce and Butter. Try it also with 'Butterflied' Leg of Lamb and with Codfish Steaks in Yogurt.

Basmati rice with spices and saffron

Serves 6

Even though this recipe is for Indian *basmati* rice, any long-grain, fine-quality rice can be used instead.

1 tsp leaf saffron, loosely
   packed, roasted and
   crumbled according to
   directions on page 44
2 tbs warm milk
12 oz basmati or long-grain
   rice

1¼ tsp salt
2 tbs vegetable oil
5 cardamom pods
2 cinnamon sticks, 2½–3
   inches long

In a small container, soak saffron in warm milk.

Wash the rice well in cold water. Soak it in a bowl with 2 pints water and ½ teaspoon salt for 30 minutes, then drain.

Heat the oil over medium flame in 2–3-quart heavy-bottomed pot (with a tight-fitting lid — to be used later), put in the cardamom pods and cinnamon sticks, and stir a few times. Add the rice, frying and stirring about a minute.

Add 18 fl. oz water and ¾ teaspoon salt. Bring to the boil, cover, reduce heat to *very* low, and cook for 20 minutes.

Lift off cover. Gently but quickly mix rice with a fork, turning it around a bit. Pour the saffron milk in 2 or 3 streaks over the rice. Cover and keep cooking another 10 minutes or until rice is quite done.

To serve: Turn the rice onto a platter with a fork (this keeps the grains whole). Serve with Chicken *Moghlai* and Yogurt with Spinach.

Sweet rice

Serves 6

This is a very simple recipe for sweet rice. It goes rather well with many English dishes, like baked ham, pork chops, roast loin of pork, lamb chops, etc. It is mild flavoured and not too sweet. If you like, you could elaborate on the recipe by adding nuts and raisins.

2½ tbs vegetable oil	1 tbs ground coriander
4 whole cloves	½ tsp ground cinnamon
3–4 whole cardamom pods	¼ tsp ground nutmeg
4 black peppercorns	1¼ pints homemade beef or
1 bay leaf	lamb stock or tinned
1 medium-sized onion,	beef broth (not bouillon)
peeled and sliced into fine	½ tsp salt (more if broth is
rings	unsalted)
12 oz long-grain rice	1 tbs granulated brown sugar

Over a medium flame, heat the oil in a 2-quart heavy-bottomed pot (with a tight-fitting lid—to be used later). When very hot, add the cloves and cardamom pods, peppercorns, and bay leaf. Fry for about 5 seconds, until the spices begin to expand and change colour. Now add the onion rings and fry for about 3 to 5 minutes, until the onions turn light brown with darkish edges. Put in the rice, coriander, cinnamon, and nutmeg, and stir for 5 minutes.

Next, pour in the broth and salt, stir, cover, and turn the flame very low. Let cook about 15 minutes.

Lift the lid, put in the brown sugar, and stir quickly with a fork. Cover again and cook another 15 to 20 minutes.

To serve: Serve plain, or garnished with slivered almonds, with *Koftas*, or Lamb *Korma*, or with English dishes as suggested above.

Sweet rice with carrots and raisins

Serves 6

In this recipe carrot strips and raisins are fried in butter and then cooked with the rice. I sweeten the rice with 2 tablespoons of sugar, but you could make it sweeter if you like.

12 oz long-grain rice	½ tsp salt
½ lb (2 large) carrots	¼ tsp ground nutmeg
3 tbs butter or usli ghee	¼ tsp ground mace
(see page 42)	¼ tsp ground cinnamon
2 tbs golden raisins	¼ tsp ground cardamom
2 tbs granulated sugar	seeds (if you keep a
1¼ pints chicken broth	pepper-grinder for carda-
(homemade or tinned)	mom seeds, use that)

Wash the rice in a colander and leave to soak in 2 pints water for 30 minutes.

Cut carrots into julienne strips. I find the easiest way to do this is to cut the carrots diagonally into long, flat slices — the kind that are used in Chinese cooking. Then I cut the slices into strips, doing two or three at a time.

Melt the butter in a heavy-bottomed frying-pan over medium heat. Put in the carrot strips and the raisins, and fry, stirring, for 10 to 12 minutes, until the carrots wilt and turn brownish at the edges. Turn off flame.

Preheat oven to 300°F., Mark 3.

Put the sugar in a 2–3-quart flameproof and ovenproof dish and heat over medium flame. The sugar will melt and then begin to turn brown. As soon as it becomes a golden-brown, pour in the chicken broth, keeping face averted. Add the rice, salt, nutmeg, mace, cinnamon, and cardamom, and bring to the boil. Keep boiling gently on medium flame for 8 to 10 minutes, until the liquid is almost absorbed. Stir frequently towards the latter half of cooking time to prevent sticking. Once the liquid is almost absorbed, turn off the heat. Cover the dish with a piece of aluminium foil 2 inches wider than the rim of the dish. Place the cover on the foil, and crinkle and arrange ends of aluminium foil so that no steam can escape. If you have a very heavy and tight-fitting lid, you can do without the foil.

Place rice dish in the oven and bake for 25 to 30 minutes. Check after 25 minutes to see if rice is done. If not, leave longer.

To serve: Spoon out onto warm platter and serve with Lamb *Korma* or *Sindhi Gosht*. Any yogurt dish would go well with it.

If you are cooking a Western meal, try eating this rice with roast duck, roast turkey, roast chicken, or baked ham.

Sweet rice with carrots and raisins
cooked in aromatic broth

Serves 6

Follow preceding recipe. Instead of chicken broth, use aromatic broth or *yakhni* (see directions on page 247). This *yakhni* gives the rice the added flavours of whole cumin and whole fennel seeds. It can be made weeks in advance and stored in the freezer.

Rice with whole spices

Serves 6

Rice is cooked with whole cinnamon sticks, bay leaves, cloves, black peppers, and cardamom pods. It is a very light and fragrant dish—and easy to make.

1 medium-sized onion	2 cinnamon sticks, about
2 tbs vegetable oil	3 inches long
6 whole cloves	3 bay leaves
10 black peppercorns	12 oz long-grain rice
5 cardamom pods	1 tsp salt

Peel onion and slice into fine rounds. Halve the rounds.

Heat the oil in a 3-quart heavy-bottomed pot (with tight-fitting lid—to be used later) over medium heat, put in the onions, and fry, stirring, until they are brown and crisp (but *not* burned)—about 8 to 10 minutes. With a slotted spoon, remove the onions and leave them on a paper towel to drain.

In the same fat, fry the cloves, peppercorns, cardamom pods, cinnamon sticks, and bay leaves for 10 to 20 seconds or until spices begin to expand and change colour. Add the rice, and fry, stirring, another minute or two. Now put in $1\frac{1}{4}$ pints water and the salt. Bring to the boil, cover, and reduce heat to very low. Cook 25 to 35 minutes, until done. Halfway through the cooking, stir once gently with a fork.

To serve: Spoon out the rice onto a warm platter, breaking any lumps with the back of a slotted spoon. The whole spices serve as a garnish—just warn your family or guests not to bite into them. Sprinkle fried onions over rice.

Serve with baked fish and almost any meat or chicken dish.

Rice with peas

Serves 6

Rice can be cooked with either fresh or frozen peas. In India, of course, it is always cooked with the fresh, hard, shelled variety, but I find that frozen peas work just as well for this dish.

2 tbs vegetable oil	1 tsp salt
½ tsp whole black mustard seeds	1 teacup shelled peas, fresh or frozen
12 oz long-grain rice	
1¼ pints chicken broth (fresh or tinned)	

Over medium flame, heat the oil in a 3-quart heavy-bottomed pot (with tight-fitting lid—to be used later). When hot, add the mustard seeds and wait until they begin to darken (10 to 20 seconds). Put in the rice, and the peas if you are using fresh ones. Stir for a minute. Add broth and salt. Bring to the boil. Cover and reduce flame to very, very low. Leave to cook for 25 to 30 minutes.

If you are using frozen peas, defrost them by placing a cupful in colander and running under warm water. Leave to drain. When rice has cooked 25 minutes, lift cover off and quickly put defrosted peas on top of rice. Replace cover and cook about 5 minutes longer or until done.

To serve: Mix the rice and peas gently and serve on large platter.

This is a relatively bland dish. It goes well with Indian lentils and meats, and equally well with almost any English meat dish.

Rice with peas and whole spices

Serves 6

2½ tbs vegetable oil
5 whole cloves
5 black peppercorns
1 cinnamon stick, 2 inches
　long
4 cardamom pods
12 oz long-grain rice

1 teacup shelled peas, fresh
　or frozen
1 tbs ground coriander
1 tsp ground cumin
½ tsp ground turmeric
1 tsp salt

Heat oil in a 3-quart heavy-bottomed pot (with tight-fitting lid
—to be used later) over medium heat. Add cloves, peppercorns, cinnamon, and cardamom. Stir for about 10 to 20
seconds, until spices begin to expand and change colour. Add
the rice, peas if using fresh ones, coriander, cumin, and turmeric. Stir for 3 minutes. Add 1¼ pints water and salt, stir
again, and bring to the boil. Cover, and turn flame very low.
Cook for about 25 to 30 minutes.

If you are using frozen peas, defrost them by placing a cupful
in colander and running under warm water. Leave to drain.
When rice has cooked 25 minutes, lift cover off and quickly
put defrosted peas on top of rice. Replace cover and cook
about 5 minutes longer or until done.

To serve: Gently mix the rice and peas and serve on large
platter. Warn diners not to bite into the whole spices. This
dish tastes good with *Koftas*, or with Chicken with Sliced
Lemon and Fried Onions. Also serve yogurt, plain or with
cut-up tomatoes, salt, and pepper.

Rice with potatoes and cumin seed

Serves 6

Rice *and* potatoes? A double starch? It's not really all *that* frightening. After all, if you were going to serve yourself a spoonful of rice, you could just as easily serve yourself a spoonful of rice *and* potatoes. The starch content is about the same, whether you're eating one starch or two, and in Britain at least the combination has the virtue of novelty.

2 medium-sized or 1 large potato	½ tbs whole cumin seeds
4 tbs vegetable oil	12 oz long-grain rice
	1 tsp salt

Peel potato, dice into ¾-inch cubes.

Heat oil in a heavy-bottomed pot (with tight-fitting lid—to be used later) over medium heat. When very hot, add the cumin seeds, and after they have begun to change colour and 'pop' (about 10 to 20 seconds), put in the potatoes. Let the potatoes brown to a nice golden colour on all sides. Then add the rice and stir for about 2 minutes. Add 1¼ pints water and salt, stir, and bring to the boil. Cover, turn the flame very low, and cook for 25 to 30 minutes. See if rice is done; if not, stir and cook for another 5 minutes.

To serve: Serve with marinated pork chops—or with *Kheema* and green beans. This is a simple yet very versatile dish that could be served with plain yogurt to an invalid or with *Korma* at a banquet.

Rice with cauliflower and cumin seed

Serves 6

This dish is very much like the preceding one, only cauliflower is substituted for the potatoes.

1 small head cauliflower	2½ tbs vegetable oil
vegetable oil (enough to have about 1½ inches in cauliflower frying-pan)	½ tsp whole cumin seeds
	12 oz long-grain rice
freshly ground pepper	salt

Break cauliflower into flowerets not bigger than 1½ inches in length and 1 inch in width at the head. Wash and drain flowerets thoroughly on paper towels.

Heat enough oil in frying-pan, wok, or *karhai* to have about 1½ inches. Keep on medium flame, much as you would for potato-chips. When hot, put in the flowerets a batch at a time and deep-fry until they are light brown on all sides and almost cooked through. Leave the insides a bit crunchy. As each batch is done, drain on paper towels, put into a dish, sprinkle with a dash of salt and a crunch of the pepper-grinder, and cover.

Heat 2½ tablespoons oil in 3-quart heavy-bottomed pot over medium flame. When very hot, stir in the cumin seeds. As soon as they change colour (about 10 seconds), add the rice and stir 2 to 3 minutes. Pour in 1¼ pints water. Add 1 teaspoon salt. Stir and bring to the boil. Cover and turn heat very low. Cook about 25 minutes.

Lift cover off rice pot and quickly (also carefully) lay the flowerets on top of the rice. Cover pot again, and cook about 10 minutes, until cauliflower is heated through.

To serve: Very carefully move all the cauliflower to one side of the pot. Spoon the rice onto a large platter first, then lay the cauliflower on top of the rice.

Serve with any combination of meats, vegetables, and lentils.

This again is a very useful and versatile dish that goes well with most English roasts and chops.

Rice with spinach

Serves 6

12 oz long-grain rice	6 tbs vegetable oil
3 tsp salt	2 medium-sized onions,
1½ lbs fresh spinach or 2	peeled and finely chopped
12 oz packages chopped	1 tsp garam masala
frozen spinach	

Wash rice thoroughly in colander. Invert into large bowl, and cover with cold water and 1 teaspoon of the salt. Leave for 2 hours.

Fill a 4–5-quart pot with water. Add 1 teaspoon salt and bring to the boil.

If you are using fresh spinach, trim and wash thoroughly, making sure all the sand is out. Wilt the spinach by dropping it, a little at a time, in the boiling water. As the spinach wilts, remove it to a colander and rinse with cold water. Squeeze the moisture out by pressing between palms of hands, and put on chopping board. When all the spinach is done, chop very finely. (*Or:* following package directions, cook frozen spinach until it is just defrosted. Drain, then squeeze out moisture.)

In a 3–4-quart flameproof and ovenproof casserole, heat the oil, add the onions, and sauté on medium flame about 5 minutes. They should just turn golden. Now put in the chopped spinach and *garam masala*. Sauté for about 30 minutes. (This much can be done in advance and the dish left covered for a few hours.)

Preheat oven to 300°F., Mark 2.

Drain rice and add to spinach with 1 pint water and 1 teaspoon salt; bring to the boil. Lower heat and simmer for 15 minutes, stirring occasionally.

Cut aluminium foil to cover top of pot snugly. Cut a hole about ½ inch in diameter in the centre of the foil to let the steam escape and the rice dry out. Place foil-covered dish in the middle of the oven for 30 minutes. Check to see if rice is done. If not, leave 5 minutes longer.

To serve: The rice is now ready to serve. If dinner is delayed, turn the oven off and leave rice in it for another 10 minutes.

Even though this dish is best served straight out of the oven, you can, if necessary, cook it 3 or 4 hours earlier. When cooked, leave it out for 5 minutes with foil on. Then cover it with a tight lid, but do not refrigerate. Fifteen minutes before serving reheat it in a preheated 300°F, Mark 2 oven for 15 minutes.

To serve: Spinach rice can be served plain or garnished with Fried Onion Rings.

For an Indian meal, serve with *Koftas*, *Seekh Kababs*, Lamb *Korma*, Chicken Cutlets, or Eggs *Moghlai*. Serve a yogurt dish with it and a vegetable, cauliflower or carrots. As for an English meal, we tried it recently with liver, bacon, and grilled tomatoes, and it was wonderful. It is also good with lamb chops or a lamb or beef roast. This is an excellent dish to impress guests with because it tastes very good and looks spectacular.

Rice with spinach
cooked in aromatic broth

Serves 6

This dish is very much like the preceding recipe, Rice with Spinach, except that instead of cooking the rice in water, it is cooked in *yakhni*, a deliciously flavoured lamb or beef broth. (Another *yakhni* recipe, using pieces of lamb, is given as part of the *pullao* recipe, on page 256.)

Follow the preceding recipe, adding 2½ cups of the following flavoured beef or lamb broth instead of water:

Yakhni

1 pint tinned or homemade
  lamb or beef broth (not
  bouillon)
1 medium-sized onion,
  peeled
4 cloves garlic, peeled
7 whole cloves
4 whole cardamom pods

2 tsp whole fennel seeds
1 tsp whole cumin seeds
1 tsp whole coriander seeds
1 cinnamon stick, $2\frac{1}{2}$–3
  inches long
6 black peppercorns
1 bay leaf

Put the broth into a pot with a lid. Tie onion, garlic, cloves, cardamom, fennel, cumin, coriander, cinnamon, peppercorns, and bay leaf in cheesecloth and drop in pot. Bring to the boil. Cover, turn heat low, and allow to simmer for half an hour. Remove the cheesecloth, squeezing out most of the liquid it holds.

When using the broth, measure to make sure you have 1 pint. If a little less, add water to make 1 pint.

If broth is already salted, use only $\frac{1}{2}$ teaspoon salt when adding spinach to rice and broth.

Serve as in preceding recipe.

Rice with black-eyed peas

Serves 6

4 oz black-eyed peas (lobhia) soaked overnight in 1 pint water with ½ tsp baking soda	**7 whole cloves**
	7 black peppercorns
	12 oz long-grain rice
2 tbs vegetable oil	**1 tsp garam masala**
	1½ tsp salt

Empty black-eyed peas and liquid into a pot. Add ½ pint water and ½ teaspoon salt. Bring to the boil. Skim off all the froth. Cover and simmer gently 4 to 5 minutes. Drain and discard liquid.

In a 4-quart heavy-bottomed pot, heat oil over medium heat. When hot, add cloves and peppercorns and fry until they expand (10 to 20 seconds). Put in the rice and black-eyed peas and fry for 5 minutes. Add the *garam masala*, 1 teaspoon salt, and 1¼ pints water. Bring to the boil, cover, lower flame to very low, and leave for 30 minutes. Lift cover to see if rice is done. If not, cover and cook another 5 minutes. Turn flame off. Covered rice will stay warm 15 to 20 minutes.

To serve: Place on a warm platter, gently breaking lumps with back of large spoon. Garnish with Fried Onion Rings (see page 258) if desired, or serve plain.

For Western meals try serving this with pork or lamb roasts and chops. It is also good with roast duck. Or try it with a German or Polish sausage accompanied with grilled tomatoes and mustard or beetroot greens!

For an Indian meal, have it with Pork Chops Cooked with Whole Spices and Tamarind Juice. Serve some kind of yogurt dish with it.

Rice with yellow split peas

Serves 4

4 oz yellow split peas	½ tsp whole cumin seeds
4 tsp salt	2–4 small white boiling
6 oz long-grain rice	onions, peeled
2 tbs vegetable oil	3 tbs butter

Soak split peas in ¾ pint cold water and leave for an hour.

Preheat oven to 300°F., Mark 2.

Bring 2 pints of water and 1 teaspoon salt to the boil. When the water is boiling rapidly, drain the split peas and put them in. Boil rapidly for 6 to 7 minutes, and drain.

In a large pot bring 5 pints of water and 3 teaspoons salt to a rolling boil, put in the rice, and boil rapidly for 5 minutes. Drain.

In a 3–4-quart flameproof and ovenproof dish, heat the oil over medium heat. When hot, put in the cumin seeds and fry for 10 to 20 seconds, until they begin to change colour. Add the onions, rolling them around once, then add the drained rice and the drained split peas and fry for 2 to 3 minutes, stirring frequently.

Cut the butter into 3 patties and place on top of rice. Cut a sheet of aluminium foil 2 inches wider than the rim of the dish. Cover dish with it. Place the lid on top. Now crinkle the protruding aluminium around the edges to seal them. Place dish in oven for 45 to 60 minutes. Check after 45 minutes and leave longer only if not yet done.

To serve: Spoon out onto warm platter and serve with *Kheema* and Yogurt with Tiny Dumplings, or with any other meat and vegetable combination you like.

Left-over rice with mushrooms

Serves 4

4 tbs vegetable oil
1 medium-sized onion,
　peeled and finely chopped
6–8 medium-sized mush-
　rooms, cleaned and
　chopped (approximately
　¼-inch squares)
½–1 fresh hot green chili,
　finely sliced (optional)

1 tsp ground coriander
1 tsp ground cumin
2 teacups plain left-over
　cooked rice (with salt)
3–4 tbs tinned beef broth,
　chicken broth, or water
¼ tsp salt (more as needed)

Heat oil in 10–12-inch frying pan on medium flame. Add first the onions and mushrooms, frying and stirring continuously, then after 3 to 4 minutes the sliced green chili, after another minute the coriander and cumin, and finally the rice, breaking any lumps there may be with the back of a slotted spoon.

Cook for 5 minutes, then put in 3 tablespoons of broth or water and the salt. Stir again, cover, lower heat, and cook for 5 minutes. Lift cover, and if rice seems to be sticking at the bottom of the frying-pan, add another tablespoon of broth or water. Allow the rice to heat through, covered, for another 5 minutes or so.

To serve: If serving this with a Western meal, you could omit the coriander and green chili. The dish goes very well with ham, pork roasts, and roast beef. Try it with bacon and eggs for breakfast or brunch. It is unusual and very good. If you are cooking this as part of an Indian meal, serve it with a simple meat like *Khare Masale Ka Gosht*. You could also serve it with Sweetbreads with Green Coriander. Serve some yogurt dish as well.

Prawn pullao

Serves 6

This pullao can be cooked with prawns or with any firm-fleshed fish like cod or halibut (see following recipe).

¾ lb fresh prawns	1 tbs lemon juice
3 tbs finely chopped fresh green coriander	½–1 fresh hot green chili, finely sliced (optional)
1 tsp ground turmeric	4 tbs vegetable oil
1 tsp garam masala	1 medium-sized onion
1½ tsp salt	12 oz long-grain rice

Peel and devein prawns (see page 147).

In a teacup, mix 1 tablespoon warm water, the chopped green coriander, turmeric, *garam masala*, ½ teaspoon salt, the lemon juice, and green chili.

Heat 2 tablespoons of oil in a 10-inch frying-pan over medium-low heat. Pour in the contents of the cup and fry, stirring, for 2 to 3 minutes. Add the prawns, and on a medium flame fry them with the spices for about 4 minutes.

With a slotted spoon, remove the prawns to a covered dish, leaving the sauce behind. Pour 9 fl. oz warm water into the frying-pan and scrape up all the spices stuck to the bottom and sides, turning up the heat if necessary.

Peel the onion, cut into fine rounds and cut rounds in half.

In a heavy-bottomed 3–4-quart pot, heat remaining 2 tablespoons oil over medium heat. Put in the sliced onions, and fry them 3 to 4 minutes until the edges begin to turn brown. Now add the rice, ¾ pint water, 1 teaspoon salt, and the liquid from the frying-pan. Stir and bring to the boil, then cover and reduce heat to very low. Cook for 25 minutes.

Lift the cover off the saucepan and add the prawns. Mix quickly with a fork and cover again. Cook another 5 minutes.

To serve: Serve with Cabbage with Onions and any yogurt side dish — Yogurt with Roasted Aubergine would be especially good.

Halibut or cod pullao

Serves 6

Follow the preceding recipe, only substitute halibut or cod for the prawns. Buy ¾ lb cod or halibut steaks or fillets. Make sure they are at least ½ to ¾ inch thick. Cut the steaks or fillets into strips, each at least 1½ to 2 inches long and about 1 inch wide.

To serve: Lift rice and fish gently out of pan and place on warm platter. You could serve it with *Moong Dal*, yogurt, and Chicken with Tomato Sauce and Butter.

Chicken biryani

Serves 6–8

Biryani is perhaps one of our most elaborate rice dishes. Of Moghul origin, it is cooked with lamb or chicken, streaked with saffron, and garnished with raisins and nuts. The chicken is first marinated for at least 2 hours in a delicious paste of ginger, garlic, onions, yogurt, lemon juice, and spices. It is then cooked briefly. Partially cooked rice is placed over it, and the chicken and rice are allowed to steam for about an hour.

6 medium-sized onions
4 cloves garlic, peeled and coarsely chopped
a piece of fresh ginger, about 2 inches long and 1 inch wide, peeled and coarsely chopped
10 whole cloves
20 whole black peppercorns
seeds from 8 whole cardamom pods

¼ tsp ground mace
4½ tsp salt
3 tbs lemon juice
10 oz plain yogurt
8 tbs vegetable oil
2 bay leaves
4 large black cardamoms, if available
2 lbs chicken legs and breasts
¼ tsp ground cinnamon
1 tsp ground coriander

2 tsp leaf saffron, loosely packed, roasted and crumbled according to directions on page 44

1 tsp ground cumin
1 tsp whole poppy seeds
2 tbs milk
12 oz long-grain rice

Garnishes (optional)

2 tbs golden raisins, fried
2 tbs blanched almonds

2 hard-boiled eggs, sliced or quartered lengthwise

First you have to make the marinade for the chicken.

Peel and coarsely chop 3 of the onions.

Place chopped onion, garlic, and ginger in an electric blender, along with the cloves, peppercorns, the seeds only from the 8 cardamoms, cinnamon, coriander, cumin, poppy seeds, mace, 1½ teaspoons salt, and the lemon juice. Blend all of these at high speed until you have a smooth paste. Place this paste in a large bowl. Add the yogurt and mix well.

Now peel the 3 remaining onions. Slice them into very fine rings, and halve all the rings.

In a 10-inch heavy-bottomed frying-pan, heat the oil over medium flame. When hot, add the bay leaves and 4 black cardamoms. Fry for about 10 to 15 seconds. Now put in the onions and fry them, stirring, for about 10 minutes or until they get brown and crisp (but *not* burned). Remove them carefully with a slotted spoon, squeezing out as much of the oil as possible. Reserve all the onion-flavoured oil, the black cardamoms, and the bay leaves. You will need them later. Mix in two-thirds of the fried onions with the marinade paste. Place the rest on a paper towel to drain. Set aside for garnishing.

Remove skin from the chicken legs and breasts. Cut the legs into two pieces each (drumstick and thigh), and quarter all the breasts. Pierce the chicken pieces with a fork and place in the bowl with the marinade paste. Mix well. Cover the bowl and refrigerate for at least 2 hours. Turn occasionally.

After 2 hours (or more), remove the bowl from the refrigerator and place all its contents in a 3–4-quart heavy-bottomed pot. Bring slowly to the boil, cover, lower heat, and simmer for 15 minutes. Remove only the chicken pieces, place them in a 5-quart casserole dish, and cover. Set aside. On a medium flame, boil down the marinade paste, stirring, until you have about 9 to 10 tablespoons left. Spoon the paste over the chicken. Cover again.

Preheat oven to 300°F., Mark 2.

Soak the saffron in 2 tablespoons hot (not boiling) milk.

Bring about 5 pints of water with 3 teaspoons of salt to the boil in a 3-quart pot, then add the rice. After it has come to the boil again, cook 5 minutes, timing very carefully (the rice must not cook through). Drain the rice in a colander, then place it on top of the chicken in the casserole. Pour the saffron milk over the rice, streaking it with orange lines. Spoon out the onion-flavoured oil from the pan, reserving a level tablespoon to fry the raisins if you like. Sprinkle the oil, cardamom, and bay leaves over the rice. Cover the casserole dish with aluminium foil, cut 2 inches wider than the rim of the dish. Now put the lid on and use the protruding foil edges to seal the dish as best you can by crinkling it and pushing it against the sides. Bake 1 hour.

Garnishes: There are several garnishes that can be used for *biryani*; you can use them all, or only what you like, but the fried onions are a must. If you wish to use raisins, you can fry them in a tablespoon of the onion-flavoured oil just after you have fried the onions.

To serve: As you lift the cover off your casserole dish, you will see beautiful saffron streaks on the white rice. Spoon the rice and chicken out onto a large platter. Sprinkle fried onions and other garnishes of your choice over, and serve hot. With *biryani*, serve *Koftas* and some yogurt dish—Yogurt with Tiny Dumplings, or Yogurt with Potatoes. If you wish to serve a vegetable, Cauliflower with Ginger and Green Coriander would be very good.

Biryani is quite definitely not an everyday dish. It is served at weddings and important dinners. Try serving it at a late supper party. It was, and is, a dish worthy of a king.

Pullao
(rice with lamb)

Serves 6

In my father's household, Sunday lunches were always rather special, as this was the only lunch we all ate together. Our family was divided into two camps: there was the group headed by my father that liked *pullao* for Sunday lunch, and there was the second group (to which I belonged), headed rather timidly by my mother, which preferred *karhi* and plain boiled rice. My mother, being very diplomatic, alternated these dishes. But also, being as awed by my father as the rest of us, she alternated the dishes in my father's favour, so we ended up by eating more *pullao* than *karhi*. And if I complained and said, 'But it was our turn to have *karhi* this Sunday,' my mother would say, 'Oh, dear, I completely forgot. You can have it next week!' 'Hmmm,' I would think, 'cheated again!' But, strange as it may seem, as I have grown older, I have begun to love *pullao*. I don't know why. The pleasures of one's palate do change—or perhaps it's the memory of my father, sitting at the head of the table, the *pullao* in front of him, surveying his wife and six children and feeling good and at peace.

Here is my mother's recipe for *pullao*, a dish of rice and meat cooked in flavoured broth. In India, the meat that is traditionally used for the dish is goat ribs, cut up in pieces about 1½ to 2 inches in length. The meat is a little fatty, more bone and less meat. Rib meat in Britain tends to be very fatty. So I would suggest you use one of two kinds of meat: if you like meat pieces with bone, ask the butcher to chop up 2½ lbs of shoulder or neck of lamb into 1½-inch cubes. If you are trying this recipe for the first time and don't want to be bothered with bones, get 1½ lbs of meat off a leg of lamb and ask the butcher to cut it into 1-inch cubes. (I usually buy a whole leg of lamb and get some cut off into chops and some boned and cut into cubes. You can freeze what you don't need.) I find that the

English prefer the boned, cubed meat. However, remember that traditionally *pullao* uses meat with bone and that *some* day, if not *today*, you should try making it that way.

1½ pints tinned or homemade lamb or beef broth (not bouillon)

1½ lbs of meat from leg of lamb cut into 1-inch cubes, or 2½ lbs of meat and bone from neck and shoulder of lamb, cut into 1½-inch cubes

2 medium-sized onions, peeled

4 cloves garlic, peeled

a piece of fresh ginger, about 1-inch cube, peeled

20 black peppercorns

6 large black cardamom pods (if available), or 14 small or greenish-yellow pods

2 tsp whole cumin seeds

1 cinnamon stick, 2½–3 inches long

2 tsp whole coriander seeds

2 tsp whole fennel seeds

4 bay leaves

2 tsp salt

5 tbs vegetable oil

12 oz long-grain rice

To make the *yakhni*, or flavoured broth: In a 3-quart pot, put the broth and the pieces of lamb. Tie up in a piece of cheese-cloth 1 peeled onion, the garlic cloves, the piece of ginger, the peppercorns, 4 of the black cardamoms or 10 of the small cardamom pods, 1 teaspoon cumin seeds, the cinnamon stick, the coriander seeds, fennel seeds, and bay leaves. Drop the cheesecloth into the pot with the broth. Add 1 teaspoon salt. Bring to the boil. Skim off the surface scum. Cover, reduce heat to low, and allow to simmer slowly for 35 minutes.

While the broth is simmering, cut the other peeled onion in half lengthwise. Now slice it finely into half-circles.

In a 10-inch frying-pan heat the oil over a medium flame. Add the onion slices and fry until they are a crisp dark brown (about 10 minutes). Don't burn them—adjust flame if necessary. Remove with a slotted spoon, draining the fat back into the frying-pan. Spread onions on paper towels and set aside for later use. Turn flame under frying-pan off, leaving its residue of fat.

When the broth is made, fish out the cheesecloth, squeeze it slightly so as not to lose any flavours, and discard. Strain the broth and set aside. Reserve the meat in the strainer.

Heat the onion frying-pan again over a medium-high flame. When hot, add remaining 1 teaspoon whole cumin seeds and either 2 large black cardamom pods or 4 small green ones. Fry for about 20 seconds or until the spices begin to expand and change colour. Now add the drained meat and fry for 3 to 5 minutes or until the meat is lightly browned on all sides.

In a 6-quart pot put 6 oz of the uncooked rice, half the meat, then the second 6 oz of rice, and the rest of the meat. Measure the flavoured broth; pour 28 fl. oz of it over the rice. If you have less (you shouldn't), add a little water. Put in 1 teaspoon salt and bring to the boil. Cover, turn flame very, very low, and leave for 20 minutes. Lift cover and stir gently with a fork; cover again and cook another 20 minutes until rice is done. (If upper layer is still uncooked, stir gently with a fork, cover again, and cook 10 minutes longer.) Turn heat off and leave covered on stove until ready to serve.

To serve: Arrange the *pullao* on a large platter. Crumble the browned onions and sprinkle all over rice. Serve with plain yogurt or Yogurt with Potatoes. Also serve a vegetable— perhaps a cauliflower dish—and a salad (tomato, onion, and cucumber salad).

Remember that this rice dish will stay hot for 20 to 25 minutes after it is cooked if you leave it covered on the stove. Also, after the rice is cooked, it is best to give the steam 5 to 10 minutes to settle before you serve.

Fried onion rings for garnishing

vegetable oil, enough to have   **1 medium-sized onion**
at least 1 inch in pan

Heat oil in small frying-pan over medium heat. Peel onion and slice very finely. Wipe onion rings with paper towels and drop into heated fat. As they fry, separate rings with slotted spoon. Fry until rich brown (they should be a rich dark brown without being burned!). Remove with slotted spoon and drain on paper towel. (This can be done ahead of time and the garnish left uncovered in a saucer.) Arrange onion rings over rice or meats.

Dals

Lentils
Black-eyed peas (lobhia)
Chana masaledar
Chickpeas with garlic and ginger
Moong dal
Kala chana aur aloo (black chickpeas with potatoes)
Masoor or arhar dal with vegetables
Cold chana dal with potatoes
Hot chana dal with potatoes
Chana dal cooked with lamb
Karhi
Tomato karhi
Whole unhulled urad and rajma dal
Baris (or vadees) with aubergine and potatoes

SEE ALSO

Dal soup (page 55)

als—lentils or pulses—are varieties of dried beans and peas. In some form or other they are eaten daily in almost every Indian home, frequently providing the poor with their only source of protein. While people in England and America speak of making their living as earning their 'bread and butter', Indians who earn a bare wage complain that they make just enough for their '*dal roti*' (*roti* is bread).

Both the rice eaters and the wheat eaters of India consume *dal* with equal enthusiasm. Each state, however, cooks its *dals* in a completely different way. Punjab excels in whole, unhulled *dals*—whole *urad* and *rajma* cooked slowly in the clay oven (*tandoor*), as well as in *chana bhatura*, a spicy dish of chickpeas eaten with puffy deep-fried bread. The fussy Delhi-*wallahs* like the hulled and split *moong dal*, delicately spiced with cumin and sprinkled with lime juice and browned onions. In Bombay, a hot, sweet and sour *toovar dal* is made by the addition of tamarind paste and jaggery (a dry, lump variety of molasses) to the cooked *dal*. In Madras, the scorchingly spicy *dal* often contains vegetables—aubergines, okra, or tomatoes.

In America and England, where a very thin watery *dal* is often served in Indian and Pakistani restaurants, people have come to the conclusion that *dal* is a soup. Well, it isn't; one of North India's favourite expressions, 'Dey dal may pani' (put water in the *dal*), refers to foods that are diluted in order to stretch them out among more people, a practice which is, naturally, deplored. A well-cooked *dal* is generally quite thick. It is hard to describe the exact consistency: it is thinner than porridge, but not quite as thin as pea soup. Having made that generalization, let me add that in some *dal* recipes the grains stay dry and almost whole, while in others, particularly some cooked in southern India, the *dal* is indeed quite soupy.

Dal is always eaten with rice or Indian breads. It can be poured over rice, especially when it is thin, or placed beside the rice, or half can be poured over the rice and the rest beside it on the plate. This way it can be eaten with the rice or with other vegetables. It leaves more options open, and is the way I prefer to do it. *Dals* can also be served in *katoris* (see page 47), which can be placed on the plates. This is the best method if you are serving *dal* with breads (see pages 307–18).

What gives *dal* dishes their final flavour or pep is the *tarka*, or *baghar* or *chhownk*. This does to the *dal* what a *rouille* does to a fish soup in the south of France. It makes it come alive! You can 'give a *tarka*' of whole mustard seeds or cumin seeds or fenugreek seeds, or of asafetida *and* cumin seeds, or of browned onions and ginger, and so on. Basically what happens is that oil or shortening (in India it is *ghee* — see page 42) is heated in a small pot or frying-pan. Whole spices are added, and the *ghee* and spices are then poured over the cooked *dal*.

Here is a list of the commonly used *dals*; you should learn to recognize them by their shape and colour.

MOONG DAL   Hulled and split: small, yellow, rectangular grains; unhulled and whole: small, green, cylindrical grain, called mung beans in health food stores.

URAD DAL   Hulled and split: small, off-white rectangular grains; unhulled and whole: small, black, cylindrical grain.

CHANA DAL   Hulled and split: round, yellow grain, larger than *moong dal*. This *dal* is of the chickpea family.

ARHAR OR TOOVAR DAL   Hulled and split: round, dull yellow grain, slightly larger than *chana dal* and often with irregular edges.

RAJMA   Whole and unhulled: red kidney bean, which comes in a medium and small size.

MASOOR DAL   Hulled and split: very tiny, round, shiny salmon-coloured grains that turn yellow when cooked.

KALA CHANA   Whole and unhulled: small black chickpeas.

CHHOLA OR KABLI CHANA   Whole: chickpeas or garbanzos.

LOBHIA   Whole: black-eyed peas.

In this chapter, I have also included recipes for the *dals* available in your supermarket (lentils, black-eyed peas, chickpeas) and for dishes made with ground chickpea flour (*Karhi*, page 276) and ground *urad dal* (*Baris*, page 281).

WASHING AND CLEANING DALS: All *dals*, with the exception of those packaged especially for supermarkets, are usually very dirty. First, they have to be *picked* clean. Dishonest wholesalers and retailers have long made it a thriving practice to add tiny stones, often the same colour as the *dal*, to boost the weight. Also, occasionally, you will find a few discoloured or deformed grains that need to be removed, or there may be stalks, twigs, and what-have-you's lurking around. The best way to remove this is to put the amount of *dal* you wish to cook at one end of a large platter. Now slide 10 or 15 grains at a time to the other end of the same platter, spotting and removing all unwanted objects as you do so. Keep your hawk's eyes open because there is nothing worse than crunching a stone as you eat your dinner! Next, the *dal* must be washed several times in cold water to remove any dust that may be clinging to the grains. After draining it is ready to be cooked.

Lentils

Serves 6–8

This is a recipe for the dry lentils as bought in an English supermarket.

1 lb lentils	1½ tsp salt
1 cinnamon stick, 2–3 inches long	⅛ tsp freshly ground black pepper
1 bay leaf	¼–½ tsp cayenne pepper (optional)
5 cloves garlic, peeled	
2 slices fresh, peeled ginger, ⅛ inch thick, and about 1 inch in diameter	3 tbs vegetable oil or usli ghee (see page 42)
1 tsp ground turmeric	a pinch ground asafetida or tiny lump asafetida
¾ lemon	½ tsp whole cumin seeds

Wash the lentils. Drain.

In a 3-quart heavy-bottomed pot, combine the lentils, 2½ pints water, cinnamon stick, bay leaf, garlic cloves, ginger slices, and turmeric. Bring to the boil. Cover, lower heat, and simmer gently until tender, about 30 to 45 minutes.

Slice lemon into 5 or 6 rounds. Remove seeds. Lift cover of pot and put in the lemon slices, salt, black pepper, and cayenne. Stir, cover and simmer another 5 minutes.

Just before serving, heat the vegetable oil in a 4–6-inch frying-pan over medium-high heat. When very hot, put in the asafetida and the cumin seeds. As soon as the asafetida begins to sizzle and expand, and the cumin seeds darken, pour the contents of frying-pan over the lentils and stir.

To serve: Serve the lentils with rice or any of the breads. A meat, chicken, or fish dish and a vegetable would complete the meal.

Black-eyed peas
(lobhia)

Serves 6

8 oz black-eyed peas soaked
    overnight in 2 pints water
    with $\frac{1}{4}$ tsp baking soda
2 tsp salt
3 tbs vegetable oil
a generous pinch ground
    asafetida or tiny lump
    asafetida
$\frac{1}{2}$ tsp whole cumin seeds
$1\frac{1}{2}$ medium-sized onions,
    peeled and chopped

$\frac{1}{4}$ tsp ground turmeric
1 tsp ground coriander
1 tsp ground cumin
1 teacup tomato sauce (see
    page 225)
$\frac{1}{4}$–$\frac{1}{2}$ tsp cayenne pepper
    (optional)
3 tbs tamarind paste (see
    page 44) or 2 tbs lemon
    juice

Empty black-eyed peas and liquid into a pot. Add $\frac{3}{4}$ pint water and 1 teaspoon salt. Bring to the boil. Skim off all the froth. Cover and simmer gently 4 to 5 minutes. Drain and discard the liquid.

In another 3-quart, heavy-bottomed pot, heat the oil over a medium-high flame. When hot, put in the asafetida and the cumin seeds. As soon as the asafetida expands and sizzles and the cumin seeds darken (this will take a few seconds), put in the chopped onions. Fry onions, stirring, for 7 or 8 minutes, or until they are lightly browned. Add the turmeric, coriander, and cumin, and cook, stirring, 1 minute. Put in the tomato sauce, lower heat, and simmer 5 minutes, stirring now and then.

Add the black-eyed peas, $\frac{1}{4}$ pint water, the rest of the salt (1–$1\frac{1}{2}$ teaspoons), the cayenne, and the tamarind paste. Bring to the boil. Cover, lower heat, and simmer gently for 25 to 35 minutes. Lift off cover, and if there is any extra sauce, turn up heat and boil it down, stirring. All the sauce must adhere to the peas.

To serve: This versatile dish can be served with pork or lamb roasts as well as with almost any Indian meal.

Chana masaledar

Serves 6

Chickpeas (large *chanas*) are cooked with onion, garlic, ginger, and the *garam* (hot) spices. This is a traditional 'snack' dish from the state of Punjab.

6 oz chickpeas (large chanas) soaked overnight in 1½ pints water with ¼ tsp baking soda

4–5 tbs vegetable oil

¼ tsp whole cumin seeds

1 medium-sized onion, peeled and chopped

1–1½ tsp garam masala

1 tsp ground coriander

2 cloves garlic, peeled and minced

a piece of fresh ginger, about ½ inch square, peeled and grated

1 tbs tomato purée

1½–2 tsp salt

⅛–¼ tsp cayenne pepper

1 tsp ground amchoor or 1 tbs lemon juice

Garnish

1 firm tomato, washed and quartered

1 medium-sized onion, peeled, halved and cut into coarse slivers

4 fresh hot green chilies (only if someone is going to eat them; otherwise use 4 long slices of a green pepper)

Empty chickpeas and liquid into a large pot. Add 1 pint water, 1 teaspoon salt and bring to the boil. Remove froth. Cover, lower heat and simmer gently for about 1 hour or until chickpeas are tender. Turn off heat, remove cover and leave chickpeas in liquid.

Heat the oil in a heavy-bottomed 10-inch frying-pan over a medium-high flame. When hot, put in the whole cumin seeds. As soon as they begin to darken, after a few seconds, add the chopped onion. Stir and fry 7 to 8 minutes or until onion begins to turn a golden brown.

Turn heat to low and add the *garam masala* and coriander.

Mix, add the garlic and ginger, and fry, stirring for 2–3 minutes. Add the tomato purée and stir again.

Drain the chickpeas, reserving about ¼ pint of the liquid. Pour this into the frying-pan. Add the chickpeas, ½ teaspoon salt, cayenne and *amchoor* or lemon juice. Mix well, cover, and let the chickpeas cook with the spices for about 30 minutes. Check the salt, adding more if necessary. Stir gently every now and then, taking care not to break the chickpeas.

To serve: Traditionally, the *chanas* (chickpeas) are placed in a bowl lined around the edge with quartered tomatoes, raw onion slivers, and green chilies, and then eaten with *bhaturas*. I have served them with *pooris* as well as with rice. A meal with Chicken Moghlai, Prawn Kerala Style, and these chickpeas as well as Cucumber *Raita* served with plain rice is very nice. This dish can be prepared a day in advance, covered, and refrigerated. Reheat gently over a low flame.

Chickpeas with garlic and ginger

Serves 6

6 oz chickpeas (large chanas) soaked overnight in 1½ pints water with ¼ tsp baking soda

10 cloves garlic, peeled and chopped

a piece of fresh ginger, 2 inches long and 1 inch wide, peeled and chopped

5 tbs vegetable oil

a pinch of ground asafetida or a tiny lump asafetida

½ tsp ground turmeric

3 medium-sized tomatoes (tinned or fresh), peeled and finely chopped

4 medium-sized potatoes, freshly boiled and peeled

2 tsp salt

⅛ tsp freshly ground black pepper

½ tsp cayenne pepper (less if desired)

2 tbs lemon juice

Empty chickpeas and liquid into a large pot. Add 1 pint water, 1 teaspoon salt and bring to the boil. Remove froth. Cover, lower heat and simmer gently for 1 hour or until chickpeas are tender. Turn off heat. Drain the chickpeas, reserving ½ pint of the liquid.

Put the garlic, ginger and tomatoes into the container of an electric blender. Add 2 tablespoons water and blend until you have a smooth paste.

Heat oil in a large frying-pan or a 10-inch heavy-bottomed pot over a medium flame. When hot, put in the asafetida. After a few seconds, as soon as it sizzles and expands, pour in the paste from the blender, keeping face averted, and add the turmeric. Stir and fry this for 1 to 2 minutes. Now pour in the ½ pint liquid and add the chickpeas. Quarter the potatoes and add them as well. Put in 1 teaspoon salt, black pepper, cayenne, and lemon juice. Bring to the boil, cover, lower heat and simmer gently for 30 minutes.

These chickpeas taste best with some kind of Indian bread — *pooris*, *parathas*, or *bhaturas*. Serve yogurt or cucumber relishes as an accompaniment. Any meat or chicken dish would go with this too.

Moong dal

Serves 6

This is North India's most popular *dal*, and it is eaten with equal relish by toothless toddlers, husky farmers, and effete urban snobs. The simple recipe given below can be used for the white *urad dal*, the salmon-coloured *masoor dal*, and the large *arhar* or *toovar dal* as well.

10 oz moong dal (hulled and split)

2 cloves garlic, peeled

2 slices peeled fresh ginger, 1 inch square and $\frac{1}{8}$ inch thick

1 tsp chopped fresh green coriander

1 tbs ground turmeric

$\frac{1}{4}$–$\frac{1}{2}$ tsp cayenne pepper (optional)

$1\frac{1}{2}$ tsp salt

$1\frac{1}{2}$ tbs lemon juice

3 tbs vegetable oil or usli ghee (see page 42)

a pinch ground asafetida or tiny lump asafetida

1 tsp whole cumin seeds

lemon or lime wedges

Clean and wash *dal* thoroughly (see page 263.) Put *dal* in heavy-bottomed 3-quart pot, add 2 pints water, and bring to the boil. Remove the froth and scum that collects at the top. Now add the garlic, ginger, parsley, turmeric, and cayenne pepper. Cover, leaving the lid very slightly ajar, lower heat, and simmer gently for about $1\frac{1}{2}$ hours. Stir occasionally. When *dal* is cooked, add the salt and lemon juice (it should be thicker than pea soup, but thinner than porridge).

In a 4–6-inch frying-pan or small pot, heat the vegetable oil or *ghee* over a medium-high flame. When hot, add the asafetida and cumin seeds. As soon as the asafetida sizzles and expands and the cumin seeds turn dark (this will take only a few seconds), pour the oil and spices over the *dal* and serve. (Some people put the *dal* in a serving dish and then pour the oil and spices over it.)

To serve: Serve with plain rice, *Kheema*, and a vegetable for a simple meal. Most meat and chicken dishes go well with this *dal*. Since some people like to squeeze extra lemon or lime juice on their *dal*, serve some wedges separately. Note: Finely sliced onion rings, fried until brown and crisp (see page 258), are often spread over the *dal* as a garnish before it is served.

Kala chana aur aloo
(black chickpeas with potatoes)

Serves 4

This is one of my favourite lunch dishes. India produces several varieties of chickpeas. *Kala chana* are small and black. They need to be cleaned and soaked in water for 24 hours before cooking. I use tamarind paste to give this dish a tart taste, but you could use lemon juice instead.

6 oz black chickpeas (kala chana)

1½ tsp salt

½ tsp baking soda

1 medium-sized onion, peeled and chopped

3 cloves garlic, peeled and chopped

a piece of fresh ginger about 1 inch square, peeled and chopped

3 tbs vegetable oil

a generous pinch ground asafetida or tiny lump asafetida

¼ tsp whole cumin seeds

4 medium-sized potatoes, peeled and quartered

1 tsp ground coriander

¼ tsp ground turmeric

1 tsp garam masala

¼–½ tsp cayenne pepper

3–4 tbs tamarind paste (see page 44), or 2 tbs lemon juice

Sort and clean the chickpeas and wash them under cold water. Drain. Soak for 24 hours in a bowl containing ½ teaspoon of the salt, the baking soda, and 1¾ pints of water.

Place chopped onion, garlic, and ginger in the container of an electric blender with 3 tablespoons of water. Blend at high speed until you have a smooth paste.

In a 3-quart heavy-bottomed pot, heat the oil over a medium-high flame. When very hot, put in the asafetida and the cumin seeds. After a few seconds, when the asafetida expands and the cumin darkens, put in the paste from the blender, keeping face averted. Fry, stirring, for about 5 minutes.

Now drain the chickpeas and add them to the pot. Also put in the potatoes, coriander, turmeric, *garam masala*, 1 teaspoon salt, the cayenne pepper, and ¾ pint of water. Bring to the boil. Cover, and allow to simmer gently for 1 hour.

Add 3 to 4 tablespoons of tamarind paste or lemon juice (you could use more or less) to chickpeas according to tartness desired. Stir. Check salt. Cook for another 10 minutes, stirring occasionally.

To serve: This dish tastes very good with hot *pooris* or *parathas*. Some kind of relish—perhaps Cucumber and Tomato with Lemon Juice—should be served with it. For a more complete meal add meat and a green vegetable dish.

Masoor or arhar dal
with vegetables

Serves 6–8

12 oz masoor or arhar (toovar) dal (hulled and split)

½ tsp ground turmeric powder

3 tbs chopped fresh green coriander

2 tsp salt

any one of the following vegetables: 2 medium-sized yellow marrows, washed and sliced in rounds or ½ lb mushrooms, cleaned and sliced or 1 medium-sized aubergine, washed and cut in ¾-inch cubes or 1 medium-sized onion, cut in half, sliced and sautéed for 5 minutes in 3 tbs vegetable oil

4 tbs tamarind paste (see page 44)

½ tsp sugar

3 tbs vegetable oil or usli ghee (see page 42)

10 whole black peppercorns

½ tsp whole cumin seeds

½ teaspoon whole black mustard seeds

10 whole fenugreek seeds

10 white urad dal grains (optional)

1–3 whole dried hot red peppers

Clean and wash *dal* (see page 263).

Put *dal* in 3-quart heavy-bottomed pot with 2½ pints water and bring to boil. If there is any scum, remove it with a spoon. Add the turmeric and green coriander and cover. Lower heat and simmer gently until tender, about 1½ hours, stirring every 15 minutes or so. Add the salt, the vegetables you are using, tamarind paste, and sugar. Cook another 15 minutes or until vegetable is tender.

In a 4–6-inch frying-pan, heat the 3 tablespoons of oil or *ghee* over medium-high heat. When hot, put in the peppercorns, cumin seeds, mustard seeds, fenugreek seeds, *urad dal*, and lastly the red peppers. When the mustard seeds begin to pop and the fenugreek and red pepper darken (this should take just a few seconds), pour the contents of frying-pan into the pot containing *dal* and vegetables. Stir, cover again and turn off heat.

To serve: Serve with plain rice and any meat, chicken, or fish dish of your choice.

Cold chana dal
with potatoes

Serves 4

In this dish the *chana dal* is first boiled and then mixed with diced boiled potatoes, salt, pepper, cayenne pepper, roasted cumin, and lemon juice. If you like, you can slice spring onions and add them as well. It is served at room temperature or, if you wish, just very slightly chilled.

3 oz chana dal, cleaned and
  washed (see page 263)
1 tsp salt
3 peeled slices fresh ginger,
  about 1 inch in diameter
  and $\frac{1}{8}$ inch thick
4 new potatoes, boiled and
  diced into $\frac{1}{2}$-inch cubes

$\frac{1}{8}$ tsp freshly ground pepper
1 tsp roasted, ground cumin
  seeds (see page 41)
2 tbs lemon juice, or 3
  tbs tamarind paste (see
  page 44)
$\frac{1}{8}$–$\frac{1}{4}$ tsp cayenne pepper
  (optional)

Put the *dal* to boil with $1\frac{1}{4}$ pints of water, $\frac{1}{2}$ teaspoon salt, and
the ginger slices. Cover, simmer gently for 1 hour. Drain.
Discard ginger slices.

In a serving bowl, combine the *dal*, $\frac{1}{2}$ teaspoon salt, and the
remaining ingredients. Mix well.

To serve: Serve with lamb roast or pork chops. Indians often
eat this as a snack, at tea-time.

Hot chana dal
with potatoes

Serves 4

This is a hot (i.e., not cold) version of the preceding recipe.

3 oz chana dal, cleaned and
  washed (see page 263)
1 tsp salt
4 tbs vegetable oil
$\frac{1}{4}$ tsp black mustard seeds
$\frac{1}{4}$ tsp whole cumin seeds
10 fenugreek seeds
2 fresh green chilies (as an
  alternative, use $\frac{1}{8}$–$\frac{1}{4}$ tsp
  cayenne pepper)

1 medium-sized onion,
  peeled and chopped
a piece of fresh ginger, about
  $\frac{3}{4}$ inch square, peeled and
  grated
4 new potatoes, boiled and
  diced into $\frac{1}{2}$-inch cubes
$\frac{1}{8}$ tsp freshly ground pepper
2 tbs lemon juice, or 3 tbs
  tamarind paste (see page
  44)

Put the *dal* to boil with 1¼ pints of water and ½ teaspoon of the salt. Cover, lower heat, and simmer gently for 1 hour. Drain and set aside.

In a 10-inch frying-pan, heat the oil over a medium-high flame. When hot, put in the mustard, cumin, and fenugreek seeds. In a few seconds, as soon as the cumin and fenugreek seeds darken and the mustard seeds begin to pop, add the green chilies. Turn them over once (this will take another second), then put in the chopped onion and grated ginger. Stir and fry the onions for 4 to 5 minutes. Now put in all the remaining ingredients, i.e., the boiled *dal* and diced potatoes, ½ teaspoon salt, the pepper, cayenne, if you are using it, and lemon juice or tamarind paste. Mix well and cook over medium flame for 5 minutes, stirring frequently but gently.

To serve: Serve with *chapatis*, *bhaturas*, or *parathas* and a yogurt relish. Any meat, chicken, or fish dish can be served with it as well.

Chana dal cooked with lamb

Serves 6

I use meat from shoulder of lamb for this recipe, but you could use leg of lamb or stewing beef. The *chana dal* cooks in an hour, or a bit less, so you will have to adjust the time when you put it in. If you use stewing lamb or beef, cook the meat for 1½ hours and *then* add the *dal*.

2–2½ lbs boned meat from shoulder of lamb, cut into 1–1½-inch cubes	1 tsp ground turmeric
	1 tbs tomato purée
	¼ tsp ground mace
5 medium-sized onions (1 peeled and chopped, 4 halved and sliced into fine half-rings)	¼ tsp ground nutmeg
	¼ tsp ground cinnamon
	¼ tsp ground cloves
	1½ tsp salt (or as desired)

5 cloves garlic, peeled and
   chopped

a piece of fresh ginger, about
   1 inch cube, peeled and
   chopped

10 tbs vegetable oil

1 tbs ground coriander

2 tsp ground cumin

$\frac{1}{8}$ tsp freshly ground black
   pepper

$\frac{1}{4}$–$\frac{1}{2}$ tsp cayenne pepper
   (optional)

4 oz chana dal, cleaned and
   washed (see page 263)

2 tbs lemon juice

Garnish

3 tbs chopped fresh green coriander

Pat the meat pieces dry with a paper towel. Set aside.

Put the 1 chopped onion, garlic, and ginger into container of an electric blender. Add 4 tablespoons water and blend at high speed until you have a smooth paste.

Heat the oil in a 10-inch heavy-bottomed casserole-type pot, over medium-high flame. Put in the 4 sliced onions and fry them, stirring, for 15 to 20 minutes, or until they are a darkish brown and crisp. Remove them with a slotted spoon and spread on a paper towel.

Drop 7 or 8 pieces of meat at a time in the onion-flavoured oil and brown them well over high heat on all sides. Remove each batch as it gets done. When all the meat has browned, turn off the heat under the pot.

When the remaining oil has cooled a bit, pour in the paste from the electric blender. Stir it well, mixing it with the juices in the pot. Turn up the heat and fry the paste, stirring all the time, 8 to 10 minutes or until it has browned. Now lower heat and add, at intervals, frying and stirring, the coriander, cumin, and turmeric; after a minute or two, the tomato purée; and after another minute, the mace, nutmeg, cinnamon, and cloves. Finally, after 5 minutes, add $\frac{1}{2}$ pint water, salt, black pepper, cayenne, the browned meat, and the cleaned and washed *chana dal*. Bring to the boil. Cover, lower heat, and simmer for 1 hour, stirring gently every 10 minutes or so. Do not let the grains of *dal* break.

When done, add the lemon juice and stir gently.

To serve: Place in a warm bowl. Sprinkle the browned onions and chopped green coriander over the *dal* and meat and serve with plain rice or *chapatis*. Serve a green vegetable (green beans or peas) and at least one relish (a yogurt relish would be good).

Karhi

Serves 6–8

This dish looks like a very thick soup with dumplings. It is usually eaten with plain rice, and it was a great Sunday favourite with my family. It is made with chickpea flour (*besan*) and buttermilk (the more sour the buttermilk, the better), flavoured with fennel, cumin, fenugreek, and mustard seeds.

N.B. Chickpea flour is very light so do weigh it.

For the Karhi

3 oz chickpea flour (besan)
¾ pint buttermilk
2 tbs vegetable oil
1 generous pinch ground asafetida or tiny lump asafetida
¼ tsp whole fennel seeds
¼ tsp whole cumin seeds

¼ tsp whole black mustard seeds
⅛ tsp whole fenugreek seeds
¼ tsp black onion seeds (kalonji), if available
2–3 whole dried hot peppers
1 tsp ground turmeric
1½–2 tsp salt
2–3 tbs lemon juice

For the pakoris, or dumplings

4 oz chickpea flour (besan)
½ tsp baking powder
½ tsp salt

½ tsp ground cumin
vegetable oil for deep frying

To make the karhi: Sift the 3 oz chickpea flour into a bowl. Add ¼ pint of the buttermilk, a little at a time, and mix well until you have a thick, smooth paste. Now add the remaining ½ pint buttermilk, mixing as you pour it in. Add 2 pints of water to the bowl, mix again, and set aside.

* In a heavy-bottomed 3–4-quart pot, heat the oil over medium-high flame. When hot, put in the asafetida. In a few seconds, as soon as the asafetida expands, add the fennel, cumin, mustard, fenugreek, and onion seeds. When the seeds darken, put in the dry peppers. When they start to darken, add the turmeric, and a second later, the liquid from the bowl. Bring to the boil, cover, lower heat, and simmer gently for 1 hour.

Add salt and lemon juice. Cook another 10 minutes covered. Turn off heat.*

To make pakoris, or dumplings (these can be made while *karhi* is cooking): Sift the 4 oz of chickpea flour and the baking powder into a bowl. Add salt and cumin. Add water slowly, mixing as you go, until you have a very thick, doughy paste — thick enough to stand in peaks. You will need about 4 fl. oz of water, perhaps a little less.

The ideal utensil for deep-frying *pakoris* is a *karhai* or Chinese wok. If you do not have one, use any other utensil you find convenient. Put at least 2½ inches of oil in and heat over a medium-low flame. Give it 10 minutes to heat. Meanwhile, fill a large bowl halfway with warm water and set it somewhere near you.

When the oil is heated, drop the doughy paste, a teaspoonful at a time, into the oil, using a second teaspoon to help release the paste. Make sure you do not drop one dumpling right on top of another. Put in enough to cover the surface and no more. The dumplings will sink first and then rise and float. Fry each batch slowly, for 6 to 7 minutes, turning them at least once; they must not brown. If they begin to darken, lower your flame. They should retain their yellowish colour, but cook through. As soon as each batch is done, lift them out with a slotted spoon and drop into the warm water. Let them soak 2 minutes, then remove from the water and squeeze them *very* gently, taking care not to break them. Set them aside, covered.

When the *karhi* is done and the heat turned off, lift the cover and put all the dumplings in. Stir gently. Do not cook the *karhi* and the dumplings together until 10 minutes before you are ready to eat. Otherwise the dumplings will disintegrate. Now you can bring the *karhi* to the boil, covered. Lower the heat and simmer gently for 10 minutes.

To serve: Take *karhi* and *pakoris* carefully out of the pot so as not to break the *pakoris*. Place in serving bowl. Serve with plain rice, *Khare Masale Ka Gosht*, a vegetable, and a relish.

Tomato karhi

Serves 6–8

This is a variation of the North Indian *karhi*. It is served in Hyderabad and is cooked with tomatoes. It can be served with or without the *pakoris*, or dumplings.

N.B. Chickpea flour is very light so do weigh it.

2 oz chickpea flour (besan)
1½ pints tomato sauce (see page 225)
2 tbs vegetable oil
a generous pinch ground asafetida or tiny lump asafetida
¼ tsp whole fennel seeds
¼ tsp whole cumin seeds
¼ tsp whole black mustard seeds
⅛ tsp whole fenugreek seeds
¼ tsp black onion seeds (kalonji), if available
2–3 whole dried hot peppers
1 tsp ground turmeric powder
1½–2 tbs salt
4 tbs lemon juice
8–10 fresh kari leaves, if available

Sift the flour into a bowl. Slowly add 3 fl. oz water, mixing as you go, until you have a thick, smooth paste. Add another 1 pint water, slowly, stirring all the time. Pour in the tomato sauce. Mix well. Set aside.

Now follow the rest of the recipe for *karhi* on page 277, the section marked between the two asterisks. Add the *kari* leaves when you put in the salt.

If you wish to make the *pakoris*, follow preceding recipe.

Instead of *pakoris*, sliced vegetables (green peppers, onions, mushrooms, marrows or aubergines) can be lightly sautéed in oil, sprinkled with salt and pepper, and dropped into the tomato *karhi* 10 minutes before the cooking time is over.

To serve: See serving suggestions for preceding recipe.

Whole unhulled urad and rajma dal

Serves 6

The whole unhulled *dals*, particularly *urad* and *rajma*, take a very long time to cook. This recipe takes 5 hours. You can, however, take comfort from the fact that they are 5 effortless hours. Once you put the *dal* on, apart from an occasional stir, not much else is required of you. In the Punjab, where the whole *urad* and *rajma dal* are specialities, they are left to cook in a slow earthen oven (*tandoor*) for 24 hours. Both *dals* can be cooked individually, using this same recipe, or they can be mixed, in whatever proportion you desire. I have mixed them half and half.

3 oz whole unhulled moong dal, cleaned and washed

3 oz whole unhulled rajma dal, cleaned and washed

a piece of fresh ginger, about $\frac{1}{2}$-inch cube, peeled and sliced

2 cloves of garlic, peeled

5 tbs plain yogurt

$\frac{1}{8}$ tsp cayenne pepper (optional)

$1\frac{3}{4}$ tsp salt

$\frac{1}{8}$ tsp freshly ground pepper

3 tbs vegetable oil or usli ghee (see page 42)

1 medium-sized onion, cut in half lengthwise, then finely sliced

a piece of fresh ginger, about $\frac{1}{2}$-inch cube, peeled and grated (see page 42)

a pinch of ground asafetida or a small lump about $\frac{1}{8}$ inch square

$\frac{1}{2}$ tsp whole cumin seeds

2 dried hot red peppers

In a very heavy-bottomed pot, combine the two *dals*, 2 pints water, the sliced ginger, and the peeled garlic cloves. Bring to the boil, cover, lower heat, and simmer gently $4\frac{1}{2}$ hours, stirring every hour or so.

Put the yogurt in a small bowl. Beat well with a fork. When the *dal* has cooked for $4\frac{1}{2}$ hours, lift off cover and mash it well against the sides of the pot with the back of a kitchen spoon. Pour in the yogurt, stirring as you do so. Also add the cayenne, salt, and pepper. Stir, bring to the boil, cover, lower heat, and simmer another 30 minutes.

Heat the oil or *ghee* in an 8–10-inch frying-pan. When hot, put in the sliced onion. Fry, stirring, over medium-high flame for about 4 minutes, then put in the grated ginger and fry it along with the onions for 1 more minute, or until onions are brown and crisp. Remove onions and ginger with slotted spoon and set aside.

In the same oil put the asafetida, cumin, and red peppers. If the oil is very hot, the cumin and peppers will darken immediately. Turn off heat and pour contents of frying-pan into the pot with the *dal*. Cover pot again and leave until you are ready to serve.

To serve: Mix the *dal* and ladle it into warm serving bowl. Sprinkle browned onions and ginger over it. At Delhi's famous Moti Mahal restaurant, a common order with this *dal* is *Tandoori* Chicken, *naan*, and Onions Pickled in Vinegar.

Baris
(or vadees) with aubergine and potatoes

Serves 6

To make *baris*, *dals* are ground, mixed with spices, made into a hard dough, and then broken off into lumps and dried in the sun. My grandmother made her own *baris*: I can still see them drying on white sheets spread over rope charpoys. These were laid out in the sunniest section of our large brick courtyard and watched over by a one-eyed hawk always perched on the telephone pole. But most people nowadays just go down to a grocery shop and buy them. Usually, two kinds are available. One is *very* hot, spiced with red and black pepper, and the other is very mild. Some groceries in America and England carry both varieties.

Since *baris* come in different sizes, the large ones need to be broken into pieces roughly an inch in diameter. Use any heavy object to break them. A hammer will do. Any smaller pieces splintering off need not be thrown away. Just add them to the pot.

Baris should be browned before they are cooked. Here is my mother's recipe for them.

4 tbs vegetable oil

1 teacup baris, broken into pieces no larger than 1 inch in diameter

2 medium-sized onions, peeled and chopped

4 cloves garlic, peeled and minced

a piece of fresh ginger, about ½ inch cube, peeled and grated

1 tsp ground coriander

1 tsp ground cumin

½ tsp ground turmeric

2 tbs tomato purée

2 medium-sized potatoes, peeled and quartered

1½ tsp salt

2 small, long aubergines (if unavailable substitute 3 teacups of the larger aubergine, diced into 1-inch cubes)

Heat the oil in a 10-inch frying-pan or 10-inch heavy-bottomed pot over a medium-high flame. When hot, put in *baris* and fry them, turning frequently, for about 2 minutes or until they turn a few shades darker. (Do *not* let them get a very dark brown.) Remove them with a slotted spoon and set aside.

To the same oil, add first the chopped onions, stirring and frying continuously, for about 4 minutes, until the onions have turned dark at the edges. Lower the heat to medium low and add the garlic and ginger; keep stirring; after 2 minutes, add the coriander, cumin, and turmeric; stir again; and after 2 more minutes, put in the tomato purée and stir; finally, after another 2 minutes, add the fried *baris*, 1¼ pint water, the potatoes, and the salt. Stir and bring to the boil. Cover, lower heat, and simmer gently for 30 minutes.

Wash the aubergines. Do not break off the stem and the green part. Quarter the aubergines, lengthwise, all the way from the stem down, and drop the quarters into the pot. Add another ¼ pint water. Stir, bring to the boil again, cover, lower heat, and simmer for 20 minutes.

To serve: Bring the *baris* to the table in a warm serving bowl. Let each person serve himself in small individual *katoris* (see page 47) or bowls. Eat with *chapatis*, *pooris*, or *parathas*. You could serve a meat dish (Lamb *Korma* would be good) and a yogurt relish with it.

Chutneys,
Pickles, &
Other Relishes

Sweet tomato chutney
Fresh green chutney with coriander leaves and yogurt
Fresh mint chutney with fruit
Tamarind chutney with bananas
Tomato tamarind chutney
Fresh coconut chutney
Carrot 'water' pickle
Turnip 'water' pickle
Carrots pickled in oil
Onions pickled in vinegar
Cucumber raita
Yogurt with tiny dumplings (boondi-ka-dahi)
Yogurt with potatoes
Yogurt with roasted aubergine (baigan-ka-bharta)
Yogurt with spinach
Cucumber and tomato with lemon juice
Tomato and onion with lemon juice
Chopped onions in vinegar
Raw onion rings

SEE ALSO

Sea bass with green chutney (page 159)
Fried aubergines with sour green chutney (page 202)
Fried aubergines with tomato chutney (page 204)
Fried onion rings for garnishing (page 258)

o Indian meal is complete without at least one kind of relish. At its simplest, this can be a small, fresh, fiery green chili, or it can be a hastily peeled and quartered onion. In lower-middle-class families, when the wife packs her husband's lunch in the early hours of the morning, she may not have any meat or vegetable to offer him with his *roti* (bread). What she will tuck in, though, with great love, ensconced between two *rotis*, will be a tiny portion of a sour spicy raw mango pickle! It may well be the climate that causes appetites to wilt and turn apathetic, especially during the blazing summer months. Relishes are, perhaps, just ways of prodding sluggish bodies into perking up and eating. At any rate, Indians seem to find them both desirable and necessary.

My grandmother used to make a lime pickle which, if I remember correctly, took years to mature. We carried it with us on the long car rides to the summer resorts Simla and Mussoori. When tossing and turning at the never-ending and ever-climbing hairpin bends made our taste buds turn green, my grandmother, like a familiar magician with his equally familiar trick, would say 'aha' and produce a small brown crock filled with her lime pickles. They were sour and pungent and black with age. One tiny bite would make the mouth pucker at first, but ultimately leave it completely refreshed.

I saw my grandmother make this pickle just once. It took five servants, the ten women of the house, and my grandmother two whole days to do all the grinding, cutting, and stuffing. Then, as the pickle matured, my grandmother would walk the length of the storeroom every day, shaking the large crocks stored in several neat rows. Every month the limes needed to be stirred by hand. Not every hand, antiseptically clean though it might be, was allowed inside the crocks. According to my grandmother, the chemistry of most hands would cause the pickle to rot. It needed a very 'special' hand, and in our household she had decided that this hand belonged to Ishri, my grandfather's personal servant. So this small wizened gentleman, and he alone, was allowed to push his gnarled hand into each crock and give the pickles a 'swish'. My grandmother must have been doing something right because she was the only lady in the neighbourhood who made this pickle successfully. All others who tried it and who, unfortunately, did not have the valuable services of Ishri, ended up with various varieties of fungi! And when my grandmother died and her valuables were being parcelled out, her famous lime pickle was also carefully distributed among selected relatives. Those lucky enough to get a jar treated it with great reverence because, by now, it was supposed to have not just taste but medicinal and even magical qualities!

The recipes for most chutneys and pickles are usually handed down from mother to daughter, each family group specializing in its own particular varieties and styles. The result is that different families will serve you completely different sets of relishes. There are now a few companies that produce and bottle relishes, but at the moment they have not quite succeeded in tearing the Indian housewife away from her own home efforts. Some of these bottled relishes are available in delicatessens. You will have to taste and check them for yourself. If you like *very* hot pickles, I will recommend one particular brand to you. The firm of Har Narain Gopi Nath has been in the pickling business for decades. (Even my grandmother bought their red chili pickle, though she bought no other.) They now sell their pickles in this country. I would recommend only their stuffed red chili pickle. It is, as I said, *very* hot, so just eat a pinhead with each morsel!

I have, very arbitrarily, I confess, divided relishes into three categories—chutneys, pickles, and 'others'. 'Others' does not seem very dignified or very exotic, but you will begin to see my problem once I get to 'others'. Meanwhile, let me start with chutneys.

There are so many different kinds of chutneys — sweet chutneys, sour chutneys, sweet-and-sour chutneys, salty chutneys, hot chutneys, cold chutneys — the list could go on and on. The ingredients used in these chutneys can include tomatoes, ginger, onions, garlic, tamarind, bananas, mangoes, raisins, coconut, fresh coriander, fresh mint, lime juice, yogurt, vinegar, sugar, etc. Chutneys can be preserves — that is, they can be bottled and kept indefinitely, like Sweet Tomato Chutney, or they can be made fresh daily, like Tamarind Chutney with Bananas or Fresh Mint Chutney with Fruit (see the following recipes). In our home we had a special woman who came in daily to grind the spices. When the spices were done, her second daily task was to grind the fresh green coriander chutney which we had at every meal.

Chutneys are generally served in small non-metallic bowls if they are to accompany a meal. Sometimes, however, they are used as a sauce to go over hot or cold foods, such as in Fried Aubergines with Tomato Chutney (page 204). Food can also be cooked in a chutney or with a chutney, as in *Kheema* Used as a Stuffing (page 80). Some chutneys are eaten not as a relish but as a vegetable. In our family we eat a chutney made with the pulp of boiled green mangoes this way.

Pickles in India are a world in themselves. A whole book could be written about them. Pickles preserve, and in a land of warm climate and little refrigeration, almost everything gets pickled in order to prolong its life — hard berries, onions, raw mangoes, green chilies, cauliflower, carrots, turnips, limes, lemons, marrows, aubergines, mutton, prawns, lobsters, quail, partridge, bamboos, and what-have-you. My very dear brother-in-law once spotted a mound of rose petals on their way out to the dustbin. Appalled by the waste, he immediately retrieved and pickled them. A week later the rose-petal pickle jar was opened for tasting. Well! Not wanting my brother-in-law's morale and pickling initiative to fade away, we all kept saying,

'Not bad, not bad at all, very interesting taste.' I decided then that pickled rose petals were one thing I intended to stay away from!

Pickling is generally done in oil, vinegar, water, or lemon juice. Oil pickles can last for years, whereas water pickles have a limited life of 2 to 3 weeks, during which there are waxing, peak, and waning periods. Oil pickles can be hot and sour or hot and sweet (jaggery — or Indian molasses — often providing the sweetness). While ceramic or glass jars are used for oil pickles, the traditional water pickles are made in *mutkas*, round pots of half-baked clay. As the water pickle matures, it picks up an earthen flavour that is very refreshing. These pickles are sour (a bit like the gherkin and cucumber delicatessen pickles) and hot if you want them to be. Before each meal, a large bowl of the pickles, both water and vegetable, is removed from the earthenware pot and put to cool — in a refrigerator if there is one. This bowl is then brought to the table at mealtime. Each place setting has a cup or non-metallic bowl into which people serve themselves both the vegetable and the water.

Fresh ginger or green chilies can be pickled in lime juice. The juice is boiled first and then added to the ginger or the chilies.

Small boiling onions are often pickled in red vinegar. These are then lifted out of the vinegar and served with dishes like *Tandoori* Chicken.

There are, of course, many other relishes as well. And here we come to my category 'others'. Chopped or sliced onions, tomatoes, and cucumbers are sprinkled with lime juice (or vinegar), salt, pepper, and cayenne, and served in varying forms all over North India. Numerous dishes made with yogurt are also very popular. I feel Britain has still to discover the versatility of plain yogurt. At the moment, yogurt seems to provide nothing more than a quick lunch for the girl on a diet. Indians use yogurt as East Europeans use sour cream. Apart from cooking with it and using it as a marinade, we use it for hundreds of relishes. *Raitas* are one of them. Here cooked or raw vegetables are added to well-mixed yogurt, seasonings are sprinkled in, and the dish is cooled before being served.

Various 'dumplings' can also be made and put into yogurt. Since they never comprise a main dish, 'relish' is a very good word for them.

Most Westerners seem to think that the usual relishes served with Indian food are Major Grey's chutney and little bowls filled with nuts, grated coconut, and sliced bananas and apples. If you have developed a taste for these items, eat them, by all means. But do experiment with some of these much more interesting local relishes.

Sweet tomato chutney

Makes enough to fill 1 pint jar

I make this chutney with tinned tomatoes. You could, if you like, use fresh tomatoes when they are in season and really tasty. To peel them, you will need to drop them in boiling vinegar. When the skin crinkles, lift them out and peel. Then proceed with the recipe. When cooked, this chutney is sweet and sour, thick and garlicky.

1 whole head of garlic, peeled and coarsely chopped

a piece of fresh ginger, about 2 inches long, 1 inch thick, and 1 inch wide, peeled and coarsely chopped

12 fl. oz wine vinegar

2, 14 oz tins whole tomatoes (or 2 lbs fresh tomatoes prepared as suggested above)

$\frac{3}{4}$ lb granulated sugar

$1\frac{1}{2}$ tsp salt

$\frac{1}{8}$–$\frac{1}{2}$ tsp cayenne pepper

2 tbs golden raisins

2 tbs blanched slivered almonds

Put the chopped garlic, ginger, and 4 fl. oz of the vinegar into the container of an electric blender and blend at high speed until smooth. In a 3-quart heavy-bottomed pot with non-metallic finish, place the tomatoes and juice from the tin, the rest of the vinegar, the sugar, salt, and cayenne pepper (or, if you prefer, add the cayenne at the end, a little at a time, stirring and tasting as you do so). Bring to the boil. Add purée from the blender. Lower heat and simmer gently, uncovered, for about $1\frac{1}{2}$ to 2 hours or until chutney becomes thick. (A film should cling to a spoon dipped in it.) Stir occasionally at first, and more frequently later as it thickens. You may need to lower the heat as the liquid diminishes. You should end up with about 1 pint of chutney, and it should be at least as thick as honey after it cools. If the tinned tomatoes you use have a lot of liquid in them, a longer cooking time may be required, resulting in a little less chutney.

Add the almonds and raisins. Simmer, stirring, another 5 minutes. Turn heat off and allow to cool. Bottle. Keep refrigerated.

To serve: Since this is one of my favourite sweet chutneys, I always spoon out a small bowl of it for all my dinner parties. It goes with almost all foods and is *very* popular. Store, bottled, in the refrigerator. It keeps for months.

Fresh green chutney with coriander leaves and yogurt

Serves 6

This chutney needs to be made the day it is eaten. It can be served in a small bowl as a relish, or it can be served over meat, cooked fish, or vegetables. If pressed to classify it, I would call this a 'sour' chutney.

1 packed teacup chopped fresh green coriander
1 fresh hot green chili, sliced, or ¼ tsp ground cayenne pepper (optional)
10 oz plain yogurt
1 tbs lemon juice

½ tsp salt (add more if you need it; the sourness of yogurt can vary with its age)
⅛ tsp freshly ground pepper
½ tsp roasted, ground cumin seeds (see page 41)

Put the green coriander and chili in the container of an electric blender with 3 tablespoons of water and blend until you have a smooth paste (you may need to push the coriander down a couple of times).

In a non-metallic bowl, combine the yogurt, salt, pepper, cumin, lemon juice, and paste from the blender. Cover and refrigerate until ready to use.

To serve: Bring the cooled bowl to the table. You could serve it with almost any Indian meal. People should take just a tablespoon at a time.

Fresh mint chutney with fruit

Serves 6

⅓–½ well-packed teacup
   washed fresh mint leaves
4 tbs lemon juice
2 fresh hot green chilies (use
   less or more as desired;
   as substitute, use ½ green
   pepper plus ½ tsp cayenne
   pepper)

1 medium-sized tart apple,
   peeled, cored, and diced
   just before blending
1 orange, peeled, seeded,
   and cubed
1 tsp salt

Combine all ingredients in the container of an electric blender. Blend at high speed until you have a smooth paste.

This chutney goes with most Indian foods. It is especially good with grilled *Seekh Kabab*, *Tandoori* Chicken, and Vegetable *Pakoris*.

Tamarind chutney with bananas

Serves 4–6

This is another sweet and sour chutney made with tamarind pulp. The addition of roasted cumin and slices of ripe bananas is, I think, very particular to Delhi dwellers. My mother's family often added raisins as well. I have not included them in my recipe, but if you wish to do so, soak a tablespoon of golden raisins in hot water for 2 hours. Then remove them from the water and add them to the tamarind pulp at the same time that you add the bananas.

Even though this chutney can be made a day in advance, it is best to add the banana slices just before serving. Banana slices that have spent a night in the refrigerator look very unhappy!

a piece of tamarind, the size of a tangerine	1 tsp roasted, ground cumin seeds (see page 41)
1–1½ tbs sugar	⅛–¼ tsp cayenne pepper (optional)
1¼ tsp salt	1 ripe but firm banana

Since the tamarind generally comes in a large block, tear off a lump about the size of a tangerine. Soak it overnight in 6 fl. oz hot water in a small non-metallic bowl or cup. (The water should cover the tamarind, so don't use a very wide bowl.) If you forget to do it overnight, do it first thing in the morning. All will not be lost! Soak it for a minimum of 4 hours.

Once it has soaked, mash down and break the lump in the water, making a thick, uneven pulp. I use my hands for this, but you could use the back of a wooden spoon.

Place a strainer over a non-metallic bowl, put the tamarind pulp in the strainer, and press down with the back of a spoon. Keep pressing until nothing but fibrous tissues and seeds are left in the strainer. Discard fibrous tissues and seeds. Make sure you scrape all the strained pulp on the outside of the strainer — it doesn't always drip down. Use extra water, if necessary, to separate all the pulp from the fibres.

Mix the strained pulp with the sugar, salt, cumin seeds, and cayenne.

Slice a peeled banana into ¼–⅓-inch slices and mix with the tamarind pulp.

To serve: Put into small ceramic or glass serving bowl and place on the table along with other chutneys and pickles.

Tomato tamarind chutney

Makes 16 fl. oz

This is, basically, a sour chutney used as a sauce for fish and stuffed vegetables. It can be made in advance, put in a jar, and refrigerated for 3 or 4 days.

4 tbs olive or vegetable oil
a generous pinch ground asafetida or ⅛-inch lump asafetida
½ tsp whole cumin seeds
½ tsp whole black mustard seeds
1 medium-sized onion, peeled and finely chopped
4 cloves garlic, peeled and minced
12 fl. oz tomato sauce (see page 225)

¼ pint tamarind pulp (see recipe for Tamarind Chutney with Bananas, page 293)
1¼–1½ tsp salt
½ tsp garam masala
⅛ tsp ground cinnamon
⅛ tsp freshly ground black pepper
⅛–¼ tsp cayenne pepper (optional)
1 tsp granulated sugar (add a bit more if you want to)

Heat the oil in a 2-quart pot over medium-high heat. When hot, put in the asafetida, and a few seconds later, add the cumin and mustard seeds. The cumin seeds will begin to darken in the hot oil within a few seconds. Put in the chopped onions and minced garlic, and fry, stirring, for about 2 minutes, or until the onions darken at the edges.

Now pour in the tomato sauce and tamarind pulp. Also add the salt, *garam masala*, cinnamon, black pepper, cayenne, and sugar. Bring to the boil. Cover, lower heat, and simmer gently for 15 minutes.

To serve: Use as a sauce with fried vegetables or with *Kheema* Used as Stuffing (for peppers, tomatoes, and aubergines).

Fresh coconut chutney

Serves 6–8

1 teacup fairly well-packed, grated fresh coconut (see page 40)

½ teacup fairly well-packed, chopped fresh green coriander

1–2 fresh hot green chilies (use as desired)

a piece of fresh ginger, about ½-inch cube, peeled and chopped

1 clove garlic, peeled and chopped

6 tbs plain yogurt

½ tsp salt

1 tsp lemon juice

1 tbs vegetable oil

⅛ tsp urad dal (the hulled, split variety) grains

¼ tsp whole black mustard seeds

Put the coconut, green coriander, green chilies, ginger, and garlic, along with 5 tablespoons of water, into the container of an electric blender. Blend at high speed until you have a smooth paste, stopping occasionally to push down the ingredients.

Pour contents of blender into a bowl. Add yogurt, salt, and lemon juice. Mix well.

In a 4–6-inch frying-pan, heat the oil. When very hot, put in the *dal* grains and mustard seeds. As soon as the *dal* darkens and the mustard seeds pop, pour contents of frying-pan into bowl with chutney. Mix well. Cover and chill until ready for use.

To serve: This South Indian chutney goes well with Vegetable *Pakoris*. It is also very good as a relish with most meals.

Carrot 'water' pickle

About 4 quarts

This is one of Delhi's most popular winter pickles. Like chestnuts, it is often sold at street corners, in large glass jars. The 'water' in the pickle turns a glorious beetroot colour because the carrot used is a special 'black' carrot which 'bleeds' like a beetroot. Enthusiasm for this pickle has now become so refined that the real gourmets do not eat the carrot at all. They just drink the juice.

Unable to find the bleeding 'black' carrot, I have substituted the ordinary orange carrot. However, I have thrown in some beetroots to supply the necessary colour. I eat both the carrot and the beetroot. The juice, of course, is the best part of all.

This pickle is good for 10 days to 2 weeks. It will get more sour as time passes. You may need to add more salt as that happens. One way to slow its deterioration is to refrigerate it.

1⅓ tbs salt	2 medium-sized beetroots
4 tbs black mustard seeds	2 hot dried red peppers
1½ lbs carrots	

Bring 7 pints water and the salt to the boil in a large pot.

Meanwhile, crush, pound, or grind the mustard seeds coarsely, so that they split at least in half, using either a heavy mortar and pestle or an Indian grinding stone or a few quick spins of an electric coffee-grinder.

Peel the carrots, removing the green top portion, and quarter them lengthwise. Halve each piece lengthwise once again.

Peel the beetroots and cut each into 3 rounds.

Place the beetroots and carrots in a clean 4–5-quart wide-mouthed jar. Pour boiling salted water over them. Add the mustard seeds and the red peppers. Allow to cool. Stir and cover.

Put a small label with the date on it so you will not forget exactly when you started the pickle. Stir once a day for 7 days with a clean wooden spoon. Keep covered. It should be ready on the seventh day.

To serve: Place in a bowl a slice or two of carrot plus half a ladleful of juice for each person eating. Cool in the refrigerator. Serve in small, individual non-metallic bowls.

Turnip 'water' pickle

About 4 quarts

Water pickles are a speciality of my family. I love them and find them very similar to the pickled gherkins and cucumbers found in good delicatessens.

This pickle takes a week to mature and then can be eaten for the next 2 weeks. It gets very sour as time passes, and you may need to add more salt to it. One way to slow its deterioration is to refrigerate it once it has matured. Both the vegetable and the juice are consumed.

5 tbs black mustard seeds	**1⅓ tbs salt**
3 lbs medium-sized white turnips	**2 whole dried hot red chilies (optional)**

Crush, pound, or grind the mustard seeds coarsely, so that they split at least in half, using either a heavy mortar and pestle or an Indian grinding stone or a few quick spins of an electric coffee-grinder.

In a large pot, bring 6½ pints of water to the boil. Add salt to the water.

Peel the turnips. Slice them into ⅓ inch rounds and place in a clean 4–5-quart wide-mouthed jar. Pour boiling salted water over them. Add crushed mustard seeds and red chilies. Allow to cool.

Stir and put lid on. Stick a label with the date on the jar.

Stir it every day with a clean wooden spoon. On the seventh day it will be ready to eat.

To serve: Place in a bowl a piece of pickle and half a ladleful of juice for each person eating. Cool in refrigerator and serve in small individual non-metallic bowls.

Carrots pickled in oil

About 1½ pints

This is perhaps the simplest oil pickle you could make. It takes about a week to mature. It can then be refrigerated and kept for months.

2 tsp black mustard seeds	1 tsp cayenne pepper
1 lb carrots of medium thickness	1 tsp ground turmeric
1 tsp salt	16 fl. oz vegetable oil

Crush, pound, or grind mustard seeds coarsely, so that they split at least in half, using either a heavy mortar and pestle or an Indian grinding stone, or a few quick spins of the electric coffee-grinder.

Peel the carrots. Cut off the coarse top and the bottom. Cut each carrot in 3 pieces. Halve or quarter these pieces lengthwise according to the thickness of the carrots.

Place carrots in clean, dry 1½ pint jar. Add salt, cayenne pepper, turmeric, and crushed mustard seeds.

Warm the oil and pour over the carrots. Put lid on tightly and shake the jar well. Leave in a warm place for 7 days. Shake the jar once or twice daily.

To serve: Shake the jar. Remove one or two carrot pieces per person, and arrange in a small bowl or on relish tray. Do not serve the oil.

Onions pickled in vinegar

About 1½ pints

This relish is served in Delhi's famous Moti Mahal restaurant. It is extremely simple to make. The onions need to marinate in the vinegar for at least 24 hours, so allow yourself sufficient time. In this recipe, I have made enough pickle to fill a 1½ pint jar. It should keep a month.

1 lb white boiling onions (pick small, clean, even-sized onions)
16 fl. oz red wine vinegar

2 cloves garlic, peeled and sliced
2 whole dried red peppers
1 tbs salt

Peel onions. Slicing only three-quarters of the way down, quarter them lengthwise. Each onion should stay whole, with the four sections attached at the bottom. Place the onions in a clean, wide-mouthed quart jar. You may have a few left over.

In a non-metallic bowl, combine the vinegar, garlic, red peppers, and salt. Mix well. Pour this mixture over the onions to cover them. Put on a tight lid and set the jar aside for 24 hours.

The pickle is now ready. Refrigerate the jar. The onions can be taken out and eaten as and when desired.

To serve: Take as many of the onions out of the vinegar as you need and place them in a glass or other non-metallic bowl. They go well with *Tandoori* Chicken and Whole Unhulled *Urad* and *Rajma Dal*.

Cucumber raita

Serves 4–6

This is a refreshing, cool yogurt and cucumber relish. In the hot summer months, it really takes the place of a salad.

1 cucumber	½ tsp roasted, ground cumin
15 oz plain yogurt	seeds (see page 41)
1 tsp salt	⅛ tsp cayenne pepper
⅛ tsp freshly ground black	(optional)
pepper	⅛ tsp paprika (for garnishing)

Peel and grate the cucumber.

Empty the yogurt into serving bowl and beat it well with a fork until it is smooth and paste-like.

Add the cucumber, salt, black pepper, roasted cumin (reserve a pinch for garnish), and cayenne to the bowl with the yogurt.

Sprinkle with paprika and the pinch of roasted cumin. Cover and refrigerate until ready to serve.

To serve: Bring bowl of cold yogurt to the table. This relish goes well with nearly all Indian meals.

Yogurt with tiny dumplings
(boondi-ka-dahi)

Serves 6–8

The only yogurt relish served at all our family wedding banquets was this one. Tiny little droplets of a chickpea flour paste are dropped into deep fat and fried. They are then softened in warm water. Finally they are combined with yogurt and spices, freshly roasted cumin being perhaps the most important ingredient used. You can make this relish as hot as you like. When I make it in Britain, I put in just a touch of cayenne pepper. But at those wedding banquets in India, it was a cool scorcher!

In India the dumplings are made by pushing the batter through the holes of a slotted spoon into the hot oil. The Indian slotted spoons have round holes about ⅛ inch wide. If you can find a spoon like that, use it. If you have a colander with holes this size, it could work as well.

For the dumplings

4 heaped tbs chickpea flour
  (besan)
¼ tsp baking powder
¼ tsp salt

¼ tsp ground cumin seeds
vegetable oil for deep frying,
  enough to have 1 inch in
  the frying-pan

For the yogurt

25 oz plain yogurt
1½ tsp salt
⅛–¼ tsp freshly ground black
  pepper

1 tsp freshly roasted, ground
  cumin seeds (see page 41)
⅛–¼ tsp cayenne pepper
  (optional)
⅛ tsp paprika

Place the chickpea flour and the baking powder in a bowl. Add a little water at a time (about 2½ fl. oz altogether) and mix to a thick, smooth paste, stiff enough to stand in tiny peaks. Use a wooden spoon or your fingers to do this. Add ¼ teaspoon salt and ¼ teaspoon cumin and mix well. Set aside.

In an 8–10-inch frying-pan, heat the vegetable oil over medium heat. Get your slotted spoon or colander, whichever you are going to use. When the oil is hot, place a tablespoon of batter on the slotted spoon or the colander and push it through with the back of a clean wooden spoon. Little droplets will fall into the oil. They should cook slowly—turning crisp, but staying a golden-yellow; they should not turn brown. This will take about 5 minutes. Adjust flame if necessary. As each batch gets done, remove it with a slotted spoon and dump it in a bowl filled with warm water. Continue until all the paste is used up. Let dumplings soak in water for 30 minutes.

Now get the yogurt ready. In a bowl, mix the yogurt well. Then add the salt, black pepper, roasted cumin, and cayenne, reserving a pinch of the cumin for garnishing later. Cover and refrigerate the yogurt until almost ready to serve.

Just before serving, take out the dumplings, a handful at a time. Lay your other palm over them and gently squeeze out excess water. Do not break them. Put them in serving bowl. Pour yogurt over them and mix well.

Garnish by sprinkling paprika and the pinch of roasted ground cumin over the top.

To serve: This yogurt dish goes very well with nearly all the lamb and pork dishes in this book. Do not serve it with other dishes containing dumplings, e.g., *Karhi.*

Yogurt with potatoes

Serves 4–6

This is perhaps the Indian version of potato salad. It is a little moister, and if I may allow myself to be prejudiced, a little tastier.

2 medium-sized boiling
   potatoes
15 oz plain yogurt
1–1½ tsp salt
⅛–¼ tsp freshly ground black
   pepper

1 tsp freshly roasted, ground
   cumin seeds (see page 41)
⅛–¼ tsp cayenne pepper
   (optional)

Garnish

⅛ tsp paprika

Boil the potatoes and allow them to cool thoroughly.

Put the yogurt in a bowl and mix well with a fork. Add the salt, black pepper, roasted cumin, and cayenne. Mix well.

Peel the potatoes and dice them into ½-inch cubes. Mix with the yogurt.

To serve: Pour yogurt and potatoes into serving bowl. Sprinkle with paprika and serve. This dish may be made several hours in advance, covered tightly and refrigerated.

Yogurt with roasted aubergine
(baigan-ka-bharta)

Serves 4–6

When I was a child and all food was cooked over coals, an aubergine was often put to bake in the ashes that fell below the grates in our stove. The aubergine would cook and soften and acquire a sumptuous smoked flavour. It was then peeled, mashed, and added to yogurt, along with minced onions and fresh mint. Here is that recipe. Instead of ashes, I use the direct flame of a gas burner!

1 medium-sized aubergine	⅛–¼ tsp freshly ground black
15 oz plain yogurt	pepper
1 small onion, peeled and	⅛–¼ tsp cayenne pepper
finely minced	(optional)
2 tbs finely minced fresh mint	1 tsp freshly roasted, ground
1 tsp salt	cumin seeds (see page 41)

Wash and wipe the aubergine. Line a burner with an aluminium protector if possible. Stand the aubergine directly on the gas burner and turn the flame on medium or medium low. Roast the aubergine on all sides, turning it over carefully. (For more detailed instructions, see Aubergine *Bharta*, page 206.) It should look fairly charred on the outside, and the inside should get soft and pulpy. This may take 20 to 25 minutes.

Peel the aubergine under cold running water, making sure all the blackened skin and the stem are removed. Now mince the pulp very finely and place in a bowl.

Empty yogurt into a serving bowl and mix well with fork. Add onion, mint, aubergine, salt, black pepper, cayenne, and roasted cumin. Mix. Cover and refrigerate until ready to serve.

To serve: Serve cold as an hors d'œuvre or as salad-type relish.

Yogurt with spinach

Serves 4–6

10–16 oz fresh spinach
2 tsp salt
15 oz plain yogurt
⅛–¼ tsp freshly ground black pepper

⅛–¼ tsp cayenne pepper (optional)
1 tsp freshly roasted, ground cumin seeds (see page 41)

Wash and trim the spinach. Make sure no sand is left.

Bring 6 pints of water to boil in large pot. Add 1 teaspoon salt. When boiling, drop spinach in it and cover. As soon as the spinach wilts, remove it and put it in a colander. Run cold water over it until it cools. Drain. Squeeze out the water by pressing spinach between your palms and then mince.

Place the yogurt in a bowl and mix well with a fork. Add the minced spinach, 1 teaspoon salt, black pepper, cayenne, and cumin. Mix well. Cover and refrigerate until ready to serve.

To serve: Serve cold with Lamb Cooked in Dark Almond Sauce or *Koftas*. Serve also with cauliflower or carrots or potatoes.

Cucumber and tomato with lemon juice

Serves 4

1 medium-sized cucumber
1 medium-sized tomato
1 tsp salt
$\frac{1}{8}$–$\frac{1}{4}$ tsp freshly ground black
  pepper
1 tsp roasted, ground cumin
  seeds (see page 41)

1–1$\frac{1}{2}$ tbs lemon juice
2 tbs minced fresh green
  coriander
$\frac{1}{8}$ tsp cayenne pepper
  (optional)

Peel cucumber and dice it finely (about $\frac{1}{4}$-inch cubes). Dice tomato as finely as cucumber. Combine all ingredients in serving bowl. Mix well. Cover and refrigerate for 30 minutes.

To serve: Bring cold serving bowl to table. This relish can be eaten with nearly all Indian meals.

Tomato and onion with lemon juice

Serves 4

1 medium-sized tomato
1 medium-sized onion
1 tsp salt
$\frac{1}{8}$–$\frac{1}{4}$ tsp freshly ground black
  pepper

1 tsp roasted, ground cumin
  seeds (see page 41)
1–1$\frac{1}{2}$ tbs lemon juice
$\frac{1}{8}$–$\frac{1}{4}$ tsp cayenne pepper

Dice tomato in $\frac{1}{4}$-inch cubes. Peel and chop the onion. Combine all ingredients in serving bowl. Cover and refrigerate for 30 minutes.

To serve: Bring cold serving bowl to table. This relish can be eaten with nearly all Indian meals.

Chopped onions in vinegar

Serves 4–6

2 medium-sized onions,
  peeled and chopped
1 tsp salt

⅛–¼ tsp freshly ground black
  pepper
¼ tsp cayenne pepper
4 tbs red wine vinegar

Combine all ingredients in small serving bowl. Mix well. Cover and refrigerate for 30 minutes.

To serve: Bring cold serving bowl to table. This relish can be eaten with nearly all Indian meals.

Raw onion rings

These are very good served with barbecued meats, chicken, and fish.

Peel onions and slice them into paper-thin rounds. Place in bowl containing cold water. Add a few cubes of ice, cover, and refrigerate. Leave an hour or two.

Drain, and scatter over meat, chicken, or fish.

Breads

Chapati
Poori
Paratha
Bhatura
Naan

I N India, we call our Indian bread *roti* and we call the Western-type loaf a *dubbul* (double) *roti*, probably because of the expansion caused by the yeast. Most of our everyday breads are unleavened—somewhat like the Mexican tortilla, but much more varied in shape, taste, and texture. They are generally made out of wholewheat flour, though barley, maize, millet, chickpea, and plain white flour are also used. We do make leavened breads like the *naan*, but they tend to be flat, rising only $\frac{1}{2}$ to $\frac{3}{4}$ inch in height.

Throughout most of North India *ata*, or finely ground whole-wheat flour, is measured out onto a very large brass platter, or *paraat*, for kneading. This *paraat* is essential because Indian kitchens do not have Formica countertops and because Indians prefer to do most of their kitchen work—chopping, cutting, grinding, and kneading—in a squatting position. Once the dough has been kneaded (this is done with clenched fists— the knuckles pressing into the dough), it is formed into a lump, covered with a damp cloth, and left on one side of the *paraat*. Just before cooking, it is kneaded again and made into little patties. These are then rolled out on a round board into *chapatis, parathas*, or *pooris*. Even though I do have a *paraat* in my kitchen, I find it just as easy to use my kitchen counter for both the kneading and the rolling. If you happen to have a marble slab, you could use that instead.

Breads are cooked on the *tava*, a heavy, cast-iron, slightly curved plate, or in a *karhai*, a wok-like utensil for deep frying, or they are baked in the clay oven known as the *tandoor*. For a *tava* you can substitute an 8–10-inch cast-iron frying-pan; for a *karhai* you can use any wide, heavy casserole-type pot (cast-iron would be excellent); and for the *tandoor*, one just has to use the oven or a charcoal grill.

309

While Indian rice can be eaten with a fork, Indian bread *must* be eaten with the hands—or rather, with one hand. A small piece of the bread is broken off, wrapped around a morsel of food, and eaten. Only one hand is used—and just the fingertips at that. The other hand has to be kept clean to pass food or pick up a glass of water.

A word of encouragement about these breads. If they do not turn out perfectly the first time, do not lose heart. There are many Indians who have not mastered them either! So much depends on how well they are rolled out, and perfection in this area comes only with long practice. If you are persistent, you will surely master them.

Here are some of the basic breads.

Chapati

Serves 4

This simple bread requires only whole-wheat flour and water. It needs to be rolled out very evenly on a floured surface. Indians keep a quantity of plain whole-wheat flour on the side and keep dusting the *chapati* with it as they roll. Next, the *chapati* needs to be cooked on a *tava*. Give the *tava* time to heat before you put the first *chapati* on. When both sides of the *chapati* are roasted, it is taken off the *tava* and placed on an open fire. This makes it puff up with hot air. A *chimta* or some flat unserrated tongs are essential for the making of the bread (see page 47). Note: Some whole-wheat flour is very coarse. Many Indians prefer to mix it half and half with all-purpose white flour.

4 oz finely ground whole-wheat flour for dough

about 2 oz finely ground whole-wheat flour to keep on the side for dusting

Place the flour in a bowl. Slowly add up to 4 fl. oz water and mix until all the flour adheres and you can knead it. (You will probably need a little less than the 4 fl. oz water.) Now knead it for 7 to 8 minutes. Roll into a ball. Cover with a damp cloth and leave for ½ to 3 hours. (If you wish to leave it longer, cover it with a plastic wrap and refrigerate. It will easily stay 24 hours.)

Dampen hands and knead the dough again. Put the *tava* or cast-iron frying-pan on a *medium* flame to heat. Knead dough while the *tava* is heating. Divide the dough into 8 balls. Keep balls covered with damp cloth. Flour the rolling surface and keep some dry flour on the side for dusting. Take out one ball. Flatten it. Dip it in the dry flour. Now roll it out evenly into a *chapati* about 5 inches in diameter. You can get it even bigger and thinner if you like. It will stick to the surface as you roll it unless you keep dipping it in the dry flour. Always keep your surface well floured.

The *tava* or frying-pan should be smoking hot by now. Place the uncooked *chapati* on it. Within half a minute or so bubbles will start rising. Now turn the *chapati* over with the *chimta* or tongs. Let the other side cook for half a minute. Both sides should have light brown spots on them. Lift off *chapati* with the tongs and lay it directly over the medium flame of another burner. (You could use the same burner, but you would have to lift off the *tava* or frying-pan every time. As a matter of fact, this *is* what most Indians do!) Keep it there a few seconds. It will puff up immediately. Now turn it over and keep the other side over the flame for a few seconds.

Either serve hot immediately, or butter on one side very lightly and place *chapati* on a large sheet of aluminium foil. Fold over the aluminium foil and shut edges firmly. Do all *chapatis* this way. They will stay warm for 20 to 30 minutes if stacked tightly and kept well covered in foil in a warm place.

To serve: Chapatis are eaten with nearly all Indian main dishes.

Poori

Serves 4–6

The dough here is rather like that of the *chapati*, only a little oil is added. Some people like to add a bit of salt as well to the dough. It is then kneaded and rolled out. Deep fat is heated in a wok, *karhai* (see page 47), or deep frying-pan, and the *pooris* are fried quickly in it. They puff up like the *chapati*. It is important that the fat be smoking hot. *Pooris* can be made ahead of time and wrapped lightly in aluminium foil. They do not stay puffed this way, but they still taste good. They can be reheated (in the foil) in a 300°F., Mark 2 oven for 10 minutes. Instead of using only whole-wheat flour for the dough you can use a combination of whole-wheat flour and all-purpose flour. I tend to use the latter, and it seems to make the *pooris* more pliable.

2 oz finely ground whole-
  wheat flour
2 oz all-purpose white flour
1½ tbs vegetable oil

oil for deep frying, enough
  to have 2–3 inches in
  frying-pan
about 2 oz finely ground
  whole-wheat flour to keep
  on the side for dusting

Place whole-wheat and white flour in a bowl. Pour the oil over it. Slowly add up to 4 fl. oz water and mix until all the flour adheres and you can knead it. (You will probably need a little less than ½ cup water.) Knead it well for 7 to 8 minutes. Form into a ball, cover with a damp cloth, and leave for 1½ to 3 hours. (If you wish to leave it longer, cover with plastic wrap or aluminium foil and refrigerate. It will keep up to 24 hours.)

Heat the oil in the *karhai*, wok, or frying-pan over a medium flame. Give it time to get smoking hot. I wait 10 minutes before I put the first *poori* in.

While the oil is heating, knead the dough again. Divide the dough into 14 balls, keeping those you are not rolling covered with damp cloth. Flatten the balls one at a time and roll them out this way: first dip the flattened ball in the whole-wheat flour that you have on the side. Now roll it evenly, sprinkling the surface and the *poori* with flour when you need to, until it is about 3½ to 4 inches in diameter. Do not allow it to stick to the surface. Whenever it does, dip it in the dry flour.

Test the hot oil by dropping a *poori* in it. It will first sink to the bottom. Then, within a few seconds, it will rise and sizzle. Now you can do one of two things. Either keep pushing the *poori* down gently—with swift but soft pushes, using the back of a slotted spoon—or, with swift strokes, baste the *poori* with the hot oil. In basting, what you actually do is push the hot oil towards and over the *poori*. Or you can do both of these things. But do it fast. Within half a minute, the *poori* should puff up. Turn it over with a slotted spoon, and cook another 30 seconds. Remove with slotted spoon, drain on paper towel, and serve immediately. If the first *poori* comes out hard, you are cooking it too long, or the oil is not hot enough, or both.

If you do not wish to serve the puffed-up *pooris* right away, deflate them as they come out of the *karhai* (watch out for that steam!) by pressing down on them; wrap tightly in a large sheet of aluminium foil. (Do not crush them, though.) As the *pooris* get done, lay them one over the other, and keep wrapping the lot with foil. This will keep them soft. If they are served this way, at room temperature, they are known as *baasi*, or 'stale', *pooris*. If you wish to reheat them, place the foil bundle in a 300°F., Mark 2 preheated oven for 10 minutes.

To serve: Pooris go well with *Kheema*, with Lamb Cooked in Dark Almond Sauce, with Chicken *Moghlai*, and nearly all the vegetable dishes.

Paratha

Serves 4–8

A *paratha* is cooked on the *tava* with butter or *ghee* rather like a pancake. In Delhi and Uttar Pradesh it is often triangular in shape, flaky, and very delicate. It can be made with whole-wheat flour or with an equal combination of whole-wheat and all-purpose white flour.

6 oz finely ground whole-wheat flour	about 4 tbs melted butter or usli ghee (see page 42)
1 tbs vegetable oil	2 oz whole-wheat flour to keep on the side for dusting
½ tsp salt	

Place the 6 oz flour in a bowl. Pour the oil over it. Add the salt. Slowly add about 4 fl. oz water (you may need a bit more), and mix until all the flour adheres and you can knead. Knead the dough well for 8 to 10 minutes. Form into a ball. Cover with a damp cloth and set aside for 30 minutes. (If you wish to leave it longer, cover with plastic wrap and refrigerate. It will keep up to 24 hours.)

Put a *tava* (page 48) or cast-iron frying-pan to heat over a medium flame. Knead dough once again for a minute. Divide dough into 8 balls. Keep balls covered with damp cloth. Take one ball out at a time and flatten it slightly. Dip it in the extra flour and roll it out evenly on a floured surface until it is about 5 inches in diameter. (You may need to sprinkle more flour on it and on the surface as you go along.) Now brush the surface of the *paratha* lightly with butter. Fold in half. Brush the surface with butter again. Fold in half a second time. You now have a triangular shape.

Roll out this triangle, with the aid of the dry flour, so that its sides are about 5 inches long (it does not have to be too even).

Brush the *tava* or frying-pan with melted butter. Place the triangular *paratha* on it. As soon as one side is a golden-brown, turn it over. Add a little more butter to the *tava* or frying-pan and cook the second side until it is also a golden-brown. A few dark spots are perfectly all right. It should not get too dark or too crisp. Adjust flame to avoid this.

As each *paratha* is done, place on a large sheet of aluminium foil and cover tightly. Put all *parathas* in the foil this way. When ready to eat, preheat oven to 300°F., Mark 2 and heat covered *parathas* for 10 minutes.

To serve: Parathas go very well with nearly all vegetable dishes, particularly peas, potatoes, and cauliflower.

Bhatura

Serves 4

The *bhatura* is a bit like a deep-fried version of the *naan*. It is very popular in the Punjab as a 'snack' bread, eaten with spiced chickpeas.

5 oz all-purpose white flour, plus a little extra flour for dusting
¼ tsp baking powder
1 egg, beaten
1–1½ tbs plain yogurt

a little vegetable oil for brushing on dough
vegetable oil for deep frying, enough to have 2½ inches in pot

Sift the 5 oz flour and the baking powder into a bowl. Add the egg and begin to mix. Slowly add the yogurt and gather together the flour. Begin kneading. Add as much yogurt as will give you a soft dough. Knead dough for 10 minutes until it is smooth. Form into a ball, brush with oil, cover with damp cloth, and keep in a warm place for 3 hours.

With moistened hands, knead dough again.

Put oil in *karhai* (see page 47), wok, or other wide utensil for deep frying. Heat over medium flame. Allow oil time to get smoking hot.

Divide dough into 8 balls and cover with damp cloth. Take one ball at a time and flatten it. Flour the rolling surface. Roll out the ball into a 4½-inch round, and drop it in when the oil is smoking. As it begins to sizzle, press down on it gently with the back of a slotted spoon. It will puff up. Turn it over and let other side brown lightly. The whole process should take about a minute. Do all *bhaturas* this way.

To serve: Serve hot with *Chana Masaledar* or any meat or vegetable dish.

Naan

Serves 6

Naan is a leavened flat bread shaped like a teardrop. It is best when cooked in the clay oven called the *tandoor*. While meats, chicken, and fish grill on large skewers inside the *tandoor*, moistened *naans* are stuck to its walls to bake.

1 lb all-purpose white flour
about 7 fl. oz milk
1 egg, beaten
¾ tsp salt
2 tsp sugar
1 tsp baking powder
½ packet dry yeast (1½ tsp)

2 tbs vegetable oil, plus a
    little more for brushing on
    dough later
4 tbs plain yogurt
¼ tsp black onion seeds
    (kalonji), or poppy seeds
    as substitute

Sift the flour into a bowl. Place the milk in a small pot and warm slightly. Remove from heat. In another bowl combine the egg, salt, sugar, baking powder, yeast, 2 tablespoons oil, yogurt, and 5 tablespoons of the warm milk.

Mix well. Pour mixture over flour and rub it in with the hands.

Add 1 tablespoon of warm milk at a time to the flour, and begin kneading. Add enough so that all the flour adheres and kneading is easy. You should have a soft dough. Knead well for about 10 minutes or until dough is elastic. Form into a ball, brush with oil, cover with damp cloth, and leave in a warm place to rise. If the temperature is above 80°F. or 27°C. it should take only 2 hours. Otherwise it may take about 3 hours.

Preheat grill.

Brush 3 baking trays lightly with oil.

Knead the dough again for a minute or two and divide into 6 balls. Flatten the balls one at a time, keeping the rest covered, and stretch them and pat them with your hands until you have a teardrop shape about 11 inches long and 4 inches wide. Do all balls this way, placing 2 *naans* on each baking tray as you do so.

Cover with moistened cloths and leave for 15 minutes in a warm place.

Remove moistened cloths. Brush the centre portion of each *naan* with water, leaving a ½-inch margin. Sprinkle the centre portion with the onion or poppy seeds.

Place trays, one at a time, under the grill, about 2½–3 inches away from the heat and grill *naans* for about 2½ minutes on each side or until lightly browned.

To serve: Serve *naans* hot with *Tandoori* Chicken, *Seekh Kabab*, Lamb Cooked in Dark Almond Sauce, or Chicken *Moghlai*.

Desserts
with a note on tea

Kulfi
Gajar-ka-halva
Grilled bananas
Fried dates
Shahi tukra
Malpua
Kheer
Gulab jamun

N Europe and America, most meals end with dessert and coffee. In India most meals end with fruit — leeches, loquats, melons, watermelons, *cheekoos*, and mangoes in the summer, and apples, oranges, bananas, guavas, and pomegranates in the winter. These are often peeled at the table by the eldest woman of the house, and then passed around, always starting with the children. Desserts or 'sweets' are served mainly at very special luncheons and dinners, at snack time and tea time, and at religious festivals (which come extremely frequently!).

'Snack time' seems to have an unusually elevated place in Indian life. I remember when I was working in television shows in Delhi. We would be deep in rehearsal when, almost every hour, there would come a desperate cry from some corner of the studio: '*Quon bhai, chai hojai?*' ('Well now, brother, how about tea?'). Every actor and technician would stop (happily) in his tracks, and the whole group would saunter off to the nearest snack shop to have sweet and savoury snacks — and tea. The very spicy hot *samosas* and the sugary-sweet *gulab jamuns* were eaten simultaneously — a bite of one balancing a bite of the other and each swallowed with a soothing sip of scalding tea.

Tea has not always been drunk in India. Until the end of the last century it was more or less unknown in the subcontinent. With their sweet and sour snacks, Indians generally drank *shurbut* — fruit juice concentrates diluted with cold water — or hot, frothy milk. This milk was, and still is, sold by the snack vendor whose status often hinges upon how much froth he can raise. Since he has no frothing machine at his disposal, he achieves his bubbly result by briskly pouring the hot milk back and forth from one tumbler to another. These tumblers are first held close to each other. Slowly they are moved to a distance of several feet. The fast-flying milk never misses its mark and the stream of milk looks like white elastic being pulled between the tumblers. This sight is responsible for one of Delhi's oldest jokes, about the visitor from the old North-west Frontier who asked if he might have 'two yards of that white thing' along with his other sweets!

Tea, which is easily North India's favourite snack beverage, has now replaced both *shurbut* and milk. It was introduced to India by the British in the early 1900's. By this time the English had already been drinking Chinese teas for over two centuries. They decided to try planting Chinese tea seeds in the hilly regions of Assam. There they discovered, much to their surprise, fully grown tea trees that turned out to be not solitary accidents of nature, but parts of whole forests of tea trees. So the English went in with their Chinese seeds, their Chinese labour, and their pruning shears to tame this 'wild' area. Soon they realized that neither the Chinese seeds nor the Chinese labour was necessary and that the native Indian tea was not only good but also proving very popular with the customers in England.

The next market they looked to was India herself. This turned out to be no problem at all. The Indians took to tea like fish to water. They learned to drink it like the English—strong, with a little milk and sugar. The milk was added to the strong tea to 'fix' the tannin content and rid it of most of its astringency.

The Indian teas come from various regions of both North and South India and are generally of the dark fermented varieties. My own favourite is the Orange Pekoe from Darjeeling, with its smoky, nutty flavour. Indians almost never use teabags. They generally brew their loose tea leaves in a warm teapot. Here is how you can make a good pot of tea: 1. Use freshly boiled water. Do not let it overboil, since water that is kept boiling tends to become de-aerated. 2. Heat the teapot by rinsing it with boiling water. 3. Put into the teapot one teaspoon of tea leaves per cup of water to be used plus one teaspoon more for the pot. (If you like your tea weak add more hot water once the tea has brewed.) 4. Pour the boiling water over the tea leaves, cover and set aside for three minutes. If you are lucky enough to have a tea-cosy, cover your teapot with it. 5. Lift cover, stir, and strain into teacups. 6. Serve plain or with lemon and sugar or with hot milk and sugar or, if you like, with just sugar or just milk.

Many of the packaged teas available in Britain are blends of teas from several regions — often from several countries. Teabags also contain blends — some being slightly better than others. Pure Darjeeling teas, labelled as such, are available in some supermarkets and most delicatessens. If you buy a pound of loose tea, store it in a tightly covered, light-proof container, away from the scent of strong spices and herbs.

Indian sweets tend to be *very* sweet. They tend also to be made of ingredients like vegetables (carrots, pumpkin), nuts (pistachios, almonds, coconut), flours (plain flour, rice flour, chickpea flour), and sweeteners (sugar, jaggery). But the most important ingredient is milk. Milk forms the base of more than half our sweets, and it is often milk in a form entirely unused in the West. Milk is boiled for hours until it forms a semi-solid dough called *khoya*. Most people do not make *khoya* at home. They go out and buy it. It is simpler. Since *khoya* is unavailable here, I have used several substitutes, powdered milk being one of them. For other desserts, milk is boiled down until it is half or a third of its original quantity. Since I do this in a few of the recipes, let me give you a few tips that may help you.

How to boil milk down

1. Use a very heavy-bottomed pot. Cast-iron or aluminium covered with porcelain is particularly good for this.

2. Since the process is slow and tedious (it may take 1 to 1½ hours), bring a chair and a book to your stove.

3. Bring the milk to an 'almost' boil. Watch it. If you let it boil over, you will have a big mess to clean. As soon as it seems that the milk will start to boil and rise, turn heat down to a medium low.

4. Adjust heat so that milk is always bubbling, but will not bubble over.

5. Once the milk has begun its slow boil, settle down with your book. Stir the milk every few minutes.

6. If a creamy crust forms on top, just stir it into the milk. It will taste fine when cold.

Kulfi

Serves 6

This is Indian ice cream at its best. Milk is boiled down to a third of its original quantity. Sugar, cardamom, and nuts are added, and the thickened milk is then poured into special conical containers and frozen. Traditionally, *kulfi* is served with *falooda*, a transparent vermicelli rather like the Japanese noodles in a sukiyaki. Since I do not expect you to have the conical containers, you could use empty tins of frozen fruit juice, or individual custard cups or paper cups or even a single bowl.

2½ pints milk
4 whole cardamom pods
3 tbs sugar

1 tbs slivered unsalted pistachios

In a very heavy-bottomed pot, boil milk down to 16 fl. oz (see note on page 324). This may take up to 1½ hours. After the first hour, lightly crush 2 of the cardamom pods and add them to the milk.

When the milk has boiled down to 16 fl. oz turn off heat. Remove and discard cardamom pods. Add sugar and nuts. Stir well.

Grind the seeds from the other 2 cardamom pods (see page 40) and add them to the milk. Leave milk to cool.

When cool, stir once and pour milk equally into six 3-fl. oz or 4-fl. oz paper cups, or similar containers, or a bowl. Cover with aluminium foil and freeze. Stir the *kulfi* every 20 to 30 minutes to help break up the crystals. It will get harder to stir as it thickens. When it becomes too thick to stir, leave to freeze solid. Keep covered.

To serve: Run a warm knife along the inside of each cup or container to remove the *kulfi*. (You may need to pour warm water on the outside to loosen it.) Serve individual portions on small chilled plates.

Gajar-ka-halva

Serves 8

In this carrot halva, the carrots are completely unrecognizable. Milk and grated carrots are cooked until they become a dryish homogeneous mass. Sugar (and, if you like, lightly fried raisins and nuts) are then added, and the dish is served warm or at room temperature.

1½ pints milk	3 tbs sugar
2 lbs carrots, peeled and grated	1 tbs each lightly fried raisins and almonds (optional)
2 cardamom pods	
10 tbs vegetable oil or usli ghee (see page 42)	½ pint clotted or heavy cream (optional)

Put the milk, grated carrots, and cardamom pods in a 10-inch heavy-bottomed pot. Bring to the boil. Lower heat to medium and cook, stirring occasionally, until no liquid is left. This may take about 30 minutes.

Add the oil, turn the heat down slightly, and start frying the carrot-milk mixture, stirring *all the time*. Continue until the carrots turn a reddish-brown. This may take 30 to 40 minutes.

Add sugar and, if you like, raisins and almonds. Cook, stirring, another 2 minutes. Turn off heat. Allow halva to cool. Cover and refrigerate until ready to eat.

To serve: This halva can be warmed or served at room temperature. In India, it is often served with clotted cream—the cream that forms when unhomogenized milk is boiled. You could, if you like, serve it with heavy cream just lightly whipped so it doubles in bulk.

Grilled bananas

Serves 4

1 tbs melted butter
2 very firm large bananas
1 tsp lemon juice
3 tbs orange juice

2 tbs brown sugar
1 tbs blanched slivered
   almonds

Preheat the grill.

Brush a small, flameproof baking dish (a small baking tray will do) with half the butter. Split the bananas in half, lengthwise, and lay them in the dish. Mix the lemon and orange juice and pour it over the bananas. Brush the bananas with the remaining butter, and sprinkle with brown sugar.

Place under grill for about 4 minutes or until bananas are lightly browned. Sprinkle almond slivers over bananas and put them under the grill for another minute or two, or until almonds are browned. Remove from grill.

To serve: Serve the bananas hot. This dish should be prepared just before eating.

Fried dates

Serves 4–6

This simple dessert is popular among the Bohris of Gujarat. If you like dates and chewy, sticky caramely things, you will love this. It takes just a few minutes to make and should be cooked just before serving.

3 tbs vegetable oil or usli ghee (see page 42)	1 tbs slivered unsalted pistachios
8 oz pitted good-quality dates	½ pint clotted or heavy cream

Heat the oil in a 10-inch frying-pan over a medium flame. When hot, put in the dates. Stir them around for 10 to 20 seconds. Remove with slotted spoon and place in serving dish.

Add pistachios to cream and put in serving pitcher.

To serve: Pass around the dates as well as the pitcher with the cream and nuts. The cream should be poured over the hot dates.

Shahi tukra

Serves 4

This popular dessert is made out of white bread rectangles, milk, and saffron.

3 whole cardamom pods, slightly crushed	4 tbs vegetable oil or usli ghee (see page 42)
1½ pints milk	3 slices of stale homemade-type white bread, ¾ inch thick, crusts removed, and each slice cut into 4 rectangles
2 tsp sugar plus 1 tbs sugar	
¼ tsp leaf saffron, roasted and crumbled according to instructions on page 44)	

Garnish

vark, if available (see page 45)	1 tbs slivered unsalted pistachios
1 tbs sliced blanched almonds	

Put the cardamom pods and 8 fl. oz of the milk into a small pot and bring to the boil. Turn off heat. Add 2 teaspoons of sugar and the saffron. Mix. Set aside.

In another pot (heavy-bottomed) bring the remaining milk to the boil. Turn heat down and reduce milk by half to a little more than a $\frac{1}{2}$ pint (see note on page 324). This may take 35 to 45 minutes.

In a 10-inch frying-pan, heat the oil over medium temperature. When hot, put in the rectangles of bread. Fry until both sides turn golden-brown. This should take about a minute on each side. You may need to add a bit more oil. Pour out oil if any is left.

Pour the saffron milk over the bread and let it sit for 5 minutes. Turn the rectangles over once during this period.

Add the remaining 1 tablespoon sugar to the boiled-down milk and pour this over the bread as well. Bring the contents of the frying-pan to the boil. Lower heat and simmer 10 minutes. Turn bread gently once or twice with a long spatula.

Lift bread gently and place on a rimmed platter for serving. Any flat dish with a shallow rim will do.

Allow to cool. Garnish with vark, almonds, and pistachios. Cover and refrigerate until ready to serve.

Serve cold.

Malpua

Serves 6

This is a pancake immersed in a sugar syrup.

6 oz sifted all-purpose white
  flour
4 fl. oz milk
6 fl. oz heavy cream
1¼ lbs sugar

2 cardamom pods, slightly
  crushed
3 tbs vegetable oil (more
  may be needed)

Mix the flour, milk, and cream with a whisk. Cover and refrigerate overnight.

Make the syrup by combining the sugar, 16 fl. oz of water, and the cardamom pods in a pot. Bring to the boil without stirring. Lower heat and simmer 2 to 3 minutes, or until all the sugar dissolves. Put syrup into serving bowl large enough to hold pancakes as well.

Heat the oil in a 10–12-inch frying-pan over a medium flame. Pour in enough batter to make two 4–5-inch pancakes at a time. Cook pancakes slowly on both sides so they get golden-brown and crisp. As pancakes are done, lift them out and put them into the syrup. Finish all the batter this way. Adjust heat so as not to burn pancakes, and add more oil as you require it. There should be about 3 tablespoons of oil in the frying-pan constantly.

Malpua can be served either at room temperature or slightly warm. Bring bowl of pancakes and syrup to table. Each person should serve himself—only the pancakes, not any of the syrup.

Kheer

Serves 4

This is my mother's recipe for *kheer*, a dessert made with milk and rice. *Please* do not call it a 'rice pudding'. This sweet has been served to kings at banquets and to brides at wedding ceremonies—in no way does it resemble the stodgy rice pudding seen around in the Western Hemisphere!

When my mother made the *kheer* she set it in shallow half-baked earthenware bowls called *shakoras*. As a result, it picked up the delicious fragrance of freshly moistened earth. You could serve your *kheer* in individual custard bowls, or, if you prefer, you could put it all in one shallow bowl from which each person would serve himself.

2 pints milk
1 tbs long-grain rice
4 whole cardamom pods,
  slightly crushed
2 tbs sugar

10 pistachios, unsalted and
  slivered, plus a few more
  for garnishing
vark, if available (see page
  45)

Combine the milk, rice, and cardamom pods in a heavy-bottomed pot. Bring to the boil. Lower heat and reduce milk until you have 1 pint (see page 324). This may take about $1\frac{1}{4}$ hours. Turn off heat.

Remove cardamom pods and discard. Add sugar and nuts. Mix well. Leave to cool.

Mix again. Pour into serving bowl. Decorate with *vark* (see page 45). Sprinkle a few more slivered pistachios on top of the *vark*. Cover bowl with light plastic wrap. Refrigerate.

Serve cold.

Gulab jamun

Serves 6–8

This is a simple, very sweet dessert which can be served warm or at room temperature. It is made with dried milk. You could call it 'fried milk balls in syrup'.

2 lbs granulated sugar
3 cardamom pods, slightly
  crushed
6 oz powdered milk
3 oz all-purpose white flour

4 fl. oz vegetable oil or
  melted usli ghee (see page
  42)
4 fl. oz milk
vegetable oil for deep frying,
  enough to have 3 inches in
  cooking pot

First make the syrup. In a 3-quart pot, combine 1¾ pints water, the sugar, and the cardamom. Lower heat. Simmer 2 to 3 minutes, or until all the sugar has been dissolved. Do not stir.

Pour half the syrup into a serving bowl (about a 2-quart size). Leave the other half in the pot, with the cardamom pods.

Combine the powdered milk, flour, oil, and milk in a bowl. Make a soft dough. Make small, smooth balls out of the dough, each about 1 inch in diameter. You should be able to make more than 2 dozen *jamuns*.

Heat oil for deep frying in wok, *karhai*, or any heavy-bottomed wide pot. You should have at least 3 inches of oil. Keep on *low* flame. The *jamuns* need to be fried *slowly*.

Put a *jamun* into the oil as a test. If it begins to brown immediately, your heat is too high. Each *jamun* should take 4 to 5 minutes to get a reddish-brown colour on all sides. If the first *jamun* does not turn out right, correct the heat. It is better to take this precaution than have a whole batch burn outside and stay raw inside.

Now put in 6 *jamuns* at a time. Turn them over as they turn reddish-brown on one side. As they get fried, put them into the syrup in the pot. Bring this syrup to the boil. Let each batch simmer in the syrup for 5 minutes. When the *jamuns* are 'syruped', lift them out with a slotted spoon and place them in the fresh syrup in the serving bowl. Keep frying and 'syruping' a batch at a time—as one batch fries, another can 'syrup'—until they are all done. When cool, cover serving bowl with plastic wrap and refrigerate. The syrup in the pot can now be discarded.

To serve: Gulab jamuns can be served cold, at room temperature, or slightly warmed. Remember, you serve yourself only the *gulab jamun*, not the syrup in the bowl!

And, to end,
would you care for a paan?

The guest has eaten well. Reluctantly, he heaves himself off a low divan and makes his way to the front door. Goodbyes and see-you-soons are buzzing about his ears. Then the hostess descends upon him with yet another large silver tray. It is the final offering—one he just *cannot* refuse. It is the *paan*, or the betel leaf. He picks one up delicately with the tips of his right thumb and forefinger, opens his mouth wide, arches his body forward so it will not catch the staining spill, if any, and then stuffs the large *paan* into his mouth. He goes out into the moonlight licking his lips and chewing contentedly.

The *paan* has rounded off his meal as nothing else could and has left him with a feeling of immense and unique well-being. He is not alone in this. After a good meal, most Indians go hunting for a good *paan*. *Paan* and cigarette stalls dot all neighbourhoods just as sweet and cigarette shops do in Britain. Indians abroad ache for it and dream of the day when they will be back on home soil, where they can buy it around the corner. I recall once, while doing an Urdu radio programme at the United Nations headquarters in New York, a group of us Indians and Pakistanis were interrupted in our rehearsal by a Pakistani gentleman who had (hush) smuggled a solitary *paan* past the X-ray eyes of a New York customs inspector. (The betel leaf, being a green living thing, is not allowed into the United States before thorough examination and, I suspect, quarantine! By that time the living thing is quite dead!) This gentleman came into the studio, waving the *paan* with a look of smug achievement. There was quiet for a second. Then, like wild demons, we all leaped upon him, snatched the *paan*, tore it into equal shreds, and devoured the scraps that fell to our lot. We were very ashamed and embarrassed afterwards as we handed the Pakistani gentleman his share, watched him eat it, straighten his tie, cough, and leave the studio without a word exchanged. There was no excuse except that it was un-premeditated! This is what a *paan* can do to Indians and Pakistanis! While *paans* are now available in parts of England, they are still a rare—and illegal—sight in America.

What exactly *is* a *paan*, and is there a substitute that can be eaten? The *paan* leaf is heart-shaped, 4 to 5 inches in length, and varies in taste from sweet to slightly bitter. The two commonest types are the *Benaresi* leaf (small, tender, sweet, and yellowish-green) and the *desi* leaf (large, crisp, slightly bitter, and dark green). A *paan* costs from a few pence up to £10 or £20, depending on what is wrapped inside it. At its simplest, this could be white lime paste, or *choona*; katechu paste, or *kattha*, a red paste made from the bark of a tree, which stains the mouth red; and chopped betel nuts. Or the *paan* can contain combinations of fennel, cardamom, clove, perfumed nuts and spices, expensive tobaccos, drugs, and aphrodisiacs. An aphrodisiac like crushed pearls naturally pushes up the price a bit! The stuffing is placed on the centre of the leaf, and the leaf is then folded over in the shape of a flat triangle or a cone. Either shape is held in place by a clove, acting as a straight pin.

In private homes, *paans* are kept in *paandaans*—brass or silver boxes with compartments and trays to hold all the spices, nuts, and leaves. (A lot of the 'Indian brass boxes' sold in English shops are really the outside shells of *paandaans*.) While the *paan* leaf is unavailable in most markets in Britain, a great many of the spices are obtainable, and can easily be served after meals to departing guests. Here are some of them. Put them into silver or glass bowls or place them in tiny mounds on a silver tray.

BETEL NUT OR SUPARI   This is a round, hard nut, requiring a special cutter (*sarota*) to cut it into sections. You can, however, get it already cut up. To the uninitiated, it seems hard, unyielding, and fairly tasteless. It does soften if sucked for long. It has a unique mild taste, which needs, perhaps, to be acquired.

Much easier on the palate are the scented and powdered *suparis* available in packages at the Indian shops. They are often mixed with other seeds, nuts, and spices. If you ever travel Air India, along with the sweets offered at takeoff and landing they will also offer you tiny packets of scented *supari*.

CARDAMOM OR ELAICHI   Indians eat whole pods as well as the separated seeds. There are two eating varieties of pods available in Britain: one slightly greenish and the other off-white. The green one is much better for eating. The seeds are sucked and chewed slowly, allowing the flavour to linger in the mouth. In India the cardamom seeds can also be bought scented and covered with *vark* (see page 45).

FENNEL SEEDS OR SONF   These are easy to buy and very refreshing to taste. Their slightly nutty, slightly liquorice-like flavour is very popular with all my English friends. Though you can eat them raw, they taste better if they are dry-roasted first. Dry-roast about a cupful at a time by placing the seeds in a heavy-bottomed frying-pan over a medium flame and stirring them until the seeds get very lightly browned. Cool and store in a lidded jar. In the Punjab, fennel is served with *misri*, grains of old-fashioned sugar candy.

CLOVES OR LONG   Indians actually suck cloves. They break off and discard the small, peppercorn-like ball on the top of the clove, which is too sharp (not all cloves have it), and pop the rest into their mouths like sweets. It is very refreshing—and not as harmful to the teeth! You will often see fashionable young Indian misses take out little silver boxes from their little silver purses, remove cloves and cardamom seeds from them, and delicately place these spices on their tongues when mouth fresheners seem suddenly called for!

Glossary

AAM PAPAR   sour mango pulp, dried in sheets

ALOO-KI-TIKIYA   potato patties

ALPHONSO MANGO   an expensive sweet variety found in the Bombay region

AMCHOOR   dried, raw mango, powdered or in slices

ARHAR DAL   a yellow, split pulse

ATA   whole-wheat flour

BAASI   stale

BABARCHI   a cook

BADAMI ROGHAN JOSH   a rich meat dish with almond sauce

BAGHAR   different combinations of spices and flavourings dropped in hot oil, *ghee*, or *usli ghee*, used for flavouring certain meats, vegetables, dals, and relishes

BAIGAN-KA-BHARTA   smoked, mashed aubergines, plain or with yogurt

BAIR   a small fruit, shaped like a plum with the texture of an apple, tasting somewhat like a combination of the two

BARIS   dried lumps of pounded pulse

BASMATI   an expensive, fine-grained, fragrant rice grown in the Dehradun region

BENARESI   from Benares

BESAN   chickpea flour

BHAPA DOI   sweetened, steamed yogurt (Bengali)

BHARTA   *see* baigan-ka-bharta

337

BHATURA a deep-fried bread made with white flour, using eggs or baking powder or both

BIRYANI a festive dish combining rice with spiced meat or chicken

BOHRIS a Muslim, Gujarati-speaking community

BOONDI-KA-DAHI a yogurt dish containing tiny dumplings made of chickpea flour

BOTI KABAB cubes of marinated meat, skewered and grilled

BRAHMIN an Indian belonging to the highest caste and traditionally vegetarian

CHANA chickpea

CHANA BHATURA a spicy chickpea dish served with *bhaturas*

CHANA DAL a split chickpea pulse

CHANA MASALEDAR a spicy chickpea dish

CHAPATI a flat bread made of whole-wheat flour

CHEEKOO a round, sweet, grainy dark-brown fruit, somewhat like a persimmon

'CHHI, CHHI, CHHI' 'dirty, dirty, dirty'

CHHOLA chickpea, green, dried or cooked

CHHOWNK same as *baghar*

CHIMTA Indian tongs

CHOONA lime (white, alkaline earth) paste

CHORCHURI a Bengali dish made with vegetables and fish-heads

DAL pulse

DALDA brand name of an Indian vegetable shortening

DELHI-WALLAH a resident of Delhi

'DEY DAL MAY PANI' 'put water in the dal'

DHANIA (FRESH) fresh green coriander

DHOKLA a savoury snack from Gujarat with a spongy cake-like texture

DO PYAZA dish, generally meat, cooked with lots of fried, sliced onions

DUBBUL ROTI Western-style, leavened loaf bread
DUMBA fan-tailed sheep, generally cooked at festive occasions

ELAICHI cardamom

FALOODA a transparent vermicelli
FALSA a tart, red berry

GAJAR-KA-HALVA a dessert made with grated carrots and
  milk
GARAM hot
GARAM MASALA a spice mixture containing black pepper,
  cardamom, cinnamon, cloves, nutmeg, and black cumin
GHEE vegetable shortening
GULAB JAMUN fried milk balls in syrup; a dessert

HALVA certain desserts made with vegetables or flours

ID Bakra-Id, a Muslim religious festival honouring Abra-
  ham's offer to sacrifice his son, Ishmael (according to the
  Koran), celebrated by animal sacrifices and feasting

JAIN member of the Jain religion, which abhors all killing
JAMUN a tart, purple, juicy plum-like fruit

KABAB skewered, grilled meat, cubed or minced. Also
  minced-meat patties
KABLI CHANA chickpea
KALONJI black onion seeds
KARHAI wide bowl-shaped utensil, used for deep frying
KARHI a soup-like dish, made with chickpea flour and butter-
  milk
KARI Tamil word meaning sauce; possible origin of the word
  'curry'

KARI LEAF small green leaf used to flavour certain dishes

KATORI small metal bowl used for serving individual portions of food

KATTHA red katechu paste, used in preparing betel leaves

KHANSAMA a chef, generally of the Anglo-Muslim tradition

KHARA MASALA a combination of whole spices, generally bay leaves, black peppercorns, cardamom pods, cinnamon sticks, cloves, and red peppers

KHARE MASALE KA GOSHT meat cooked with *khara masala* (see above)

KHATTE ALOO sour potatoes

KHEEMA minced meat, raw as well as cooked

KHEER a cold dessert made with thickened milk and rice

KHITCHERIE a word meaning 'hodgepodge', it could be used for scrambled eggs or various combinations of rice and *dals*

KHITCHERIE UNDA scrambled eggs

KHOYA a substance formed by boiling milk down until all the liquid evaporates, used as a base for many Indian desserts

KOFTA meatball

KORMA a rich meat dish

KULFI an Indian ice cream made with thickened milk and nuts

LOBHIA black-eyed peas

LONG cloves

MALPUA Indian pancakes in syrup; a dessert

MASOOR DAL a salmon-coloured split pulse

MILAGUTANNIR Tamil word for 'pepper water' and origin of the name 'mulligatawny' soup

MISRI old-fashioned sugar candy

MOGHLAI of Moghul tradition

MOGHULS Muslim Mongols or Tartars who ruled India in fact or in name from the sixteenth to the nineteenth century and who introduced to it Persian-style foods, jewellery, furnishings, etc.

MOONG DAL   a small yellow split pulse

MULLAH DO PYAZA   a dish made with meat and often an equal quantity of onions

MURGH MUSSALLAM   a whole chicken cooked in a thick sauce

MUTKA   a round pot of red clay used for storing and cooling water as well as foods pickled in water

NAAN   a large, tear-shaped leavened bread, generally baked on the walls of a clay oven, or *tandoor*

NARGISI KOFTA   meatball stuffed with a hard-boiled egg

NIRAMISH VEGETABLES   'vegetarian' vegetables, cooked without onions and garlic (Bengali)

OM   'I am' (Sanskrit)

PAAN   betel leaf; betel leaf stuffed with quicklime paste, katechu paste, betel nuts and other spices, nuts or tobaccos, according to desire

PAANDAAN   a metal box with trays and compartments, designed to hold the green betel leaves as well as the various nuts and spices needed in their preparation

PAKORI   dumpling or fritter

PAPAR   pulse wafer

PAPPADUM   a South Indian word for *papar*

PARAAT   a large, round, wide-rimmed tray used for kneading bread

PARATHA   a flat bread made with whole-wheat flour and cooked on a griddle with a little shortening, *usli ghee*, or butter

PARVAL   a small marrow-like green vegetable, with crisp egg-like seeds

PHIRNI   a cold dessert made with thickened milk and crushed rice

POORI   a puffy, deep-fried bread made of whole-wheat flour

PULLAO   a rice and meat dish

PURAN POLI a sweet Maharashtrian bread
PYAZ onion
PYAZWALA KHARE MASALE KA GOSHT meat with whole spices and onions
PYAZWALE SOOKHE ALOO dry potatoes with onions

QAVVALI poem sung in a particular style by a group of people
'QUON BHAI CHAI HOJAI?' 'Well now, brother, how about tea?'

RAHU a large fresh-water fish
RAITA a dish made with yogurt and a vegetable
RAJMA DAL red kidney beans
ROGHAN JOSH meat cooked in a Muslim style to look dark red and rich
ROTI bread

SA'AB short spoken form of the word 'sahib', or master
SAFED SARVO white soup (Gujarati)
SAMBAR a South Indian *dal* dish
SAMOSA triangular cones of dough, stuffed with meat or vegetables and deep fried
SAROTA betel nut cutter
SEEKH same as *seekh kabab*
SEEKH KABAB minced meat, mixed with spices, stuck around a thick skewer and grilled
SHAHI TUKRA a cold bread dessert
SHAKORA disposable bowls of red clay used for holding individual portions of food
SHAMI KABAB minced-meat patties, generally stuffed with minced onions, green chilies, and mint
SHARAB liquor
SHARABI KABABI one who likes to eat and drink
SHURBUT fruit juice or other flavouring syrups, diluted with ice-cold water and drunk throughout India

SIL BATTA   the two parts to the North Indian grinding stone
SINDHI GOSHT   meat cooked in the style of Sindh
SINGHARA   a fresh-water fish
SONF   fennel seed
SOOKHE ALOO   dry potatoes
SUPARI   betel nut

TANDOOR   clay oven used for baking and broiling
TANDOORI   cooked in a *tandoor*
TARKA   same as *baghar*
TAVA   a slightly curved, cast-iron plate used for cooking breads
THAL   a metal tray
THALI   a metal plate
THANDAI   a cold drink made with milk, almonds, and cardamom
TOOVAR DAL   same as *arhar dal*

UNDA   egg
UNDHYA   a vegetable dish from Gujarat cooked in an earthenware pot placed upside down over live coals and damp hay
URAD DAL   a yellow split pulse that turns slightly viscous when cooked
USLI GHEE   clarified butter

VADEES   same as *baris*
VARK   gossamer-thin edible silver or gold foil, used for garnishing foods, particularly desserts and festive rice

YAKHNI   flavoured meat broth used for cooking rice

ZAAFRAAN   saffron

Index